Principles and Practice

of Textual Analysis

Principles
and Practice
of Textual
Analysis

BY VINTON A. DEARING

UNIVERSITY OF CALIFORNIA PRESS
Berkeley Los Angeles London
1974

001.552
D34P
92575
Mar. 1975

University of California Press
Berkeley and Los Angeles, California

University of California Press, Ltd.
London, England

Copyright © 1974 by The Regents of
the University of California

ISBN: 0-520-02430-3

Library of Congress Catalog Card Number: 73-76122

Printed in the United States of America

TO MY WIFE

Contents

Preface

The method of analysis described in the following pages may be applied to the transmission in any form of any idea or complex of ideas, but it grew out of textual criticism, and particularly out of an interest in developing textual criticism to deal better with the Greek New Testament. My indebtedness to my predecessors in textual criticism and bibliography is for the most part documented in the notes, but I ought perhaps to add that I know and respect the work of Paul Maas, Bruce M. Metzger, D'Arco Silvio Avalle, and Dom J. Froger, to whom I have not had occasion to refer. I have cited a number of scholars only to disagree with them, but this should not be taken to imply blanket disagreement or any lack of admiration for the texts and collations they have provided for us. Even Housman, the Jonathan Swift of textual criticism—intense of feeling, expert in invective, blind to the promise in uncertain first steps toward scientific method—I honor more than my notice of him would suggest, though I believe absolutely that the time is not far distant when his famous simile of the dog and the flea will be recognized as being, like Swift's simile of the spider and the bee, simply wrong.

My *Manual of Textual Analysis* appeared before I had fully freed myself from the influence of the old way of looking at the problems of textual criticism and before I had more than a vision of the usefulness of computers. The present work carries out to the full the distinction introduced in the *Manual* between the genealogy of manuscript and other books as physical objects and the genealogy of the ideas or complexes of ideas that these physical objects transmit. In addition it provides much more detailed instructions as to how to perform textual analysis with computers and without, and for the first time formulates the axioms of textual analysis and demonstrates their inevitability. Since the methods given in the *Manual* for resolving conflation by overlays and locating archetypes by a theory of simplicity do not fit the developed theory and practice of textual analysis, they have been abandoned.

Wherever possible, however, I have incorporated passages from the *Manual* without or with very little change. I therefore wish to repeat my acknowledgment in its preface that I received deeply appreciated help of various kinds from Hugh G. Dick, John J. Espey, Earl R. Miner, H. T. Swedenberg, Donald F. Criley, Everett S. Calhoun, Thomas H. Southard, Sir Walter Greg, and Silva Lake. In preparing the present work, I have had help from Alvin R. Goldsmith, Robert Zachary of the University of California Press, the anonymous readers of the manuscript when it was submitted for publication, and a great many people in the Western Data Processing Center, now the Campus Computing Network, at the University of California, Los Angeles, especially William P. Anderson, Kenneth Tom, and Kenneth Marvin. Research grants from the University of California, the John S. Guggenheim Foundation, and the International Business Machines Corporation have paid for my use of computers and my research in British libraries. I am particularly indebted in this connection to Edmund A. Bowles of IBM and R. Clay Sprowls of UCLA. But by far my most important debt is to ideas that have come to me from no human source and through no mental powers of my own, when I expectantly watched for them. If this book has any validity, it is almost entirely owing to these ideas, which have ranged from the most broad and fundamental to the most minute and particular. Wrong ideas have come unsolicited as well, but my hope is that I have been able to distinguish wheat from tares and have gathered only the former into my barn.

After this book had gone to press, Eldon Jay Epp, Irving Alan Sparks, and Paul R. McReynolds were kind enough to ask me to apply textual analysis to the apparatus for chapter 20 of the Gospel of Luke prepared by the International New Testament Project, and to discuss the method in the Textual Criticism Seminar of the Society of Biblical Literature. Work with the apparatus led me to correct and expand in proof the opening of chapter 2, section 2. There too, and elsewhere, members of the seminar will recognize the effects of their comments.

In his Hatch Memorial Lecture in 1973, Professor Epp spoke of the "twentieth-century interlude" in New Testament textual criticism, during which essentially no progress has been made. Were I to choose a metaphor for the twentieth century in textual criticism generally, I should compare it to the horse latitudes, where the winds, if any, are light and fickle. When I wrote my *Manual*, I thought that such head-winds as I might encounter would come from those who wished no limitation upon individual judgment. I now think I am more likely to meet headwinds from those who yearn for complete objectivity. Be that as it may, if I am right about the steady course of textual analysis it will bring textual criticism out of the horse latitudes into the full Gulf Stream or Humboldt Current of progress. It is thus my earnest expectation that the "twentieth-century interlude" is drawing to a close.   V. A. D.

I

Preliminary Distinctions

Textual analysis as defined in this book determines the genealogical relationships between different forms of the same message, to use the terminology of information theory, but not the relationships between the transmitters of the different forms. A message is a mental phenomenon, originating in one mind and more or less perfectly receivable in others depending on the effectiveness with which the physical transmitters function. Messages are not confined to words or even to sound, but may consist wholly of visual images, or they may be metamessages, making explicit the form, content, or style of other messages. There is no limitation whatsoever in textual analysis on the type or types of transmitters. Textual analysis is therefore, like information theory, a completely general discipline of very wide specific applicability in the arts and social sciences.

In a conversation with Robert A. Fairthorne I once said that machine translation would be a nearer possibility if we stopped trying to translate each natural language into every other and developed an artificial language into and from which the rest could be translated, for then each natural language could be translated into all the others through the common intermediary. An artificial language is not necessary, said Fairthorne; any of the natural languages can be the intermediary between the rest. With this fact in mind, I have chosen here not to develop a wholly generalized account of textual analysis, which textual critics, historians, cartographers, musicologists, iconographers, and so on, would have to translate into terminology familiar to them, but instead to adopt the language of textual criticism for the most part, with apologies to those who will still have to translate from the more literary terminology and examples into their own. For this reason, I shall hereafter normally use the word *text* instead of *message, variant* instead of *different, state* instead of *form,* and *record* instead of *transmitter.* In this terminology, textual analysis determines the genealogy of the variant states of a text, when variant states exist, but not the genealogy of their records. To favor textual critics in this way is not unjust: textual analysis was developed by textual critics.

The goal of textual analysis is not, however, merely to provide a genealogy of the states of a text, but more importantly to identify the state from which all the others have descended or, if such a state is not known to be extant, then to reconstruct the latest state from which all the extant states have descended. This identified or reconstructed state is in most respects the closest we can approach to the author's original intention. James Thorpe has similarly defined the "ideal of textual criticism" as "to present the text which the author intended," immediately warning, however, that attainment of this ideal is not easy.[1] A difficult task can hardly be easy to learn. Therefore, although I have sought to lead the reader by easy steps to an understanding of textual analysis, mastery will still require hard study and perhaps much unlearning of favorite misconceptions. The experienced textual critic will also recognize that advancing by easy steps means ignoring at the beginning some fundamental problems, but he will find at the end that no problem has been dodged.

From time immemorial, copyists and readers have attempted to rectify errors in the records that fall under their eyes. It is easier to see that something has gone wrong than to decide how to emend it, to use the technical term. Still, the redundancy in most messages often makes accurate emendation certain. Everyone who reads newspapers has successfully resolved puzzles like the following:[2]

> There are two promisings, however. Seamus Twomey, "provisional" IRA leader in agree to a new cease-fire if Britain provided written guarantees that Catholic areas would not be harassed and if mutual observers were provided for.

---

[1] James Thorpe, *Principles of Textual Criticism* (San Marino, Calif., 1972), p. 50.

[2] Condensed from *The Christian Science Monitor,* western ed., July 15, 1972, p. 10. Actually the misplaced line was between paragraphs in the preceding column.

> Belfast, has indicated that the IRA would
> A second promising sign comes from the
> most extreme of Protestant loyalists.

The foregoing may not seem a very interesting example, but there appears to be an inverse relationship between the certainty of an emendation and its interest. The foregoing example stands at one end of the scale; at the other stands the most famous emendation in English literature. In the unemended text of *Henry V*, Mistress Quickly describes the death of Falstaff in part in these words: "his Nose was as sharpe as a Pen and a Table of greene fields." Whose heart is not stirred by Lewis Theobald's emendation, "and a babl'd of greene fields"? Yet soberer thought reveals that "talk'd" is as likely as "babl'd," given the handwriting of the period, and that, in fact, since one meaning of "table" is "picture," no emendation is needed at all.[3]

Emendation of texts is not a part of textual analysis itself; rather it operates upon the results of textual analysis to produce textual states that are in all respects the closest we can approach to the authors' original intentions. But the same kind of reasoning sometimes allows us to tell with the same relative certainty when one state of a text is descended from another, and such conclusions are important to textual analysis. Everyone is familiar in typewriting with evidence amenable to reasoning of this kind. When the typist's eye has skipped from a word to another occurrence of the same word farther along, the reader may not be able to restore the full text without consulting a record in which it is preserved. In such a case, the shorter state is clearly a descendant of the longer state and not the reverse.

Part of Hamlet's meditation on one of the skulls thrown up by the gravediggers (not Yorick's but another) disappeared in this way from the second quarto, 1604, which reads:

> . . . this fellowe might be in's time a great buyer of Land, with his Statuts, his recognizances, his fines, his double vouchers, his recoueries, to haue his fine pate full of fine durt, . . . ?

Between "recoueries" and the comma following belongs, as we learn from the first folio, 1621:

> : Is this the fine of his Fines and the recouery of his recoueries

---

[3] Discussions of this famous passage are innumerable. I picked up the alternative "talk'd" from Gerald E. Bentley and the fact that no emendation is needed from Ephim G. Fogel.

The reader will notice that we find the more authorial state of the text in a later edition. The first quarto, 1603, has only a fragment of this passage, "vouchers and Double vouchers," cemented between earlier and later fragments of the scene.

More than two thousand years ago, editors of Homer began comparing the states of his texts as recorded in their libraries and deciding, when they found a place where the states varied, which state was correct. This procedure, now called the eclectic method of textual criticism, continues to have a large following. Almost all biblical texts printed today have been prepared by the eclectic method, and medieval texts extant in many manuscripts are likely to be as well. Now, in most places where states of a text differ, no state is on the face of it preferable. The textual critic may then choose on the basis of the antiquity of the records (although he knows that antiquity and correctness are not necessarily concomitants); or the number of states in agreement (although he knows that numbers and correctness are not necessarily concomitants either); or the correctness of the states in places where their correctness is immediately determinable; or their conformity to the style of that part of the text which is the same in all states; or their aesthetic or other appeal at individual places or in general.

For example, we find the gravediggers talking as follows in the second quarto of *Hamlet*:

> *Clowne.* . . . there is no auncient gentlemen but Gardners, Ditchers, and Grauemakers, they hold vp Adams profession.
> *Other.* Was he a gentleman?
> *Clowne.* A was the first that euer bore Armes.

When we turn to the first folio we find that the dialogue continues:

> *Other.* Why he had none.
> *Clo.* What, ar't a Heathen? how dost thou vnderstand the Scripture? The Scripture sayes *Adam* dig'd; could hee digge without Armes?

Our first impulse may be to say that the shorter state resulted from eye-skip because the longer state ends with the same word. But we observe that the joke is complete in the shorter state; the longer merely adds an explanation. Furthermore, both the joke and the explanation would be quite likely to end with the key word, no matter which state was the more authorial. Under the circumstances, the shorter state is not clearly a descendant of the longer state. If we are using the eclectic method, however, we may decide that the state in the quarto is the descendant here because, as we have seen, it certainly is a few lines later.[4]

Textual critics of the eclectic school do not attempt to justify each of the many decisions of this kind which they must make. It is impossible, for example, to disentangle the interlaced motives that led Konstantin von Tischendorf to set so high a value as he did on Codex Sinaiticus, the earliest of the great uncial manuscripts of the Greek Bible, which Tischendorf himself discovered at Saint Catherine's monastery in the Sinai peninsula. Some eclectics then resort to counting the noses of other eclectics. For example, the Nestle editions of the New Testament, long standard, originally followed at least two of the three great editions of Tischendorf, Westcott and Hort, and Weymouth or Weiss.

Textual analysis never has to depend upon nose counting, but it may sometimes have to avail itself of the better kinds of reasoning used in the eclectic method.

The first genealogical method was devised by Karl Lachmann early in the nineteenth century and was applied by him to medieval, classical, and biblical texts. It is still the only genealogical method known to many textual critics. Lachmann's rule for textual genealogy is that states of a text having a common error have a common ancestor from which they have derived the error; that when there are no common errors, states agreeing in a striking way have a common ancestor from which they have derived their striking agreement; and that when there are no striking agreements, states often agreeing have a common ancestor from which they have derived these agreements. What this rule means in practice may be seen from a hypothetical example. Suppose we have a text in four states, A, B, C, and D, as follows. Only state A is given in full here, with line numbers supplied; the rest are represented in a summary called an apparatus criticus, critical apparatus, or merely apparatus. Brief designations of states are called their sigla; thus the siglum of state A is A.

> 1 J'admire, Madame, comme le Ciel a pu former
> 2 deux âmes en qui l'on ait vu une plus grande
> 3 conformité de sentiments, qui aient fait
> 4 éclater, dans le même temps, une résolution à
> 5 braver les traits de l'Amour, et qui, dans le

---

[4] Thus the source from which I picked up these examples, A. C. Clark (*The Descent of Manuscripts* [Oxford, 1918], p. 3), cites both as eyeskips.

6 même moment, aient fait paroître une égale
7 facilité à perdre la réputation d'insensibles.

1 Madame] A, C-D; Madame (c'est à dire, Madame Pompadour) B.
1 Ciel] A-C; bon Dieu D.   1 former] A-C; créer D.   2 ait vu] A-B;
voit C-D.   2 âmes en] A; âmes aussi semblables en tout que les nôtres,
deux âmes en B-D.   3-6 aient fait . . . fait paroître] A-B; aient fait
paroître C-D.   7 réputation] A-B, D; renommée C.   7 insensibles]
A, C; impitoyables B; endurcis D.

In the apparatus, the words to the left of the brackets are called
lemmas and those to the right are called variants. When the nature of
the text makes it appropriate, as here, variants are often called variant
readings or merely readings. A lemma and its variant or variants constitute a variation. The first variation above indicates that where A,
C, and D have only "Madame," B has "Madame (c'est à dire, Madame
Pompadour)," and the meaning of the others is similar.

Obviously, the choice of lemmas is determined by the choice of the
state to be recorded in full as a reference datum, so that a lemma is
essentially only another variant. Therefore, the general definition of a
variation is that it consists of two or more variants. Since definition of
a variant is much more complicated than definition of a variation, we
leave it until later. The examples provide a sufficient intuition of the
matter for our present purposes. We need here note only that the
terms "variant" and "variation" are used for the things themselves in
the states of the text as well as for the records of them in the apparatus.
The invariant parts of the states make up what is called the context
of the variations.

Now, by Lachmann's rule, the variation in lines 3-6, where the eyeskip is a striking error, supported by the other variation (in line 2)
where A agrees with B and C with D, indicates the following genealogical
tree, stemma, or diagram:

This tree shows a common ancestor for A and B (represented by the
juncture of lines just above them), from which they derived their readings of "ait vu" and "aient fait . . . fait paroître"; a common ancestor
for C and D (represented by the juncture of lines just above them) from
which they derived their readings of "voit" and "aient fait paroître";

and a common ancestor for these ancestors (represented by the juncture of the lines at the top), called the archetype.

A, B, C, and D in this tree are said to be terminal, their ancestors are said to be intermediary. The descent from the archetype through the immediate ancestor of A and B to A (or to B) is said to be direct, or successive, and the descent to A and B from their immediate ancestor is said to be independent or radiational.

The lines of descent for each of the variants in a variation must be entirely separate if we are to explain all the agreements of the states in the same way. If we were to interchange B and C in the tree above, for instance, we might explain the readings of "voit" and "aient fait paroître" in C and D as derived from the archetype, but we should then be unable to explain the derivation of the readings of A and B in these variations. States of a text which must be included in a tree to give a consistent genealogical explanation of the distribution of the variants among the extant states of a text are called inferential intermediaries.

The construction of a textual tree marks a real advance over the eclectic method. In the first place, the states of a text have not come into existence spontaneously and independently; they have a genealogy. Even the probabilist who imagined a monkey chancing to type out *War and Peace* never envisioned generations of monkeys producing the same text over and over. Second, having established the genealogy by consistent reasoning, we can if necessary reconstruct the archetype, at least in large part, with comparable consistency. Turning back to the tree we have drawn, we observe that the archetype will agree with A and C in reading "insensibles" in line 7 because A and C have no other common ancestor from which to derive the reading. For the same reason, the archetype will never have the readings found in only one of the extant states, for there is no other common ancestor for all three of the other states. The archetype will presumably agree with A and B in lines 3-6, since the reading of C and D is an error resulting from eyeskip. But we cannot tell whether the archetype will have "ait vu" with A and B in line 2, or "voit" with C and D. In this instance, therefore, we must reason about the archetype in the same way as an eclectic critic, whose principles, as we have seen, are not necessarily consistent.

This is not to say that the archetype is necessarily an authorial state of the text; it is not. We may, for instance, be able to come closer to an authorial state by emending the reconstructed archetype. But in our example the archetype is closer to an authorial state than any of the extant states of the text, which are all an eclectic critic has to work with.

Though interest will normally focus on the archetype, other states may be worth reconstructing if one is interested in the full history of the text. When two states have the same reading, any state intermediary between them will have this reading. Thus, in our example, not only the archetype but the common ancestors of A and B and of C and D will have "insensibles" in line 7.

Our gain over the eclectic method is then not double but triple. First of all, we have determined a fact about the text, namely the genealogy of its states. Second, we have then been able to determine in most cases which of the variants are preferable without resort to the eclectic critic's less consistent methods. And, third, we can reconstruct other states besides the archetype, which the eclectic method cannot do at all.

To these claims for the genealogical method many readers will at once be able to raise objections. In the first place, satisfactory results are not always obtainable by the Lachmannian rule and, in this particular instance, have in fact not been obtained. As we shall see, the correct tree here is as follows:

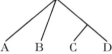

But this correction serves only to underline the value of a satisfactory genealogical method, for with this correct tree we never have, in our example, to fall back on the same kind of reasoning as the eclectic critic. We see that the archetype, like A and B, has "ait vu" in line 2, because A and B descend from it independently.

Besides failing to locate the archetype satisfactorily, the loose phrasing of the Lachmannian rule allows the textual critic to choose among the variations from which to reason about his trees. Since each critic makes up his own mind on this fundamental matter, books and articles on the method are never very explanatory of actual practice. Brief as they tend to be, they are almost wholly given over to peripheral matters, such as paleography, emendation, the major records and the romance of their discovery or previous ownership, the great editions of the past, and genealogical trees currently respectable. Because my interest in textual genealogy centered upon the Bible, as it does now, I began my studies with Kirsopp Lake's *The Text of the New Testament,* a more or less standard work which I read in the last of its six editions. I can still recall my surprise at discovering that Lake's exposition of the genealogical method would not explain the derivation of the genealogical trees in his little volume. Nevertheless, the Lachmannian method continues popular and is often employed as if there were no other, that is, with no explanation at all. Whenever a textual critic parcels out the states of his text into groups and without further ado assigns to each group an inferential ancestor and an archetype as the ancestor of the groups' ancestors, he is a Lachmannian.

The first work to attempt a foundation in formal logic for what textual critics had been trying to do by the Lachmannian rule was Sir Walter Greg's *Calculus of Variants* (1927). This book did not have the influence it deserved, perhaps because Greg's enormous stature as a thinker and doer in bibliography tended to draw attention away from his very great abilities in textual criticism, but more likely because the title and the mathematical symbols used in the calculus caused readers to reject it before they understood it.

A calculus in this sense is simply a system of notation and a precisely formulated step-by-step procedure (an algorithm) which facilitate accuracy of reasoning. Since everyone now understands that the foundations of mathematics are in logic, the reader will recognize that in choosing a simple example from arithmetic I am nevertheless illustrating a practice fundamentally logical. The task of addition is reduced to a calculus by decimal notation and an algorithm too familiar to require exposition:

$$\begin{array}{r} 55 \\ \underline{129} \\ 184 \end{array}$$

We have only to compare this sum with the task of adding LV and CXXIX to see why the Romans have given us the word *calculus* ("pebble"); they devised a kind of abacus, using pebbles, to do what we do so much more easily. It is perhaps worth noting that neither the notation nor the algorithm is absolutely binding on the other. We could attain the same results with binary notation, for instance, or with the Trachtenberg algorithm.[5]

[5] Binary numbers are explained in almost any book about computers; for the Trachtenberg algorithm see Ann Cutler and Rudolph McShane, trans. and adapt., *The Trachtenberg Speed System of Basic Mathematics* (Garden City, N.Y., [1960]), pp. 105-131.

It is impossible to design an effective calculus without making explicit to oneself exactly what operations are to be performed. In the process of designing his calculus, therefore, Greg made a number of discoveries of major importance to a full understanding of textual analysis. He recognized the fundamental division of variations between types he called simple and those he called complex. Simple variations have only two variants. These Greg divided into type 1 and type 2. In a type-1 variation, one state stands alone against a "true" group of the others. (Greg recognized that a single state is also a group, just as we now know that a "set" can have a single "element," or even, if it is an "empty" set, none at all. In the present book a single-state group is called a singleton.) In a type-2 variation there are two true groups. This classification is very useful, and we shall continue to employ it. Greg hardly explored complex variations, and his numbering of their types (type 3 for a variation with three variants, type 4 for a variation with four variants, and so on) is not useful. We shall employ a different classification for these when we need it later on.

Greg recognized that the groups in simple variations, as distinct from those in complex variations, are always terminal, and that they must all be taken into account. Thus, to revert to our example, the type-1 variations make A, B, C, and D terminal groups. Similarly the type-2 variations make AB a terminal group and CD another. On the other hand, the complex variation does not make AC a terminal group. Greg also recognized that the terminality of the two groups AB and CD does not establish the form of the textual tree. If we think carefully about terminality, we see that the variation that makes A a terminal group also makes BCD a terminal group, and so on with the other type-1 variations. In short, the terminality established by a simple variation is not with respect to the archetype but with respect to the other group in the variation. Greg thus demonstrated that textual analysis is a two-stage process. First one establishes the terminality of the groups and then one locates the archetype.

So much of Greg's effort went into demolishing the Lachmannian way of locating archetypes that many of his readers have supposed he left textual analysis in a worse state than he found it, but that is not so. Greg was aware of the principle of parsimony (as we shall see, genealogical reasoning is impossible without this principle). And of course he was aware of the effect of directional variations, as they are called, in which one variant can be recognized as certainly descended from another.

Only states agreeing in variants certainly descended from other variants, that is, only states sharing what are called later, worse, or less authoritative readings, need have ancestors of their own which are not the archetype. Then, by holding the number of ancestors to a minimum (applying the principle of parsimony), we locate the archetype.

To return to our example, the eyeskip in C and D in lines 3-6 will not allow them or the common ancestor from which they derived the error to be the archetype. In the same way, the eyeskip in A in line 2 prevents it from being the archetype. The parenthetical note found in B in line 1 would also appear to be nonauthorial, and yet it is not the kind of addition that would cause a copyist to eliminate it if he found it in the record from which he was copying. This prevents B from being the archetype. The common ancestor of A and B, however, can be the archetype and therefore by the law of parsimony must be. Thus we derive the corrected tree above, in which the common ancestor of A and B is also the ancestor of the common ancestor of C and D. It will be seen that the lines of descent for each of the variants in each variation are still entirely separate.

Notice, too, that in the Lachmannian tree we had to suppose that the archetype and the immediate common ancestor of A and B both read "aient fait . . . fait paroître" in lines 3-6, and that both could read "ait vu" in line 2. If the immediate common ancestor of A and B need not differ from the archetype, we need not suppose they are different states of the text. But might not the archetype read "aient fait paroître" with C and D in lines 3-6, so that it might be their immediate common ancestor instead? No. To suppose that the archetype can have less authoritative readings than other states is to ignore the evidence by which we tell ancestors from descendants.

Greg devoted almost no attention to extant states of a text which are not terminal but intermediary. Not so his contemporary, Dom Henri Quentin. Quentin examined the states of a text three at a time. His rule was that if two of the three never or almost never agreed against the third, it was intermediary between them. Let us turn again to our sample text. Taking the triad A, C, D, we might by Quentin's rule decide that C was intermediary between A and D, because C and D agree against A three times, in lines 2 (twice) and 3-6, and A and C agree against D three times, in lines 1 (twice) and 7, but A and D agree against C only once, in line 7. The rule leaves it up to us to decide how small the number of the latter agreements must be in proportion to the others to qualify as "almost never" occurring. This freedom is the equivalent of the Lachmannian's freedom to ignore some variations. If we decided that C was an intermediary, we should then set up a partial tree accordingly. Some of the possibilities are:

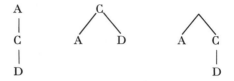

Considering the eyeskips in A (line 2) and in C and D (lines 3-6), we should choose the last of these. Taking then the triad A, B, C, we should find all three terminal and set up another partial tree. Some of the possibilities here are:

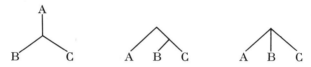

Considering the eyeskips, the annotation in B (line 1), and the principle of parsimony, which outlaws unnecessary ancestors, we should choose the last of these also. Putting the two partial trees together we should have:

In some situations, Greg's method gives the same results as Quentin's without requiring that the states be analyzed in threes. The principle of parsimony, when applied to extant states of a text, means accepting as intermediary any that are not necessarily terminal. This acceptance gives the same effect as Quentin's rule when two states never (not "almost never") agree against a third. In our example, if C did not stand alone against all the other states in having "renommée" in line 7, so that no type-1 variation made C and the true group ABD terminal, Greg's method would give the last tree above.

On the other hand, Greg never devised a method for analyzing complex variations, whereas Quentin, by taking the states three at a time, and so never dealing with a whole variation, could treat all alike. It is rather fitting, therefore, that I was studying Quentin's method in his

Mémoire sur l'Établissement du Texte de la Vulgate (1922) when I discovered a principle that allows us, without taking the texts in threes, to determine not only when groups in complex variations are terminal but also when groups not actually appearing in any variation are terminal. If the lines of descent for each variant in a variation must be entirely separate, as we have said, then the members of a group in any variation exclude all the other extant states and any unrecorded states intermediary between them from being intermediary between any members of the group. As the term "intermediary" is used here and hereafter in this book, an ancestor is intermediary between its immediate descendants. In the trees above, for example, the immediate ancestor of C and D is intermediary between C and D as well as between them and the archetype. I named my discovery the principle of exclusion.

At about the same time that I discovered the principle of exclusion, I also became aware that the genealogy of the states of a text was distinct from and not necessarily even parallel to the genealogy of its records. To the determination of the first kind of genealogy I gave the name "textual analysis." The genealogy of records I assigned to the separate province of bibliography. No doubt I was led to this second discovery by reading discussions of whether the dates of manuscripts should be considered in drawing up their genealogies.

When Isaac Newton was asked how he had discovered the law of gravity, he replied, "By incessantly thinking about it." Many years of incessant thought have intervened between my discoveries and my present understanding of their application. In the interval I have sometimes reached wrong conclusions and sometimes wrongly thought that reasoning was at an end, but I have been rescued again and again by better insights, graciously given and gratefully received.

The principle of exclusion explains why the groups in simple variations are always terminal. As there are only two groups in these variations, the groups are mutually exclusive. In a type-1 variation, the single state cannot be intermediary between the states in the true group, and since there are no other extant states, the single state is perforce terminal. In a type-2 variation, the states in each group exclude those in the other and any inferential states intermediary between them, and as there are no other extant states each group is perforce terminal. The principle also explains why, given the complex and type-2 variations in our example, B and D would have to be recognized as terminal even if neither stood alone in a type-1 variation. B, for instance, cannot be intermediary between A and C or between C and D. The full set of these rules will appear later.

At first I thought it sufficient to sketch out the rules without a calculus for applying them, but in due course I discovered that I could not apply them satisfactorily myself without one. Greg's calculus, however, I felt was incapable of extension from simple to complex variations. In the end, I worked out not one calculus but three, a method with pencil and paper for simple problems, a method with key sorting and an abacus for more complex problems, and a pair of computer programs for problems of any complexity whatsoever.

One cannot work long with computers before discovering that satisfactory results remain problematical until a program rests on sound theory. I therefore set to work on the axiom system of textual analysis, and was able to show that genealogical reasoning is impossible on any but a limited set of principles, most of which I have mentioned already without calling special attention to them. One can use the calculi, however, without understanding the axioms on which they rest, and he will probably grasp the axioms more easily after some experience with one of the calculi, so I have put off for some pages coming to grips with the formal theory of textual analysis.

We need not, however, and in fact must not, put off further discussion of the distinction between textual analysis and bibliography. That the states of a text and their records have different genealogies is obvious from the facts that one record may transmit more than one state of a text and that the same state of a text may be transmitted by different records. More than one state of a text occurs in the same record when it is corrected in such a way that the corrections do not obliterate what they replace. Sometimes, too, the same record preserves two or more states of a text completely separately, either because they have different purposes (e.g., one state for reading, one in score for singing), or for comparison (e.g., a parallel text edition), or by accident (e.g., the same poem appearing twice in an anthology).[6] Different records transmit the same state of a text when they are produced by a mechanically perfect reproductive process, such as Xerox copying, and whenever it is deemed vital to preserve the text without change, as in statute books,

---

[6] States for reading and singing occur, e.g., in John Dryden, *An Ode, on the Death of Mr. Henry Purcell* (London, 1696). Dryden's epilogue beginning "Oft has our Poet wisht" appears twice in *Miscellany Poems* (London, 1684), on S7, and T2.

state documents such as the Constitution of the United States, religious documents such as the Book of Common Prayer, and careful scholarly reprints of all sorts. The many identical copies produced by printing from the same setting of type, however, provided they are uniformly bound and readied for sale as a single lot, are usually counted as one record.

These facts are obvious to all, yet textual critics have in the past almost always confused the two genealogies when they did not devote their attention exclusively to the genealogy of records. It is, in fact, extremely difficult to free oneself from the bibliographical spell once one has fallen under it. I have myself only gradually recognized how fundamental and important it is to exclude bibliographical thinking from textual analysis.

It is most important of all in dealing with textual states that are commonly said to be conflated or contaminated, that is, to have more than one independent ancestor. Greg identified the evidence for conflation as a mutual exchange of members between groups in different variations. For instance, if the groups in a type-2 variation are AB and CD, as in lines 3-6 of our example, and the groups in another type-2 variation are AC and BD, the groups in the second variation have mutually exchanged members with respect to the groups in the first (it does not matter whether we think of B and C or of A and D as exchanged). Such an exchange, if accepted, indicates a tree with a "ring" in it, such as:

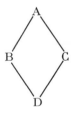

The same kind of exchange occurs between complex variations as between simple, and between simple and complex, and where complex variations are in question the ring may involve more than two variations. On the other hand, no variation with fewer than two true groups can be part of such an exchange, for a group with only one member has nothing to exchange.

Both Lachmann's and Quentin's rules break down when exhanges of this kind occur. Greg precisely identified but made no attempt to solve the problem. Yet it occurs all the time, and it is one reason that the eclectic method, which never has to deal with it, has maintained itself so easily. The phrasing of Lachmann's and Quentin's rules is designed to let the textual critic ignore some of the agreements in such exchanges on the grounds that they have occurred by chance or through emendation, but this does not solve the problem in enough cases to mean much. What is worse, both rules allow the critic to see evidence for conflation in variations with fewer than two true groups, thus compounding the problem instead of simplifying it. In fact, as we shall see, no method can be devised to determine the genealogy of the records or states of a text if some of them may have more than one immediate ancestor and all ancestries are to be accounted for.

It is possible, as we shall see, to treat a conflated record as having a prime ancestor and to build a tree reflective of the prime ancestries by the usual rules, but this approach is to deal with conflation as if it did not exist. On this basis, a textual tree becomes not a representation of a real state of affairs but a mathematical model of reality, the most parsimonious explanation of how a series of events might have occurred. Yet as I completed the axiom system for textual analysis I could see nothing more as possible.

Then one night as I lay in bed reading my eye fell on a new statement of a proposition long familiar to us all, namely, that the motions of the sun and earth are the same, no matter which we say is revolving about the other, our choice in the matter being only between simpler and more complex equations. The parallel with textual criticism struck me at once. I saw that the actions of copyists are the same, whether or not we choose to call the results conflation, and that the choice between the two points of view is even more definite than in celestial mechanics, for it lies not between simpler and more complex equations but between, so to speak, equations—simple enough, fortunately—and no equations at all, a mere wandering in error's wood.

I was then led to consider whether one view of conflation might be true in the sense that the heliocentric theory is true. As I pondered the matter, it came to me that this was a special case of the general question: Is a copyist manufacturing a record or is he recording a state of a text? And after further thought I realized that for textual analysis to accept the copyist as a manufacturer of records is, like the geocentric theory, in a real sense fundamentally wrong. If we are to derive the genealogy of the states of a text, we must view copyists as producing states of this text. The distinction between the genealogy of the states of a text and the genealogy of its records is absolute.

Mentally observe, if you will, a scribe at work copying a manuscript. From time to time he becomes dissatisfied with what he reads and consults another manuscript, from which he copies if what he finds there satisfies him better. Those are his actions. What is he "really doing"? Making one manuscript out of two others, has been the standard answer. He is producing a conflated manuscript. Would the scribe agree, if asked? Not at all. He would say, I am recording a message, and when I find that the message has reached me imperfectly I look for a better record of it. I am not making up a third state of this message out of two others, I am trying to record a state of this message which neither of my sources has transmitted perfectly to me. If I am successful, my manuscript will transmit the archetypal state of the message. If I fail, then if all my errors are my own I shall have produced a completely independent descendant of that archetype. Or it may be that I shall not remove all the errors in one of my sources; in that event, I shall at least have produced a state of my text intermediary between the archetypal state and the state in my source. Otherwise I shall have produced a state of the message more or less related to that transmitted by one of my sources, or if equally like both then relatable to either without prejudice, having some of the errors in that source, some of the archetypal readings not in that source, and some errors not in that source. Whatever my success, however, I have not manufactured one state of the message out of two others. To say so would be to confuse means with ends.

In short, from the point of view of one who deals with states of a message instead of with its records, and the textual analyst is such a one, conflation does not exist at all. He does not treat conflation *as if* it did not exist, any more than a heliocentrist treats the sun *as if* it did not revolve around the earth.

The light of truth blinded Saint Paul. New insights are not always easy to understand, much less to accept when understood. The reader, then, may well still have objections. The scribe we have just imagined followed now one of his manuscripts, now another. (Strictly, this procedure is contamination.) Imagine now a scholar who has before him two more or less parallel accounts of the history of his people, upon each of which he sets a very high value. Where the accounts run parallel, he copies one or the other; where they do not he copies first one and then the other. (This last procedure is conflation in the strict sense.) Surely he is compiling one history out of two?

The answer to the question is no, but a textual critic may have to be born again before he will understand it, especially if he is a worshiper of the two-personed god Graf-Wellhausen and sees in our scholar his "R^{JE}."[7] Be that as it may, our scholar is compiling one history out of two only from the bibliographical point of view. To say that he is compiling a history rather than producing a manuscript is not to take a textual view of his activities.

From the textual point of view, our scholar is attempting to transmit the archetypal history of his people by including every detail in the manuscripts before him, even at the risk of including mistaken information. Should his method succeed, he will have reproduced the archetypal state of his text. Note carefully that we must not suppose that he will automatically fail. We have no more information about the archetypal state than he. His work may appear from the literary or historical point of view redundant, inconsistent, and even self-contradictory, but so may the archetype have been, and the manuscripts before him may be efforts by different copyists to produce a more artistically pleasing narrative. And if he fails to reproduce the archetypal state of his text, he fails in one of the same ways as the scribe we imagined before: he produces an independent descendant of the archetypal state, or a state intermediary between the archetypal state and one of his sources, or a state more or less related to one of his sources. Like the scribe, he can never manufacture one state of the history out of two others. Once again to say otherwise would be to confuse means with ends.

The less experienced textual critic is more likely to understand this textual point of view than the more experienced, because he has less to unlearn, even though the other ought to see more clearly how this new understanding lightens and brightens his tasks. The more experienced critic must unlearn the doctrine of conflated readings. A conflated reading is one supposed to have resulted from miscopying first one manuscript and then another, or, to put the best possible light upon it, from harmonizing the two. As we shall see, these two-headed monsters do not exist. Besides that, one must decide that conflation exists before

---

[7] For the Graf-Wellhausen theory, see any treatment of the text of the Book of Genesis.

he can think he has discovered a conflated reading, so that they could not be cited as evidence for conflation even if they did exist. But suppose I decide to harmonize two manuscripts? Do I not know what I am doing? You know your actions, but you interpret them for yourself. Would a bibliographer be bound to accept our scribe's interpretation of what he was doing when copying from two manuscripts? Not at all.[8]

Finally, the bibliographer, seeking to relate means (transmitters) genealogically, can never fully answer the antinomian objection that he may be wrong by rule. A record whose immediate independent descendants do not record different states of its text can vanish without a trace. Agreements can result from normal copying, from conflation, from emendation, from independent errors (as for instance making the same eyeskip twice), or just by accident. Who is to say what combination of circumstances produced the agreements or failed to produce the differences the bibliographer analyzes? What check is there on his estimate of the most probable circumstances? The best reply he can make is that his procedure is rational and that the objection is fundamentally antirational and subversive of good order. Science itself can make no better reply.[9] But the textual analyst, relating effects (messages) genealogically, is not subject to the antinomian objection, neither indeed can be. He is describing not what was but what is and therefore what all can agree upon. He cannot be wrong by rule.

---

[8] After this book was in type I found the following remarks by William T. Powers: "Behavior . . . is not something self-evident. . . . The point of view of the observer defines the behavior he sees . . . and he must find an objective way to discover the *right* point of view—namely, that of the behaving system [e.g., scribe]. The observer must try to find out which of the infinity of potential controlled quantities [e.g., message, transmitter] is the one that the behaving system is actually sensing and controlling. Only when the controlled quantity has been correctly identified can the observer see that the system's outputs are always such as to counter the effects which environmental disturbances [e.g., imperfect transmitters] would otherwise have on the controlled quantity [e.g., the message to be transmitted]" (*Science*, CLXXXI [1973], 1116-1118). I am willing to admit the validity of bibliographical interpretation within its own sphere, that is, as long as it is not asserted as a statement of scribal purpose or as the only statement of the result of scribal behavior.

[9] "The public must learn that scientific findings are always tentative and may prove erroneous or obsolescent, but that their tentative guide is more valid and safe than any other approach to the world" (Amitai Etzioni, "Understanding of Science," *Science*, CLXXVII [1972], 391).

"Awake, awake," cries the textual analyst to his fellow textual critics; "lead thy captivity captive." There is a real sense in which conflation does not exist, a way never to be wrong by rule. In Milton's words, "Methinks I see in my mind a noble and puissant [discipline] rousing herself like a strong man after sleep, and shaking her invincible locks: methinks I see her as an eagle mewing her mighty youth, and kindling her undazzled eyes at the full midday beam, purging and unscaling her long abused sight at the fountain itself of heavenly radiance."

II

Algorithms and a Calculus

The solution of a textual problem by textual analysis has seven steps, two of which are preliminary to textual analysis itself and one subsequent. The first step is deciding on the states to analyze. The second step is deciding on the variations to analyze. The third step, which is the first in textual analysis proper, is rewriting any variations that would introduce rings into the tree. The fourth step is finding any terminal groups not in the simple variations. The fifth step is connecting the terminal groups: it produces a "preliminary diagram." The sixth step, the last in textual analysis proper, is locating the archetype: it produces the "final diagram" or tree. The seventh step is emending the archetype.

1. DECIDING ON THE STATES

In order to be recognized as states of the same text, states must be more alike than different. Thus historians of literature distinguish between Shakespeare's *Hamlet* or *Macbeth* as altered by Davenant, and the Davenant-Dryden *Tempest*, which is no longer Shakespeare's even though it preserves some of Shakespeare's wording. There is no standard way of measuring the difference between states. The most convenient and therefore the normal level of likeness and unlikeness in literary texts is the word as conventionally written. For example, "inform" and "conform" are normally treated as wholly different, in spite of the fact that the last five letters in each are the same. But a textual critic may wish to include as one text an original with its translations, a source with the works deriving from it, several analogues or examples of a literary type, and so on, and then his concern is with literary characteristics that are to a lesser or greater degree mental abstractions or impressions that may be stimulated by various strings of words. Some of these abstractions are what folklorists call *motifs*, and the term may conveniently be employed generally. Motifs are most easily examined for likeness and unlikeness if they are translated or "mapped" into standard expressions, in which case word-for-word comparison once more becomes the normal level for analysis. In mapping we may phrase all but one of the states in the wording of that one, but if all states are very different an artificial phrasing may be more satisfactory. Both procedures are illustrated in a large-scale example later. Here is a smaller example, with the states in different languages and with one in verse and one in prose:[1]

> In sterculino pullus gallinacius
> dum quaerit escam margaritam repperit.
> "Iaces indigno quanta res" inquit "loco!
> hoc si quis pretii cupidus vidisset tui,
> olim redisses ad splendorem pristinum.
> ego quod te inveni, potior cui multo est cibus,
> nec tibi prodesse nec mihi quicquam potest."

> As a cock was turning up a dunghill, he espied a diamond: Well (says he) this sparkling foolery now to a lapidary would have been the making of him; but for any use of mine, a barley corn had been worth forty on 't.

At first the states are much alike, and either can be rephrased in terms of the other. That is not the same thing, however, as translating one into the language of the other. Rather, it involves deciding where the phraseology of the two is essentially synonymous. It is easy enough to see that *margaritam*, "pearl," is not synonymous with "diamond," perhaps harder to decide that *pullus gallinacius*, "young cock," is not synonymous with "cock," and still harder to decide that *repperit*, "discovers," is not synonymous with "espied." In the last instance, the difference in tense is not significant because the languages are different and it is clear that the present tense in the Latin is doing duty for the

---

[1] The first state given here of this Aesopic fable is Phaedrus, Book III, Fable 12, Ben Edwin Perry's text in the Loeb Library edition of Babrius and Phaedrus, but omitting the title and epimythium; the other state is Sir Roger l'Estrange's *Aesop*, Samuel Johnson's text in his Dictionary, s.v. "lapidary."

past, just as in the English with "says he" later on. The rest of the Latin—"while he seeks food on a dunghill"—and the English may be accepted as synonymous, each making explicit an aspect of the action that the other only implies. We can, then, render the English of the first sentence in terms of the Latin as follows: In sterculino mas gallinacius dum quaerit escam adamantem videt.

The next sentence in the Latin—"You lie in an unworthy place," says he, "[for] such a thing !"—has no parallel at first in the English, but we can say that there is no essential difference between "such a thing" and "this sparkling foolery," the English merely making explicit the implication of the Latin. We can ignore the English "Well" and "now" as colloquialisms of no essential meaning at all.

The third sentence in the Latin—"If anyone desiring your price had seen this, you had long since been restored to your pristine splendor"—has a more remote parallel in the English, but we can see that both concern the great price that a polisher of gems would receive. We can still phrase the English in terms of the Latin, but we might decide rather to rephrase both. The fact that "margarita" and "adamans" have different genders in the Latin allows us conveniently to introduce some difference into the motifs, in place of the subtler differences that vanish when we reduce the states to their lowest common denominators:

[Latin:]   Hac politor gemmarum magnum pretium recipisset.
[English:] Hoc politor gemmarum magnum pretium recipisset.

The fourth sentence in the Latin—"That I, to whom food is of much greater interest, have found you, can be of no advantage to you or to me"—has again a parallel in the English which is phrased quite differently, so that both could be rephrased as motifs. Obviously there is a degree of freedom in rephrasing states of a text which is not possible when working with the states themselves, and therefore not really desirable, but it may be possible to obtain a reasonable consensus by submitting one's work to referees.

A bibliographer may say that to belong to the same genealogy records must have been brought into existence in the same way. Thus, if B has been copied from A, and D from C, but C was written out from memory, he may say that A and B have one genealogy and C and D another. The textual analyst, however, treats indifferently a memorized message, a voice recording, a manuscript, or any other type of record in any combination.

A different problem in delimiting a text is posed most often by titles and other superscriptions and subscriptions. Less often there may be a question of how much of a state besides any superscription or subscription belongs to a text, as when Sir Henry Wotton's "The Character of a Happie Life" in Harl. MS 6057 in the British Museum is run in without title or a break of any kind after another poem. Subscriptions and superscriptions do seem to lead a life of their own, presumably because the information they contain is easily remembered and so may have a different genealogy from the rest of the work. In the past, textual critics have tended to treat them separately if at all, but there is no absolutely compelling reason to do so. Treating them as part of the text may introduce problems with rings which would otherwise be avoided, but we now have a well-defined and effective method of dealing with rings.

One text may include another. The Lord's Prayer, for example, existed before it was recorded in Matthew and Luke (in variant states), and is to be found in other works as well, while still maintaining a separate existence. Extracts, too, may have genealogies independent of the works from which they are extracted. It may, however, seem better to treat an extract with the same passage in the whole work, as though the passage were not included in the work, for a copyist may attempt to improve the transmission of an extract by consulting a record of the whole work or to improve the transmission of the whole work by consulting a record of the extract, in which case treating the two genealogies as one may be the most convenient way of showing their relationship. The alternate possibility of treating the extract as a fragmentary state of a whole work makes for more complex variations, as we shall see, and these are harder to work with than simple variations. A quote may be treated like an extract.

The worker with printed books has an extra task in identifying his states. Completely different settings of type may be hidden away among copies that reputedly or seemingly are duplicates.

Sometimes a textual critic deliberately deals with only some of the states of a text, most obviously in editions of modern works, where reprints that do not show revisions by the author are often ignored. With manuscripts the tendency is to take only the final corrected state in each record. British scholars have not taken much account of manuscripts unless the author never saw his work in print, but American scholars have commonly treated any disregard of the manuscript evidence as a silent invitation to supplement or supersede a previous analysis.

The enormous mass of biblical texts makes it reasonable to investigate only a "family" of manuscripts, that is, a selection sharing distinctive characteristics. Biblical scholars also deal sometimes with only a part, say a chapter, of a text. Again, these limitations result from the mass of manuscripts to be considered and are adopted with an awareness of the dangers. An increase in the parts or states analyzed may have the same effect as finding a new state: rings unrecognized before may upset the previous analysis. That is to say, no analysis based upon selected parts or states is guaranteed to be as satisfactory as analysis of them all. The advent of the computer has made it unnecessary to deal with small selections and also reduced the labor if the work must be done again. But even when the states are few, not every textual critic makes an exhaustive search for them.

I leave until the chapter on textual editing an explanation of how to search for states of a text and how to choose sigla for them. For the present, we shall continue to use the letters of the roman alphabet as sigla for the states of the texts used as examples.

2. Deciding on the variations

As we shall see in a moment, variations may be context-defined or agreement-defined, or partly context-defined and partly agreement-defined. Insofar as a variation is context-defined, its variants are alternates. A simple variation can then be classified as a substitution, add-omission,[2] or transposition. A complex variation may be any combination of substitution, add-omission, and transposition. Insofar as a variation is agreement-defined, however, the variants are not alternates and so are neither substitutions, add-omissions, nor transpositions. Variations may have smaller variations nested within them, they may overlap, they may occur in sequence, without intervening context, and we may have a choice of contexts. There appear to be no other factors affecting the forms of variations, but the appearance may be deceptive. If a variation is discovered with a different form than those illustrated below, its form should be analyzed in the light of two principles that underlie the following discussion. The first principle is that

---

[2] This most useful term was introduced into textual criticism by Archibald A. Hill, "Some Postulates for Distributional Study of Texts," *Studies in Bibliography,* III (1950-51), 63-95.

variations should be held to as few variants as possible, even if this means increasing the number of variations recognized. The second principle is that only context or agreement or both define the form of a variation; the possible cause of a variation or the possible synonymity of its variants does not define its form.

Let us suppose we have four states of a text, with variants as follows:

urbium oppressione infinita auri et argenti copia ditatus est.

infinita] A; infinitaque B; et infinita C; infinita et D.

Taking the variants in pairs, for the moment, *infinita | infinitaque* is a substitution, *infinita | et infinita* is an add-omission, and *et infinita | infinita et* is a transposition.

We should note first that when the variants are in the same language, we work with the words as commonly written, even though the variants are synonyms, as in *infinitaque | et infinita*.

Next, we should note that the pair *infinitaque | et infinita* taken by itself is not both a substitution and an add-omission. The pair *infinita | et infinita* taken by itself is an add-omission because "infinita" is part of the context, that is, it is invariant in A and C with respect to each other. On the other hand, the pair *infinitaque | et infinita* taken by itself does not include any invariant part of the text in B and C with respect to each other; it is therefore a substitution only.

What is the context when we take the first three variants together, *infinita | infinitaque | et infinita*? Clearly "infinita" is not part of the resulting context, which must be invariant in A, B, and C with respect to each other. We have, then, a variation A:B:C defined by the context in the three states. The context makes each variant an alternate of each of the others.

But just as clearly, A and C both have "infinita," even if there is no alternate to it in B because there is no defining context. We have, then, an agreement-defined variation AC:B within the context-defined variation A:B:C.

We can see more clearly that B has no alternate to "infinita" when we take all four variants together, as we must, since all exist. We have, then, a context-defined variation A:B:C:D, with the same context as before, and within it two agreement-defined variations, ACD:B, because A, C, and D have "infinita," and A:B:CD, because C and D have "et." A and B do not have "et," but they do not agree in any alternate to "et," because there is no defining context.

Sequences may also result in agreement-defined variations. Suppose we have three states of a text, with variants as follows:

Mais de ço vus afi ma fei
Que unc ne li fist plus qu'a mei.

unc ne li fist] A; unc li fist ne B; ne li fist unc C.

Here we have a context-defined variation A:B:C, and within it an agreement-defined variation AC:B, because A and C have "ne li fist." It might seem that A and B have "Que unc," but we ought not to confuse variation with context.

The foregoing is also an example of overlapping transpositions, which, we see, make a single larger variation. Substitutions of more than one word may similarly overlap, and with the same result, a larger variation. It follows that an overlap of a transposition and a substitution will also have the same effect. Overlaps of add-omissions with themselves or with transpositions or substitutions, however, have a different effect, which is discussed below.

If some of the variants in a complex variation include alternates when their states are taken separately, then any agreement in other variants with any of the alternates may be accepted as alternates. Suppose we have three states of a text, with variants as follows:

þerof we mowe wel y-wyte
þaȝ þer be nauȝt of hyt y-wryte.

þer be] A; be þer B; þer he C.

Here we have a context-defined variation A:B:C and within it a variation AB:C that is partly context-defined, because "be" and "he" are alternates in A and C taken separately, and partly agreement-defined, because both A and B have "be." With three variants, nothing would be changed by viewing the variation AB:C as agreement-defined only, but with more than three variants, recognizing agreements with alternates as also alternates can reduce the groups in the variations and the number of variations. Variants that have no agreements with alternates are grouped as they are grouped in the larger variation.

When variations are wholly agreement-defined, so that their variants are not alternates, the same word may stand alone in one agreement and in a sequence of words in another agreement, or the same word or words may occur in two different sequences. If, however, two wholly agreement-defined variations within the same context-defined variation divide the states in the same way, we record only one, by analogy with the contexts for context-defined variations within a larger variation, which contexts are not counted every time they agree, and in fact are not separately counted at all, but only as parts of variants making up the larger variation.

The foregoing rules can be applied to all nests of variations, and are particularly useful in analyzing the more complex nests. Simpler nests, however, are sometimes easier to think of in different ways.

When variations are nested, the groups established by the outer variations retain their identity when the inner are written, unless the inner specifically reassemble them because of agreements or divide them further because of differences. If an outer variation has two groups each of which has smaller variations within it, we record each group as a whole when recording the smaller variations in the other.

If the outer variations are large enough, they may be represented in part by dummy variants giving a summary account of the real variants, and these may be separated in the apparatus from the representation of the inner variations. The reader must then remember the nature and extent of the outer variations as he works with the inner.

Suppose we have three states of a text with variants as follows:

δούλους παρακάλει πᾶσαν πίστιν ἐνδεικνυμένους ἀγαθήν.

πᾶσαν πίστιν] A; πᾶσαν B ; om. C.

The use of "*om.*," i.e., "omission," as a dummy variant is a convenience only. C omits words with respect to A, but A adds words with respect to C. Here we have a variation AB:C, because C does not have πᾶσαν πίστιν, and within this variation another, A:B, because B does not have πᾶσαν, to which we add the group C from the outer variation, giving A:B:C. Instead of nested add-omissions, we might equally well see here a context-defined variation A:B:C and within it an agreement-defined variation AB:C because A and B have πᾶσαν. It might then seem that we ought also to have a variation A:BC because B and C do not have πίστιν. But we can only recognize agreements when words occur; we cannot recognize them when words do not occur. Archibald Hill was the first to point out that nothing (i.e., the absence of certain words) cannot be divided.

If in the above example C had supplied the lemma, the apparatus would have read:

παρακάλει] C; + πᾶσαν πίστιν A; + πᾶσαν B.

And if B had supplied the lemma the apparatus would have read:

πᾶσαν] B; + πίστιν A; *om.* C.

From this we see how the nature of the variation will sometimes seem to change according to which variant appears in the lemma. With a little practice, however, we can recognize, no matter how the variation is written, that we have nested add-omissions.

Where a state is too fragmentary to be dealt with conveniently by recognizing a series of add-omissions, we write a dummy variant, say, "*frag.*," for the section where the text is badly broken up. Within the resulting variation, if other variations occur and the fragmentary state includes their contexts we treat the variations as if they were not nested in the larger variation, and if any other variations occur we treat the variations as we would if they were nested in an add-omission.

Nested variations within a transposition are not always easy to distinguish from other kinds of variations. We must first keep in mind that a transposition is in effect two contiguous complementary substitutions. Therefore, if A has "rising up early" and B has "early rising" or "early morning rising," and in general wherever the same variants seem simultaneously to produce a transposition and another transposition, substitution, or add-omission nested within it, we do not have a transposition but a substitution. For a nest, a third variant must differ slightly from one of the first two; for example, *then he said | he said then | he then.* We can easily identify a variation within a transposition as long as the ends of the transposed elements are unaffected, for we have then what is in effect another context-defined variation, even though the context in one variant has been displaced with reference to that in the other. In fact, each variation can then be written as though the other did not exist. Otherwise, an inner substitution or transposition can be identified only if it produces a partly context-defined, partly agreement-defined variation, as already illustrated. Under all other circumstances the inner variations are only agreement-defined, that is, neither substitutions, add-omissions, nor transpositions, again as already illustrated.

Nesting of variations within a substitution always produces agreement-defined variations, although it may sometimes seem more natural to think of it as similar to nesting within an add-omission. Suppose we have four states of a text, with variants as follows:

Meu filho, tu sempre estás comigo; tudo o que é me é teu.

Meu filho, tu sempre estás . . . me] A; Filho meu, tu sempre estás . . . me B; Filho meu, tu estás sempre . . . me C; Meu tempo D.

Here we have a context-defined variation A:B:C:D, within which we have three agreement-defined variations, A:BC:D, because B and C have "Filho meu," AB:C:D, because A and B have "sempre estás," and ABC:D, because A, B, and C have "tu" and "comigo; tudo a que é me." If we wish to, however, we can say that we have a variation ABC:D because D has "Meu tempo" instead of "Meu filho (*or* Filho meu) tu sempre estás (*or* estás sempre) comigo; tudo o que é me." The two transpositions then give us A:BC, to which we add the group D from the outer variation, giving A:BC:D; and AB:C, to which we add D, giving AB:C:D.

When one variant is not so much different as it is shorter than another, it is often more natural to recognize an add-omission. If, in the foregoing example, D had only "Meu" instead of "Meu tempo," we should recognize the overlap of an add-omission with a transposition. Add-omissions retain their individuality when they overlap other variations, so that the effect is the same as if they were contiguous. In the foregoing example as modified, then, we should have a variation A:BC:D for *Filho meu | Meu filho | Meu*, two variations ABC:D, one because A, B, and C have "filho" and one for the add-omission in D, and a variation AB:C for *sempre estás | estás sempre*, to which we should add D, giving AB:C:D. We should treat the overlap of an add-omission with a substitution similarly.

If two add-omissions overlap, each is a separate variation. Let us suppose we have three states of a text with variants as follows:

The rules of architecture are reducible to three or four heads.

three or four] A; four B; three C.

Here we do not have A:B:C. Instead we have AC:B because B omits "three or," and AB:C, because C omits "or four." If the add-omissions are large enough, there may be smaller variations within each. The states omitting these parts of the text then stand alone in the smaller variations, that is, if two states omit overlapping parts of a text, each stands alone in any smaller variation in the part it omits and both stand alone in any smaller variation in the part they both omit. But the part they both omit does not make a variation itself. In the example, the presence of "or" in A does not make a variation A:B:C.

We come now to contiguous variations. Suppose we have three states of a text with variants as follows:

> Und sie kehrten sich um, und weg war gerufen der Richter.

> weg war gerufen] A; weg war gehalten B; war weg gerufen C.

Here we might be tempted by the apparatus to see a context-defined variation A:B:C, in which event we should see within it two agreement-defined variations, AB:C, because A and B have "weg war," and AC:B, because A and C have "gerufen." But in fact we have here a transposition, *weg war | war weg*, followed by a substitution, *gerufen, | gehalten*. There is no need to see a complex variation as well.

In the same way, if A has "dat," B has "wij," and C has "dat wij," we have contiguous add-omissions, of "dat" (AC:B) and of "wij" (A:BC). If A has "hum hadde," B has "jeg hadde," and C has "jeg bekreftet," we have contiguous substitutions, *hum | jeg* (A:BC), and *hadde | bekreftet* (AB:C). Contiguous transpositions may also occur. Care is necessary in reading these variations from an apparatus, because the nature of the variation will seem to change, depending upon which state provides the lemma or lemmas.

Care is necessary, also, in recognizing contiguous add-omissions and substitutions. Suppose we have three states of a text with variations as follows:

> Kjærlighet er der vi finer den når vi søker den.

> finer den] A; finer B; søker den C.

Here we have a substitution, *finer | søker* (AB:C), followed by the add-omission of "den" (AC:B). But if C had "søker" here instead of "søker den," we should have a context-defined variation A:B:C and within it an agreement-defined variation AB:C, because A and B have "finer." What is the reason for the difference? In the first instance "finer" is context for the add-omission in A and B, and "den" is context for the substitution in A and C. In the second instance, however, where C did not have "den," the add-omission and the substitution had the same context. We can only recognize an add-omission next to a substitution, in other words, when each has its own context.

A transposition, on the other hand, preserves the same or essentially the same text in a different order, so that it gives a feeling of context for any contiguous add-omission, no matter which element of the transposition is contiguous to it. Thus, to modify the foregoing example once more, if C had "der finer vi" instead of "der vi søker den," we should have a transposition, *finer vi / vi finer* (AB:C), followed by the add-omission of "den," (A:BC), even though "den" was found only in A.

The examples may be easier to understand in tabular form. We have, then, first a substitution and an add-omission; then a substitution only; and finally a transposition and an add-omission:

finer den	finer den	vi finer den
finer	finer	vi finer
søker den	søker	finer vi

If in the second example D had "søker er" we should still have only a single variation.

So far we have examined variations in which the invariant words on each side (the context) clearly delimit the variants. Sometimes the invariant words appear to be mixed in with the variants. Suppose we have three states of a text with variants as follows:

Formano un dolce suon diverse Chorde.

dolce suon] A; alto suon B; suon le mie C.

This is not a single variation, but two, the first delimited by "un" and "suon" (A:B:C), and the second by "suon" and "diverse" (AB:C).

We are most likely to be misled when we have variants that are synonymous in meaning. Alternate ideas do not make alternate variants. If A has καὶ ᾿Ιησοῦς and B has ᾿Ιησοῦς δέ, the phrases are synonymous, but we do not have a substitution or transposition; ᾿Ιησοῦς is context, and we have two add-omissions. If A has οἱ γὰρ ἑπτά and B has πάντες γάρ, the phrases will be essentially synonymous if the persons or things referred to as οἱ ἑπτά and πάντες are the same, but we do not have a substitution or transposition; γάρ is context, and we have a substitution and an add-omission. If A has ἀρχιερεῖς καὶ γραμματεῖς and B has γραμματεῖς καὶ ἀρχιερεῖς, the sense is essentially the same whichever word comes first, but we do not have a substitution or transposition; καί is context, and we have two substitutions.

Variations where the differences are small act as context within variations where the differences are large. As we have just seen, transpositions are small differences in this sense. Suppose we have three states of a text with variants as follows:

Thar grysly bodeis lynkit mony fald.

bodeis lynkit] A; bodeis lynk thame B; bakis war lynkit C.

Here *lynkit* / *lynk* is a sufficiently small difference to serve as context for the other variations. We have, then, AC:B for the smaller difference, AB:C for *bodeis* / *bakis war*, and AC:B for the add-omission of *thame.*

The rule that small differences may act as context for larger differences does not, however, mean that the small differences always make context. In the first example in the present section, as we have seen, *infinitaque* / *et infinita* is a substitution; it is not an add-omission followed by a substitution.

Breaks in the sense also act as context. If A has, "The girls anointed themselves, they dressed their hair, or looked over their finery, and compared together their trinkets," and B has "they" before "compared" instead of before "dressed," we have two add-omissions, not a transposition, because common breaks in the sense act as context. When both of the apparently transposed elements have breaks, the one with more breaks acts as context.

We are sometimes tempted also to match nouns with nouns, verbs with verbs, and so on, but this is not legitimate. If A has "He said, ' I will go,' " and B has "He said that he would go," we have a substitution, *I will* / *that he would*, we do not have an add-omission followed by two substitutions. Nor, on the other hand, are A and B variants because one has direct discourse and the other indirect, unless this kind of motif is the subject of our investigation.

If the variations are at all complicated, and especially when they are drawn from an apparatus, it is always wise to write them in a column before analyzing them. It is usually helpful also to write the longest variant first, even if it is not the variant used as the lemma. It may then appear that there are alternate ways of expressing some of the variants, one of which ways may be especially useful. For example, suppose A has προσέθετο πέμψαι ἕτερον καὶ προσέθετο πέμψαι, B has ἕτερον καὶ προσέθετο πέμψαι, and C has προσέθετο πέμψαι. When we write the variants in a column we see that there are three ways to think of the variant in C:

$$\text{προσέθετο πέμψαι ἕτερον καὶ προσέθετο πέμψαι}$$
$$\text{ἕτερον καὶ προσέθετο πέμψαι}$$

(1) προσέθετο πέμψαι

(2)   προσέθετο πέμψαι

(3) προσέθετο   πέμψαι

If we accept (1) we have two separate add-omissions; if we accept (2) we have nested add-omissions; and if we accept (3) we have overlapping add-omissions. With only these variants, we might accept (1); but if D has προσέθετο ἕτερον πέμψαι καὶ . . . , it might be easier to accept (2) or (3) because C can then be made a singleton in the resulting variation; and if in addition E has . . . καὶ ἔθετο πέμψαι, it might be easier to accept (3), for the same reason.

If a corrector has altered a record of C to make A, he may have thought of C as (1) or (2) or (3). If two records of C have been altered to A, one may have been altered as if C were (1), the other as if C were (2), and the two alterations may then have been listed separately in an apparatus, one as the omission of ἕτερον . . . πέμψαι, the other as the omission of προσέθετο . . . καὶ. The textual analyst using the apparatus will still treat both A and C in any single convenient way.

Lastly, we may note that it is reasonable to let order establish context. If A has "peace and joy and power" and B has "truth and love," we may take the first "and" in A as context, and so recognize the two substitutions as *peace / truth* and *joy and power / love*.

It should be clear from the foregoing that we need to be careful when making up lists of variations from an apparatus. Even if we have compiled the apparatus ourselves, there will be a temptation to take as one variation what appears as one in the apparatus, when there are in fact two or more at this place, or to take as two variations what appear as two in the apparatus, when there is in fact only one. We need to keep both the apparatus and the full text in mind constantly.

The textual analyst divides his variations into *substantive, quasi-substantive*, and *accidental* and ignores the latter class. A substantive variation is a difference in words, in grammatical forms, and in word order. A quasi-substantive variation is a difference in spelling, punctuation, and so on which affects the sense. Thus capitalization may mark personification, a comma may alter the sense of a word or a sentence ("Next to [Next, to] the sacred temple you are led"), a hyphen or an apostrophe may do the same ("His brows thick fogs, instead of glories, grace [Glories-Grace]," "As oils on water's [waters', waters] flow"), and so on. Accidental variations are those in which the sense is not affected.

Deciding when the sense is affected is not always easy, so that consistency is not easy to attain. It is particularly hard when some scribes have a system of accidentals, say of punctuation or accentuation, and others do not or omit them altogether. Many variations of the quasi-substantive kind will then be ambiguous; within the same variation some differences may be real and others only apparent. The problem may be solved by treating a difference of uncertain significance as a true difference, but the temptation is to ignore the whole variation.

Names raise another difficulty: What is the boundary between variation in spelling and variation in name?

Dialectal variants and translations offer special problems. It would seem to be simpler to treat translations separately from the states in the original language and, if there is more than one version in any one language, to treat each by itself. Each will have its own earliest state, which may be connected to the state of the text in the original language that it most resembles. Of course the scholar must be alert for indications that some states in one translation have been influenced by another translation or by a fresh comparison with the text in the original language. Biblical collations, however, normally include the versions, the more unfamiliar languages sometimes cited in translation, and there seems to be no insuperable objection to analyzing all at once. This gives a hint concerning dialectal variants: if they are regular alternates for the original readings, they are the equivalents of the original readings and so may be ignored by the textual analyst. The following, for example, are the same state:

> An preost wes on leoden,   Laȝamon wes i-hoten
> A prest was in londe,   Laweman was hote

Still other problems arise when word-for-word correspondences are few but not so few as to demand rephrasing of the states in artificially standardized motifs. For example, in the eleven states of Chaucer's *Complaint to his Purse* collated by George B. Pace,[3] the title and the first fourteen lines are wanting in his CC[1], the title is wanting in A, CC[2], Ff, and H[1], and the title varies in the rest as follows:

The complaynt of	Chaucer	to	his		Purse	F
The complaynt off	Chaucers	vn-to	his		purse	M
The compleint of	chaucer	vnto	his	empty	purse	Cx
La Compleint de	chaucer	A	sa	Bourse	Voide	P
A supplicacion						
to Kyng Richard by	chaucier					H[2]
	Chaucer					A[2]

[3] George B. Pace, "The Text of Chaucer's *Purse*," *Studies in Bibliography*, I (1948-1949), 103-121.

Disentangling the variations here requires some thought.

If we treat the title as part of the text, then the omission in CC^1 is a type-1 variation in which CC^1 is the singleton, and the omission of the title alone is a complex variation in which CC^1 is again a singleton:

A CC^2 Ff H^1:A^2 Cx F H^2 M P:CC^1

The first and last groups here will appear as well in all variations within the title. If, on the other hand, we treat the title separately from the text, these groups, and in fact the two preceding variations, will not appear at all.

In what follows we shall treat the title as part of the text. Aside from the omissions, the variants in the next variation are the words to the left of the author's name, "The complaynt of" (including variant spellings and French synonyms), "A supplicacion to Kyng Richard by," and nothing:

A CC^2 Ff H^1:A^2:CC^1:Cx F M P:H^2

The variants in the next variation, again aside from the wholesale omissions, are "Chaucer" and "Chaucers" (understood as a possessive rather than a variant spelling):

A CC^2 Ff H^1:A^2 Cx F H^2 P:CC^1:M

The next variation is the omission of the words to the right of the author's name:

A CC^2 Ff H^1:A^2 H^2:CC^1:Cx F M P

We now have an omission within a second omission within a third and two more variations within that. In the first, the variants in wording are "to," "vnto," and "A," which must stand alone because it might equally well be a translation of either of the first two, and vice versa:

A CC^2 Ff H^1:A^2 H^2:CC^1:Cx M:F:P

In the last variation the variants in wording are "Purse" and "empty purse" (including the French synonyms):

A CC^2 Ff H^1:A^2 H^2:CC^1:Cx P:F M

There are a number of important points here. First, as we have seen, an add-omission results in a simple variation only if it is not wholly within the range of another add-omission and there is no exactly corresponding substitution. Second, again as we have seen, states that omit a passage in which other states vary are treated as varying individually unless they omit exactly the same passage. Unless two states omit exactly the same passage, the fact that other states vary where they both have nothing tells us nothing more about their relationship, and neither does treating them as separate groups in the inner variations.

Third, the French title, which reads "Bourse Voide" instead of "empty Purse," nevertheless gives an exact translation of the phrase, which therefore is counted as agreeing with the English even though the adjective is in a different position in the translation. But the French "A" is ambiguous; it tells us nothing about the relationship of the states, and so we group it by itself. We can deal similarly with abbreviations, including initials in personal names, and, I believe, with the substitution even of pictures for words, and the reverse. Here we have another example of difficulties that may arise with the recovery of additional states of a text. If we did not know of F, we should lump P with Cx and M because "A" and "vnto" are synonyms.

Fourth, and finally, the principle by which we recognize "Bourse Voide" as the equivalent of "empty Purse" allows us to recognize that states with the same words agree even when they have the words in different places. In the case of Wotton's poem, for example, where some states are anonymous, others have his name at the head, and one has his name at the foot, the states with his name form a group.

When working with a list of variants compiled by someone else we sometimes find that the readings in certain states are recorded only sporadically or are omitted by accident. In the former instance we may decide to ignore the states as probably having readings that would cause them to be differently placed in the tree if we knew the readings; in the latter we can treat the states as singletons in the variations from which their readings have been omitted, for in this way we are not implying a special relationship for them. The resulting variations may turn out to be crucial when we come to place the states in the tree, but if we keep a record of the possibly crucial variations we can annotate the tree accordingly.

Fragmentary states can be treated with the rest, but if they are very fragmentary they make many complex variations, which are always harder to work with than simple ones. In that event it may be easier to treat the completer states by themselves first, and then, after the preliminary diagram has been constructed for them, to work with all the states in the passages where the fragmentary states are present, in fitting these states into the diagram.

When word-for-word correspondences occur between works commonly regarded as distinct, it is not satisfactory to limit the analysis to motifs. For example, since the Synoptic Gospels report some of Jesus' sayings and activities in the same or almost the same words, it is not satisfactory to base an analysis of their relationships merely on the order in which the different authors place these sayings and activities. Such works must first be divided into sections, and in the sections where there is word-for-word correspondence variations in wording must be sought for. The motifs also must be divided into levels of abstraction and the appropriate variations looked for at each level. This is not to say that the analysis must be pushed to the highest level of abstraction. It will be quite satisfactory, for example, to examine the biblical records of Jesus' life without regard to the fact that some information occurs in the Gospels, some in Paul's letters, and so on. How to decide where to divide the sections is not a question that can be solved by abstract reasoning, but it seems likely that the places to divide will come at breaks in the sense commonly recognized or likely to be commonly recognized.

A bibliographer should limit his analysis to variations that show the descent of books and manuscripts, and these may include many distinctions that do not convey meaning in the way that words and phrases do; for instance, line-for-line correspondence in prose texts. The more minute or unusual the correspondence between records, the more certain the close physical relationship. A bibliographer is likely to lay particular stress on common errors as evidence. He is also likely to give weight to unusual spellings. On the other hand, mutilations in a manuscript which destroy some of the words are not counted as evidence unless there are corresponding lacunae in other manuscripts. A bibliographer will freely attribute to chance those agreements among his records which cannot or which he feels need not be explained as the result of the copyists' intentions to reproduce their exemplars. If he finds that a copyist feels free to vary from his exemplar, as medieval scribes were prone to do with secular texts, he is much exercised to separate out the evidence he needs and may even speak of his problems as being different from those of other textual critics.

A bibliographer may also delimit variations differently from a textual analyst. For example, he may decide that ἀρχιερεῖς καὶ γραμματεῖς /

γραμματεῖς καὶ ἀρχιερεῖς is a transposition, not two substitutions. But such decisions must be made with caution. A scribe might, indeed, have mentally rearranged the three words in the example before he wrote them down. He might also, however, have written the third word in place of the first, recognized his mistake, and made up the deficiency by writing the first word in place of the third. There is really no way to prove whether the difference or differences resulted from one or three processes, and no way to decide, then, even from the causal point of view, whether the example should be viewed as one variation or two. It will also be clear that a thoroughgoing causal approach will need a special set of rules for identifying context before it can produce as consistent analyses of variations as the rules set forth above.

Nonsense words and illegible words may have bibliographical meaning, but they have no textual meaning. The textual analyst does not simply ignore them, but he may deal with them differently from the bibliographer. Suppose A has *ἴσως*, B has *ἴσως* followed by the nonsense word *οὔγως*, and C has *οὔγως* instead of *ἴσως*. The textual variation is AB:C, because C does not have *ἴσως*. The fact that *οὔγως* occurs in B and C may have significance to the bibliographer, however, in which case he would write two variations, AB:C, because A and B have *ἴσως*, and A:BC, because B and C have *οὔγως*.

Bibliographers and textual analysts necessarily differ in the way they treat the dates of their states or records, for the dates of manuscripts and other records are only the terminal dates, if that, of the states they record. If the purpose of a copyist is to reproduce his exemplar, a successful copyist produces a record that postdates the state of the text it records. If the purpose of an editor is to remove scribal errors from his text, a successful editor produces a state of the text which antedates his exemplar.

Let us suppose that we have three manuscripts, A, B, and C, datable in that order. Let us suppose as well that the only textual variations they record are A:BC and AC:B, and that directional variations show that A is the archetype. As we shall see, the textual analyst must then draw the tree

A
|
C
|
B

The bibliographer cannot, because C did not come into existence until after B. He must draw the tree

What has happened is that the copyist of C has produced a duplicate of the text of the intermediary. As we shall see, the textual analyst's rules forbid him to multiply duplicates. The bibliographer recognizes that the dates of the manuscripts are included in the variations which he must take into account. These variations may be expressed as *before* time[1], *before time*[2], and so on: for example, *before the fifth century, before 1501*. In the present instance, he would write A:BC for *before time*[1] and AB:C for *before time*[2], and this later variation would lead to the construction of his tree by the usual rules.

Now let us suppose that the textual variation A:B:C occurs in our example as well. Then the textual analyst might adopt the bibliographer's variation in the dates of the records. He might reason that in the variation A:B:C the inferential intermediary agreed either with A or B, in either event making C terminal. He would in these terms be justified in so concluding if he thought that circumstances, such as the length of the text, made a duplicate unlikely, for human and mechanical inefficiency in copying is the main cause for variations. But the textual analyst would do better to stick to what is rather than what was, if he is to avoid the uncertainties the bibliographer must live with.

Laboratory methods of dating records are of two kinds. Minute analysis of chemical properties may give direct evidence of age, for certain substances alter with time at known rates. The dating will be approximate, with an approximate range of possible error specified. Other chemical or microscopic analysis of ink or paper may identify products whose dates of manufacture and general use are known from other sources.

More often records are dated by extrapolation. Exemplars are collected which may be dated, either because they bear dates themselves or because their origin or early existence is determinable from other sources (any conflicts in the evidence must be resolvable). According to the theory of consistent evolution, these establish an order of development of the material, design, and letter forms used. Therefore undated records that have the same characteristics as dated records are given the same dates. Those having characteristics intermediate between those of dated records are dated between them. Those apparently more primitive or more developed in their characteristics than any dated record are dated earlier or later. Sometimes the theory of constant rate of evolution is also followed. The datings so determined may be only very rough approximations. If they depend, for example, on the script, a range of several centuries may be possible, so little did the professional book hands change for some alphabets. For example, manuscript 017 of the Greek New Testament has been assigned both to the ninth and eleventh centuries.[4]

Occasionally there is clear evidence that conclusions based on evolutionary theories would be incorrect: carbon-14 analysis of the wrappings of the Dead Sea Scrolls showed that the script found in some scrolls is not archaic but archaized. Obviously, too, the conclusions are no truer than the theories. Carbon-14 analysis itself once rested in part on an incorrect theory, namely, that the amount of carbon 14 available for absorption by living things has been constant through time.[5] Thus we see that theories of constant rates of change are not always tenable even in the physical sciences. Consistent evolution seems to obtain in many fields, but historians cling to a pendulum, poets to a cyclical, theory of human behavior.

A refusal to accept straight-line evolution may be seen in Lester A. Beaurline's analysis of Dryden's spelling habits.[6] Having to estimate what these habits were in an interval where we have no autograph documents, Professor Beaurline assumed that they would conform to Dryden's known earlier habits. In this particular instance, enough of Dryden's earlier and later autographs have survived so that it would be possible to examine the evolution of his spelling and apply the

---

[4] Silva Lake, *Family II and the Codex Alexandrinus* (London, 1936), pp. 10-11.

[5] The textual critic who wishes to use carbon-14 dating will find the following useful: *Radiocarbon Variations and Absolute Chronology*, ed. Ingrid V. Olsson (New York, [c1970]); and *Dating Techniques for the Archaeologist*, ed. Henry N. Michael and Elizabeth K. Ralph (Cambridge, Mass., 1971). According to the review in *Science*, CLXXVII (4 August 1972), 419, the latter is complete but needs correction from the former with regard to short-term perturbations established from European medieval samples.

[6] John Dryden, *Four Tragedies*, ed. L. A. Beaurline and Fredson Bowers (Chicago, 1967), p. 32.

results by analogy to the period where documents are lacking. But rejection of the straight-line theory would not establish Beaurline's countertheory, which must always remain an assumption. Why, for instance, should not Dryden's habits in the interval in question conform instead to his known later habits, if straight-line evolution is to be abandoned?

Still other methods of dating depend upon evidences of physical disturbance in one manuscript or book which will explain the condition of another. Such dating will be only relative—earlier, later—but may be all that is needed. This evidence constitutes a type of directional variation and is discussed more fully below. Contrariwise, sometimes the fact that one manuscript is older than another is taken as a directional variant. This is an assumption of last resort, and no historical argument should be based on it.

The bibliographer, as opposed to the textual analyst, can sometimes recognize what are called *potential* intermediaries, though he does not usually trouble to express the evidence for them in the form of variations. A potential intermediary leaves some bibliographical trace of its existence without independent descendants, as for instance when omissions of standard length in a text indicate that a copyist skipped whole lines in his exemplar but no exemplar with this lineation is known. The textual state of a potential intermediary has vanished, however, and other intermediaries may vanish without leaving even a bibliographical trace. This is why textual critics, whether textual analysts or bibliographers, are careful to say that their archetypes are not necessarily the authors' originals; it is not merely that they wish more freedom to emend them.

Textual critics are not always aware, however that the same fact makes it impossible to talk about the habits of a particular scribe when only one of his manuscripts is known. If he has apparently been careful, we are justified in assuming that he was careful, but if he has apparently been careless, he may in fact have carefully copied the work of a careless predecessor or may have been preceded by a succession of average workers. For the same reason we cannot be sure of his linguistic or other preferences. Even his handwriting may have been determined for him by his predecessors. This dismal circumstance denies a constant human tendency to reach across time to a fellow creature whose marks on paper make him seem very close and interesting.

Directional variations require further discussion. The examples in chapter 1 from the graveyard scene in *Hamlet* have already shown us the difference between an ideal directional variation and one superficially the same but not truly directional. The ideal directional variation depends very little on the surrounding context for recognition. The eyeskip in Hamlet's speech is dependent on the context only to the extent that the shorter state strikes a careful reader as slightly ungrammatical and the longer state makes up this deficiency. But it is the add-omission itself that is convincing. The shorter state does not specifically require or even suggest the insertion of "Is this the fine of his Fines and the recouery of his recoueries"; this is why we accept these words as not an attempt at emendation but as belonging to a state of the text from which the shorter state has descended because of a mechanical error.

An example more dependent upon the surrounding context for recognition occurs in Chaucer's *Complaint to his Purse*. Most of the states of the poem say that the sun "of yelownesse had neuer peer." One manuscript, however, has "the lewdnesse" instead of "yelownesse." We can see from the rest of the poem that "yelownesse" is correct; Chaucer says he wants his purse's color to be like the sun; that is, he wants it full of what Huck Finn called "yaller-boys." We can see how "the lewdnesse" could result from "yelownesse" by way of "yelowdnesse," spelled "yelewdnesse," even though no known state preserves the intermediary. We cannot, on the other hand, imagine a scribe who would do more with "the lewednesse" when he found it in his exemplar than perhaps omit the article, for since everyone knows that the sun is yellow no one would miss an explicit statement of the fact, and a scribe of any learning would not at once reject the idea of the sun's wantonness, remembering Apollo and Daphne, and the monsters engendered in the Nilotic mud.

Directional variations become progressively less satisfactory the more difficult it becomes to tell correct variants from incorrect. At the lower end of the scale are those where the choice between variants is purely aesthetic. Bibliographers also find directional variations progressively less satisfactory as the wrong variants more strongly suggest the right ones. From the bibliographical point of view, an emendation is a descendant of a wrong reading, so a wrong reading that looks as if it would have been easy to emend is correspondingly less certain to be a descendant of a correct reading. The textual analyst, however, as we have seen, regards emendation as an attempt to record the archetypal state of a text, so to him successful emendations are archetypal readings.

The following list of possible directional variations has special reference to manuscripts (including typescripts) and printed books, where the variations occur in contexts otherwise identical. Other records will provide additions to or require subtractions from this list because of the different mechanical processes by which they have been produced, and so will variations in contexts only generally parallel in different states or different texts. Whatever critics may have thought at various times, we have not had the foggiest notion of how to recognize directional variations when the variants are motifs. The higher criticism of the Bible, for example, where rules for recognizing directional variations in motifs are much to be desired, displays instead only examples of the logical error *post quod ergo propter quod*, suppositions that ideas will only be elaborated, and so on; but see Appendix C.

Confusion of similar letters. The first examples result from transcription from majuscule to minuscule and the reverse:

ΠΑΡΕΤΗ′ΡΟΥΝ   ἔκφοβοι
γὰρ ἐτήρουν (114, etc.)[7]   ″ΕΜΦΟΒΟΙ (K)[8]

A majuscule *Π* with a defective right leg could be mistaken for a majuscule *Γ*, but a minuscule *γ* would not suggest either the majuscule or a minuscule *π*. The minuscule *κ* was often written in a form closely resembling the minuscule *μ*, but a majuscule *M* would not suggest either the minuscule or a majuscule *K*.

The remaining examples result from peculiarities in the hand or type. The first results from the form of open capital P:

CLAVDVNT
PLAVDVNT (R)[9]

C might be misread as open capital P, but once the closed capital P was written, it would not suggest C. The second example results from long s. It is taken from printed books but the same confusion can result in manuscripts.

savors
favors (Gregory Smith's ed.)[10]

[7] Silva Lake, *op. cit.*, pp. 17-18; Mark 3:2.

[8] Silva Lake, *op. cit.*, p. 26 n. 10; Mark 9:6.

[9] F. W. Hall, *A Companion to Classical Texts* (Oxford, 1913), p. 162; Virgil, *Aeneid*, vi.139.

[10] Donald F. Bond, "The Text of the Spectator," *Studies in Bibliography*, V (1952-1953), 110 n. 2; *Spectator* 262.

Long s is easily misread as f, but once long s has gone out of use f
will not suggest it. Thus a knowledge of paleography and typography
is necessary for determining between random error, which has no directional value, and confusions of this kind.

Misinterpretation of contractions. The first example results from a
common "head-and-tail" contraction:

$$\overline{\iota\varsigma} \; ['I\eta\sigma o\tilde{v}\varsigma]$$
$$\varepsilon i\varsigma \; (346)^{11}$$

The second involves a name and a number:

CL [i.e., Claudius]
centesimo quinquagesimo $(\beta)^{12}$

G. B. Harrison has suggested that "O, Glendower" in *l Henry IV*,
II.iv.373 resulted from a misreading of "O." (i.e., "Owen").[13] It is also
possible for a scribe to suppose a contraction where none exists:

constantissimo
consulibus tantissimo (Vindobonensis)[14]

As before, a knowledge of paleography and typography is necessary
to interpret the evidence.

Confusion of words generally resembling each other. Here again it
must be clear that a real confusion has arisen and not just the chance
substitution of one word for another. A knowledge of paleography and
typography is again required, because confusions possible in one type
face or hand may be impossible in another. If it is impossible or unlikely that the confusion could have occurred in the process of transcribing the copy, the possibility of confusion in an intermediate copy
needs still to be taken into account. Many confusions of this kind have
their source in incorrect division or combination of words (see below),
and some are apparently assisted by similar formations in the neighboring context.

Progress   Scream
Process (8vo ed.)   Stream (8vo ed.)[15]

---

[11] Kirsopp Lake and Silva Lake, *Family 13 (The Ferrar Group)* (London, 1941),
p. 93; Mark 10:18.

[12] Aulus Gellius, *Noctivm Atticarvm*, ed. Carolus Hosius (Lipsiae, 1903), I, x.

[13] *Major British Writers* (New York, [c1954]), I, 215.

[14] Hall, *op. cit.*, p. 169; Livy, iii.35.9.

[15] Bond, *op. cit.*, pp. 123, 112; *Spectator* 267, 376.

Names may appear, disappear, or replace each other for this reason

Lucullorum

iucoliorum (R) [16]

Numbers are also subject to errors of confusion with other numbers (∞, 1,000, and X, 10) and with similar words or parts of words (*iii* seems once to have been mistaken for *vir*; and *OI Λ*, where *Λ* = 30, for *OIΔE*).[17] Confusion of similar sounding words is called *homophony*. In the following example the standard text is apparently in error; the margin and, in many manuscripts, the text itself give the more correct reading, upon which the Greek is based:

לֹא (Qere)

לוֹ (Kethib)[18]

Mistaken combination or separation of words. More specific terms are *fusion* and *fission*. In manuscripts these conditions often result from mistaken interpretation of continuous script:

| εἰν ’Αρίμοις *Iliad* ii.783 | all together |
| Inarime *Aeneid* ix.716[19] | altogether (8vo ed.)[20] |

False punctuation may result in the grouping of words out of their proper context, and sometimes in insertions to patch up the sense:

He grieved the land he freed should be oppressed

He grieved the land, he freed, should be oppressed (1668)[21]

Transposition. Transposition of letters is called *anagrammatism* or *metathesis.* Once again, familiarity with paleography and typography is essential; in type, ligatures prevent transposition of the individual letters of which they are composed, and it seems likely that ligatures would be thought of by the scribe also as compound letters. McKerrow gives as an impossible transposition in type the words "file" and "life" in founts in which the former is made up of three sorts, the latter of four.[22] Of course, both compositors and scribes may conceivably mis-

---

[16] Hall, *op. cit.*, p. 182; Cicero, *Verrine Orations*, 2.*Act.* iv.49.

[17] On the whole subject of numbers see Hall, *op. cit.*, pp. 180-181.

[18] *Biblia Hebraica*, ed. Rud. Kittel, ed. alt. amend. stero. (Lipsiae, 1909), p. 370; I Samuel 2:16.

[19] Hall, *op. cit.*, p. 173.

[20] Bond, *op. cit.*, p. 125; *Spectator* 113.

[21] Dryden, *Annus Mirabilis*, 39.

[22] Ronald B. McKerrow, *An Introduction to Bibliography for Literary Students* [2d imp.] (Oxford, [1928]), p. 257.

read their copy. Hall records that anagrammatism is especially common in the transcription of proper names. Further, he says that although anagrammatism in a name often results from general resemblance, it probably results also from the scribe's failure to pronounce correctly to himself while writing. In verse, scribes sometimes write in prose order; in prose, they sometimes reverse familiar antitheses. Scribes generally prefer to insert omitted words later in the context if the structure of the language and the sense of the passage will allow. It is common also for scribes, finding omitted passages supplied in the margins of their exemplars, to insert them in the wrong places in the copies:

ἄγοντες ἥκομεν   τἀμά δ'οὐκ
ἥκοντες ἄγομεν (R)[23]   τὰ δ' ἀμ' οὐκ (C)[24]

correct Love, and elegant Desires
corrects Love, and elegant Desire (8vo ed.)[25]

A leaf or a multiple of leaves may also be transposed.

Mistranscriptions from one alphabet to another. In the following example the earliest reading has had to be established by retranscription:

ἰχθὺν et ἵππον
ἰχθὺν et ippon
ἰχθὺν καὶ ἵρον (ꓤ)[26]

The reading "Oncaymeon" (i.e., ὂν καὶ μὴ ὄν) in Marlowe's *Dr. Faustus*, i.12, resulted in a similar way; here the original reading was recovered only by emendation.

Retention of once meaningful signs in contexts where they have no place. In the first example the original is restored from a parallel passage; here the marginal notation of an omission (τά) has been inserted in the wrong place, catchword (περὶ) and all:

θεάσασθαι τὸν οὐρανὸν καὶ τὰ περὶ αὐτὸν ἄστρα
θεάσασθαι τὰ περὶ τὸν οὐρανὸν καὶ περὶ αὐτὸν ἄστρα[27]

In the second example a marginal note has (twice) been misunderstood and taken into the text:

---

[23] Hall, *op. cit.*, p. 176; Aristophanes, *Acharnians*, 91.

[24] Hall, *op. cit.*, p. 176; Euripides, *Iphigenia in Aulis*, 396.

[25] Bond, *op. cit.*, p. 125; *Spectator* 224.

[26] Aulus Gellius, *ed. cit.*, I, 94.

[27] Hall, *op. cit.*, p. 179; Iamblichus, *Exhortation to Philosophy*, chap. 9.

q̄ [= quaere] (F)
quae (H)[28]

The last example is from printed books:

fran-/tick
fran-tick (1592C)[29]

Imperfect corrections.

τῶν γε ζώντων
τῶν τε ζώντων (C)
τῶν πεζῶν τῶν (A, G)[30]

genu esset aut talus
genuisset aut talus (B)
genuisset aut sibi aut aliis (F)
genu esset aut tibia aut talus (u)[31]

The confutation of Citizens obiections against Players
The confutation of Citizens against Players (4th ed.)
The coniuration of Citizens against Players (5th ed.)[32]

It is normally necessary to have a chain of at least three readings to determine direction, but even with two readings, if one occurs in a damaged archetype or in a manuscript that clearly indicates a damaged archetype, the necessary conditions will be met. In other words, if the scholar has only a correct and an incorrect reading, he cannot be sure but that the "correct" reading is merely a plausible emendation of the incorrect; but if he has an *imperfect* reading that is not otherwise incorrect, he may conclude that it is earlier than the incorrect reading. Hill refers to the example of the *Dialogues* of Epictetus of which the archetype has a stain on the text; the descendants either leave a blank at this place or run together the context on each side of the stain.[33] Hall's term for imperfect correction is *interpolation*, which in this sense does not necessarily imply insertion.

[28] A. C. Clark, *The Descent of Manuscripts* (Oxford, 1918), p. 35; Nonnius, 107.27 and 114.25.

[29] McKerrow, *op cit.*, p. 196; Nashe, *Pierce Penilesse.*

[30] Hall, *op cit.*, p. 188; Xenophon, *Cyropaedia*, v.5.23.

[31] Hall, *op cit.*, p. 188; Pliny, *Epistles*, i.20.14.

[32] McKerrow, *op. cit.*, p. 198; Nashe, *Pierce Penilesse.*

[33] Hill, *op. cit.*, p. 82.

Failure to repeat. This is called *haplography* and may involve a letter (often when letters are used for numerals), syllable, word, or phrase. The repetition in the following example is a peculiarity of the author:

'Αμὴν ἀμὴν λέγω ὑμῖν
'Αμὴν λέγω ὑμῖν (28)[34]

Omissions resulting from similarities in words or syllables. These are sometimes called *eyeskips*, sometimes *homoeoteleuta* (same ending, so that skips caused by similar beginnings of words are sometimes called *homoeoarchy*); they are called ὁμοιότης (abbreviated ὁμ.) by Clark and *homoeographa* by Postgate. The resemblances causing the skip need not be exact. In the first example, the error was noticed and corrected in the margin of the papyrus:

οἱ ἄνδρες ἐν τῇ νήσῳ ἐπολιορκήθησαν ἀπὸ τῆς
ναυμαχίας μέχρι τῆς ἐν τῇ νήσῳ μάχης
οἱ ἄνδρες ἐν τῇ νήσῳ μάχης (Oxyrhynchus pap. no. 16)[35]

In the second example the correct text is known only from a quotation in Donatus:

qui in hortus fuerit, qui unguenta sumpserit
qui unguenta sumpserit[36]

As we have seen, the context may suggest that an apparent eyeskip is not one in fact. When a scribe or an editor recognizes an eyeskip, he may insert the omitted matter to the left or to the right of its true place, resulting in a transposition. When an apparatus records a transposition, therefore, the content to the left or to the right ought also to be examined for evidence of an eyeskip.

Simple omission. More technical terms are *lipography* and *parablepsia*. Normally these variations are not directional, since it cannot be determined that the fuller reading is not a plausible emendation. But if, as Clark has pointed out, the omission corresponds exactly to a line or group of lines in the manuscript with the fuller state of the text, the fuller state is doubtless earlier; it is unlikely that an emendation or interpolation would exactly fill a line or group of lines in a manuscript, if the lines are written from margin to margin:

---

[34] John 1:52; collation in Lake and Lake, *op. cit.*, p. 148.
[35] Clark, *op. cit.*, p. 1; Thucydides, iv.391.
[36] Clark, *op. cit.*, p. 1; Cicero, *In Behalf of Caelius*, § 27.

. . . qui hac ratione
philosophentur ii nihil habeant quod sequantur. Dictum est omnino
de hac re alio loco . . . (Leid. Voss. 86 [B])
. . . qui hac ratione de hac re alio loco . . . (Flor. Marc. 257)[37]

. . . pos-
sent et ex sese similia sui gignere. Sunt autem qui omnia naturae nomine appel-
lent ut Epicurus . . . (Leid. Voss. 86 [B])
. . . possent ut Epicurus . . . (Flor. Marc. 257)[38]

The second example is not as good as the first, but it gains strength
from the fact that the first occurs in the same pair of manuscripts.
Most of the manuscripts of 1 John in the British Museum (and many
others) omit

ὁ ὁμολογῶν τὸν υἱὸν καὶ τὸν πατέρα ἔχει

from 2:23. In Harl. MS 5557 (manuscript 321 of the New Testament
in the standard numbering), the words occupy exactly one line, as
follows:

ἀϱνού
μενος τὸν υ̅ν̅, οὐδὲ τὸν πϱᾱ ἔχει · ὁ ὁμο
λογῶν τὸν υ̅ν̅, καὶ τον πϱᾱ ἔχει · ὑμεῖς

I am inclined, however, to regard this as a coincidence and to ascribe
the omission, if it is one, to homoeoteleuton. The difficulty here is
that John's style is so repetitious that if one wished to forge a sentence,
he would be very likely to produce the variant in 321 (and many other
manuscripts).

Omissions of standard lengths. Clark has shown that when the text
is written from margin to margin, omissions of the same or nearly the
same number of letters, or of multiplies of the base number, indicate
that whole lines of an ancestor have been omitted. The shorter state
will then be later than the longer, even when neither happens to have
been preserved in the specific ancestor and descendant between which
the loss occurred. Errors running to more than one standard length in
the same manuscript are evidence of the line lengths in a series of ancestors. Since individual lines will often vary from the standard, the
latter will be more readily calculable from errors of several lines in
length. Sometimes the omission will be exactly one line in the manu-

---

[37] Clark, *op. cit.*, p. 8; Cicero, *De Natura Deorum*, i.12.
[38] Clark, *op. cit.*, p. 8; Cicero, *De Natura Deorum*, ii.81.

script under observation, indicating that the manuscript has been copied line for line from its ancestor. Examples are necessarily too lengthy for reproduction here; Clark provides a large number, mostly from classical Latin texts.[39]

Note, however, that scribes copying line for line often saved themselves trouble when working from manuscripts in two columns by copying the first line of the second column on a page before copying the second line of the first column. A succession of copies might thus be made with exactly the same lineation, so that here the bibliographer cannot always be sure he has identified an immediate and not a more remote ancestor. And various possibilities may disturb the calculations. An ancestor written not in standard lines but in sense units will obviate any numerical relation among additions and omissions of lines or multiples of lines in its descendants. Only when there is evidence in the descendant of a correction of the lineation is there a clue. Indentation for paragraphs in the ancestor will produce occasional short lines which, if they fall within omissions or accidental repetitions in the descendants, will upset the usual numerical correspondences. Since the scholar normally must estimate on the basis of the uncorrupted text and with assumptions as to abbreviations and spelling, his calculations will be thrown off by passages in the ancestor which are already corrupt or corrected by insertion or where his assumptions do not hold. A passage in the ancestor which is interrupted by flaws in the parchment will have the same effect. Sometimes the scribe of the ancestor will have expanded or contracted his script; sometimes several scribes with varying hands will have worked on the same manuscript; sometimes quaternions will have been formed from a different number of leaves; sometimes one of the columns on a page (normally the left one) will have been wider than the other or others. Similar irregularities occur when the manuscripts are scrolls instead of codices.

Repetition from neighboring contexts. Repetition from the immediate context (*dittography*) is usually either obviously wrong and easily correctible or not certainly wrong and so not satisfactory directional evidence. It may occasionally happen, however, that a dittography, although not obviously wrong, is sufficiently uncharacteristic of the writer, or is obviously wrong but suggests no easy emendation. The first two examples are of this kind:

---

[39] Clark, *op. cit.*, pp. 1-48.

> Ἀμὴν λέγω ὑμῖν
> Ἀμὴν ἀμὴν λέγω ὑμῖν (106, 579)[40]

iussu eius Romam
iussueiussuromam (Vind. lat. 15)[41]

The next example, although apparently easy of correction, was not in fact corrected until the editions were collated by Bond:

> to bound his Existence
> to bound to his Existence (8vo ed.)[42]

When the repetition occurs after a longer interval, it may displace some other part of the text. Hall notes that when the scribe's eye travels forward, the repetitions are likely to be shorter than when it travels backward. The repetition need not be exact.

Some were dazzling, like the sun,
Shining down at summer noon.

Some were dazzling like the sun,
Some shining down at summer noon. (*Poet. Wks.*, ed. Shorter)[43]

Insertions from the margin.

uetus est tutela draconis
non potuit legi uetus est tutela draconis (Neapolitanus 268)[44]

Insertions of variant readings, glosses, and explanations of the construction are often called *adscripts*; these often replace the original reading. Before a variation can be identified as a gloss, Hall warns, it must be ascertained that one of the alternates invites annotation and that both are in the same construction. Obviously the easier alternative is the gloss. In the first example the original is restored from Harpocration:

> πρὸς τὸν λίθον ἄγοντες καὶ ἐξορκίζοντες
> πρὸς τὸν βωμὸν ἄγοντες καὶ ἐξορκίζοντες[45]

The swalow mordrer of the foules smale
The swalow mordrer of the flyes smale (R)[46]

---

[40] Mark 3:28; collation in *Nouum Testamentum Graece Secundum Textum West-cotto-Hortianum: Euangelium Secundum Marcum*, ed. S. C. E. Legg (Oxford, 1935).

[41] Hall, *op. cit.*, p. 192; Livy, xlii.17.8.

[42] Bond, *op. cit.*, p. 125; *Spectator* 210.

[43] Emily Bronte, "Through the Hours of Yesternight," from Hall, *op. cit.*, p. 193.

[44] Hall, *op. cit.*, p. 194; Propertius, iv.8.3.

[45] Hall, *op. cit.*, p. 196; Demosthenes, *Conon*, § 26.

[46] Chaucer, *Parlement of Fowles*, 353, from Hall, *op. cit.*, pp. 196-197.

Additions or substitutions from similar writings. In the first example one of the Gospels (Matt. 24:29) has influenced the transcription of another—but only if Matthew as a whole derives from Mark:

καὶ οἱ ἀστέρες τοῦ οὐρανοῦ ἔσονται ἐκπίπτοντες
καὶ οἱ ἀστέρες πεσοῦνται ἐκ τοῦ οὐρανοῦ (389, 565, 700)[47]

In the second example the scribe has remembered the passage alluded to (Cowley's *Davideis,* I, 79) and has substituted quotation for allusion:

Where their vast courts the mother-strumpets keep
Where their vast courts the mother waters keep (H)[48]

The influencing passage must be archetypal in its text; otherwise it may be either influencing or influenced. See also Appendix C.

Miscellaneous bibliographical evidence. If two manuscripts correspond page for page but one has fragmentary last lines, runovers from the last lines in the lower margin, or expansion or contraction of the script, that one is the later. The Bodleian manuscript of Primasius on the Apocalypse has short lines at the foot of each page, but its ancestor is lost. Manuscripts may also correspond quaternion for quaternion, with spacing out or contraction coming at the end of quaternions only. Here scribes have evidently each been assigned a certain part of a text to copy, the ancestor having been broken up and distributed by quaternions among them. Evidence from spacing out and crowding together is equally useful with printed books.

In printed books, if paragraph breaks omitted in one edition correspond to those following a full line in another, the omissions mark the later edition; there has not been enough white space in the earlier edition to attract the compositor's eye. If in two editions, corresponding page for page but not sheet for sheet, signatures correct in one appear also in the other but are there incorrect, the edition with the erroneous signatures is the later. If in one issue the watermarks are all the same, and in another they differ at just the places where the typesettings of the issues differ, the consistent series marks the earlier issue. A sharp eye will detect many another sign of priority of the same sort. In fact, with bibliographical evidence, rules cannot cover all the possibilities, and the bibliographer with no ability to make deductions for himself is lost.

---

[47] Silva Lake, *op. cit.,* p. 135; Mark 13:25.
[48] Dryden, *Mac Flecknoe,* 72.

A single example must serve for a host. In the 1730 edition of John Gay's *Wife of Bath* it is clear that the octavo impression preceded the quarto, which is printed from the same type as the octavo except for the signatures. Even one of these is the same in both. The abnormal appearance of the octavo type page on the quarto leaf shows that the type was set for the former. It would be a safe deduction that the octavo was printed first; it is a sure deduction, because the signature common to both is correct for the octavo only.

Other probabilities and possibilities. Griesbach has furnished some additional rules:[49] the shorter reading, the harder reading, the harsher reading, the rarer form, the reading at first glance apparently wrong, are probably the earlier; emphatic expressions, pious expressions, the more orthodox expression, are probably the later; the reading repeating a neighboring word or idea, the reading that smells of a gloss, the reading dependent upon the Fathers or the scholiasts or first found in a lectionary or in a translation, are almost certainly later.

R. B. McKerrow has furnished some additional rules for printed books.[50] Other things being equal, the handsomest edition, or the edition with the fewest errors in the mechanics of typography, is probably the first. If the preliminaries have a separate or an interrupted run of signatures in one edition and not in another, the single series probably marks the later edition; the indications are stronger if there is a reference in the preliminaries to the printing of the text, or if in the edition with the single series of signatures the first page of the text falls in the same gathering with the end of the preliminaries. If one edition exactly fills a number of sheets whereas another is short or long by a leaf or two, the first, representing an economy easy to obtain when one has printed copy, is probably the later.

Griesbach's and McKerrow's rules are based on assumptions about the scribe's or compositor's actions under certain circumstances. Our knowledge of scribal practice has not increased since Griesbach, but our knowledge of printing has much increased since McKerrow. We now know that his rules are rules of last resort; the chances that they are correct are not large. This knowledge strengthens the arguments against Griesbach's rules which one encounters from time to time. The

---

[49] Conveniently summarized in Henri Quentin, *Essais de Critique Textuelle (Ecdotique)* (Paris, 1926), p. 31.

[50] McKerrow, *op. cit.*, pp. 184-199.

rule that the longer reading is the later seems to me entirely indefensible. Obviously, too, what one critic will see as merely hard, harsh, or apparently wrong, another will see as wrong altogether.

Too often the critic is forced even further back upon the assumption that the better reading is the more authoritative, or the reverse if the author is revising. James Thorpe has shown how weak these assumptions are.[51] Many authors are bad revisers and all authors make the same kinds of mistakes as copyists. English authors began to seek improvements from friends before 1700 and by the nineteenth century had to accept improvements thrust upon them by editors and publishers—real improvements, not just corruptions. Improvement of dramatic manuscripts by actors, directors, managers, and producers has no doubt gone on since the origin of the drama. One may decide that a witticism found in some Chaucerian manuscripts and not in others is not scribal but authoritative, but this is only because one knows Chaucer better than his scribes. How many Yoricks there have been among scribes we shall never know.

Bibliographers are inclined to ignore the less certainly directional variations when so doing will simplify their family trees. Faced with several variations A:B, A having the archetypal reading in some and B in others, they do not feel bound to accept the two states as independent descendants of a lost archetype but may take the one with the most more certainly authoritative readings or with even a single striking example as the ancestor of the other. If the textual analyst lets the form of his family tree influence his analysis of the directional variations, he reasons in a circle.

One kind of variation often cited as directional is A:B:C where one of the readings is the same as the other two laid end to end. The one so-called conflated reading can in fact only be identified as conflated if the genetic relationships of the states are already decided upon. Critics who cite conflated readings as evidence of converging transmission are quite likely to cite the same kind of readings as evidence of diverging transmission. Thus Streeter, finding ἐκεῖ ἐν τῇ ἐρήμῳ in the Byzantine manuscripts of Mark where ἐκεῖ appears in the Sinaitic Syriac and ἐν τῇ ἐρήμῳ in the Alexandrian or Neutral manuscripts, argues that the Byzantine reading is therefore later; but finding Ὀψίας

---

[51] James Thorpe, *Principles of Textual Criticism* (San Marino, Calif., 1972), pp. 3–49.

δὲ γενομένης, ὅτε ἔδυθεν ὁ ἥλιος in Mark, Ὀψίας δὲ γενομένης in Matthew, and Δύνοντος δὲ τοῦ ἡλίου in Luke, he argues that Mark is therefore earlier.[52] In fact he had already decided that the Byzantine reading was later and Mark earlier. The critic must use all his evidence to determine his family trees, and he cannot then find additional support for his reasoning in variations of previously obscure significance.

Directional and partially directional variations should be written at least twice, the second time with arrows instead of colons as necessary to indicate which groups have readings descended from the readings found in other groups. For example, if we have a complex variation in which it is clear that the reading of A and B is a descendant of the reading of C, and that the reading of D and E is also a descendant of the reading of C, we should write both AB:C:DE and AB←C→DE.

A complex directional or partially directional variation has a relationship between the ancestor and descendant readings which must be indicated by one or more "synthetic" variations, that is, variations not occurring in fact but set up by the textual analyst to record facts about the states. We preface these variations with an asterisk to show that they do not exist explicitly in the data, a symbolism borrowed from historical linguistics. Inasmuch as no states that do not have the ancestor or descendant readings can interrupt the connections between those that do, we represent the fact by making one group out of the latter, as follows: if we have A→B:C or A←B:C we write *AB:C; if we have A→B→C or A←B→C, we write both *AB:C and *A:BC; if we have A→B→C:D or A←B→C:D we write both *AB:C:D and *A: BC:D; and so on. In other words, for every pair of groups connected by an arrow there must be a synthetic variation in which these two groups are one, and the other groups are as they occur in the variation as normally written.

If the variations are at all numerous, it is best to sort them, so that they can be analyzed systematically and so that none will be overlooked. The variations are easiest to sort if they are written out on separate cards. Variations with arrows should be sorted separately, but the corresponding synthetic variations should be sorted with the other variations.

---

[52] Burnett Hillman Streeter, *The Four Gospels*, 4th imp. rev. (London, 1930), pp. 115-116, 163-164.

We need at this point to introduce more types for the variations. As we know, a variation A:BCDE is type 1, a variation AB:CDE is type 2. A variation A:B:CDE, that is, a complex variation with only one true group, is type 3. A variation AB:CD:E, that is, a complex variation with more than one true group, is type 4. A variation A:B: C:D:E, that is, a complex variation with no true groups, is type 0.

The following rules are for an absolutely fixed sort sequence of variations written with colons only and need not be followed in every detail if one is working by hand and is willing to put up with some inefficiency. Small adjustments can be made for variations written with arrows, or the arrows can be drawn in above or below the sigla of the states.

Always write the sigla in the same order. In the following examples, the order is alphabetic, but if there is a more meaningful order it may be employed. Thus, if the first edition of a work is given the siglum F1, the second the siglum Q1, the third the siglum F2, and the fourth the siglum Q2, the sigla can always be written in the order of the editions. It will be found, however, that an alphanumeric order, F1, F2, Q1, Q2, is easier to follow consistently.

In the simple variations, write the smaller group first. If the groups are the same size, write the one with the first member first, for example, ABD:CEF, not CEF:ABD. In the complex variations, write the groups in order of the first member in each, for example, AB:CD:EF, not CD:AB:EF or some other way. Be sure that every siglum is present in each variation, for it is easy to forget states omitting a passage where other states vary, when writing the latter variation.

Arrange the variations by type, from 0 to 4.

Arrange the simple variations according to the number of sigla in the first group. If two variations have groups of the same size, arrange them according to the order in which the sigla are written; for example, AB:CDEF before AC:BDEF before BC:ADEF.

Arrange the complex variations according to the number of groups in each. If two variations have the same number of groups, treat the colon as preceding all the sigla in the sort order and arrange them according to the order in which the sigla (now including the colon) are written; for example, A:BCD:EF before AB:CD:EF before AB: CDE:F before ABC:DE:F.

When there are duplicates, count them and discard all but one. Keep the count attached to the one not discarded.

Assign serial numbers to the variations not discarded.

In addition, list the true groups from the type-4 variations, attaching to each the serial number of the variation from which it was taken. Arrange the groups in order of the number of sigla in each, and if two have the same number of sigla, then arrange them in order of the sigla in each; for example, AB before ABC before CDE. Mark the duplicates but do not discard them.

For an example let us take the apparatus from the first example in chapter 1, in which each variation is indeed a single variation and not a convenient way of indicating more or less than one:

1 Madame] A, C-D; Madame (c'est à dire, Madame Pompadour) B.
1 Ciel] A-C; bon Dieu D.   1 former] A-C; créer D.   2 ait vu]
A-B; voit C-D.   2 âmes en] A; âmes aussi semblables en tout que
les nôtres, deux âmes en B-D.   3-6 aient fait . . . fait paroître]
A-B; aient fait paroître C-D   7 réputation] A-B, D; renommée C.
7 insensibles] A, C; impitoyables B; endurcis D.

We have two examples of D:ABC in line 1, and two of AB:CD, in lines 2 and 3-6. Sorting the variations therefore gives us:

1	A:BCD	(1)
2	B:ACD	(1)
3	C:ABD	(1)
4	D:ABC	(2)
5	AB:CD	(2)
6	AC:B:D	(1)

3. REWRITING VARIATIONS THAT WOULD INTRODUCE RINGS

The preceding steps in the solution of textual problems by textual analysis are preliminary to textual analysis itself, but they are not less important. Textual analysis is a logic engine, like a computer. As Appendix B shows, it can be and, as we shall see, in large problems it can only be performed by a computer. A computer is a number cruncher and textual analysis is a reading eater, and with both it is what goes into the mouth which defiles. Computer users have an acronym, GIGO, "garbage in, garbage out," which exactly fits textual analysis. If the textual states and their variants are not correctly chosen, the results of textual analysis will be unsatisfactory, even if the analysis itself is performed perfectly. In this age of blaming "the computer" for all kinds of office failures, it behooves us to recognize that the failures are not in the machines but in the people who feed them, just as errors in typing are not the fault of the typewriter. So in textual analysis. Its rules are absolutely logical, as we shall see, so that failures can result only from improper choice of states and variations or from failure to follow the rules.

To make the rules easier to follow, I now introduce a calculus that can be carried out with pencil and paper and is entirely suitable for small problems. It is in theory if not in fact suitable for problems of any magnitude, if one has the time and the patience to carry it out. Faster calculi for larger problems may be found in the appendices.

In what follows it is assumed that the variations have been sorted as described above and that the copies of the directional variations written with arrows have been set aside for the time being. These last are not used until the last step of textual analysis.

In order to be used in later steps, type-2 and type-4 variations (i.e., simple and complex variations with more than one true group) must meet a simple test. Suppose we have variations AB:CDE, DE: ABC, and AB:CD:E. We want to know whether we can write the first two so that each siglum of the second is directly under the corresponding siglum of the first without disturbing the groupings themselves. We may have to vary from the normal sort order of the sigla to do this, and we let the colons fall where they may as long as they separate the groups of sigla just as in the previously written variations. We have no trouble with the first two variations if we rewrite the second:

$$A\ B:C\ D\ E$$
$$A\ B\ C:D\ E$$

We can do the same with the first and third and the second and third of our variations, with more or less rewriting:

$$A\ B:C\ D\ E \qquad E\ D:C\ B\ A$$
$$A\ B:C\ D:E \qquad E:D\ C:B\ A$$

These variations, then, have all passed the test.

It may happen, however, that no amount of rewriting will permit us to keep the groups intact and still line up all the sigla. For example, AB:CDE and AE:BCD will not line up:

$$A\ B:C\ D\ E \qquad A\ B:C\ D\ E$$
$$E\ A:B\ C\ D \qquad B\ C\ D:E\ A$$

The same sort of thing can happen with simple and complex variations:

$$A\ B:C\ D\ E$$
$$D\ A:B\ C\ \ :E$$

Or with complex variations only:

A B: C D:E
D A:B C   :E

One variation in each of these pairs has failed the test, and a further test is necessary to determine which one.

We shall do best to make the first test in two operations. First, take the type-2 and type-4 variations in sorted order and test each with all the others after it in the order. Thus, if we had two type-2 and two type-4 variations, we should test the first type 2 with the second and with the two type 4s, the second type 2 with the two type 4s, and the first type 4 with the second.

The next operation results from a peculiarity of the type-4 variations. Two or more complex variations may have the effect of locking the sigla into an unalterable sequence. For example, we can line up A: BC:DE or AB:CD:E under AE:BCD, as follows:

B C D:E A   E A:B C D
B C:D E:A   E:A B:C D

But the two complex variations lock the sigla in a sequence that prevents us from lining up the simple one under them:

A:B C:D E
A B:C D:E
E A:B C D

Locking takes place when sigla have different partners in the complex variations. In the following example, B and C are locked with respect to A and D, but not with respect to each other:

A:B C D:E F   A:C B D:E F
A B C:D E:F   A C B:D E:F

And in the next example, the group AB is not locked, nor are the two sigla:

B A:C:D E:F   C:D E:F:A B
B A:C D:E F   C D:E F:A B

Complete locking may require more than two variations. The second variation below does not lock A, and the third with the second would not lock F:

A:B:C D:E F
A:B C:D E:F
A B:C D:E:F

The second testing operation will then have two parts. First we test for locked sequences. Take the type-4 variations one at a time. Test each against all the others to see if locking results. If incomplete locking results, test the sequence established so far against all the other type-4 variations. Repeat until there is a complete lock or until no more locking results. Remove the last variation from the locking sequence and try for another lock with another variation. (*a*) If no other lock results, remove another variation from the original sequence and try again. (*b*) If a new partial lock results, try to extend it as before. Repeat the whole as necessary.

The various sequences can be recorded as found without immediate further processing, or further processing can follow as each sequence is found. Either way, the second part of the operation is to test each sequence against all the type-2 variations and all the type-4 variations not making the sequence to see if they will line up.

If there is never a failure in lining up the variations, no variations would introduce rings into the tree, and we can proceed to the next step of textual analysis.

If a failure occurs, we have a choice in the order of the next three operations. We need a count of the agreements of the states, each with each, in the variations. This can be the second operation, but if we make it the first we can combine the two others. We can list the pairs of states in a Cartesian triangle, but if there are many states, the pair counts will be easier to find if we list every combination. Suppose, then, that we have variations with occurrences as follows: AE:BCD (3), A:BC:DE (1), and AB:CD:E (2). In the first variation, we see that A agrees with E, B with C and with D, and C with D. Since there are three examples of this variation in the text, the count for each agreement is three. The second variation increases the count of the BC agreement to four. The third variation, since it occurs twice, increases the count of the CD agreement to five. We can tally the agreements in any way we wish, producing finally one of the following:

AB 2				AA	AB 2	AC 0	AD 0	AE 3
AC 0	BC 4			BA 2	BB	BC 4	BD 3	BE 0
AD 0	BD 3	CD 5		CA 0	CB 4	CC	CD 5	CE 0
AE 3	BE 0	CE 0	DE 1	DA 0	DB 3	DC 5	DD	DE 1
				EA 3	EB 0	EC 0	ED 1	EE

In the second table, positions for the agreement of each state with itself are not strictly necessary, but they make it easy to read down as well as across; even in a large table, where listing the agreements of A, let us say, with the other states requires several lines, reading down is made easier.

The next operation is writing the rings indicated by the variations that will not line up. For example, the ring indicated by AB:CDE and AE:BCD is:

A B: C D E   A———B

E A:B C D   E———CD

The two variations lock the sigla into a sequence of the same kind that we have seen earlier, except that the sequence now curls back upon itself and so can be thought of as beginning at any point in the sequence. Sigla that are differently grouped in the variations are in different elements. Thus A, grouped alternately with B and E, is an element. So is B and so is E, for the same reason. C and D, however, are grouped together in both variations, so they are in the same element. Because A is grouped alternately with B and E, its element belongs between theirs. Similarly with CD. Thus the ring is established.

There are various possible ways of writing the rings, but duplicates will be easier to identify and sorting will be facilitated if a standard way is used. The method here is to start with the earliest state, according to the sort order, and to put to the right of its ring element the element beginning with the next state not in the first element. This automatically determines the sequence of the rest of the elements.

The elements and their sequence can be determined from the calculus by reading the variations from left to right. The state or states which both line up and are in the first group in the variations or in the first group after colons that line up comprise the first element. The state or states which line up and are in the preceding group in one variation and in the next group in another variation comprise the next element, and so on until we come to a state or states found in all variations but which do not line up; the latter comprise the last element. Or we can start with the same element but proceed in the reverse direction.

The rings indicated by AB:CDE and AD:BC:E and by AB:CD:E and AD:BC:E are as follows:

A B: C D E   A—B   A B: C D:E   A—B
                   | | | |
D A:B C   :E   D— C   D A:B C   :E   D— C

E is not an element in either ring because it is not differently grouped in the two variations. In the first example it stands alone in the second variation, in the second example it stands alone in both. Any number of states may be omitted from a ring for this reason.

As we have seen, several type-4 variations may lock the states into a sequence. In such a situation, there may be more than four elements in a ring. Thus the ring indicated by AE:BCD, A:BC:DE, and AB:CD:E has five elements:

```
A:B C:D E          A—B—C
A B:C D:E          |     |
E A:B C D          E————D
```

A state that is not locked into a sequence will not be an element in such a ring. If we have AB:CDE:F and A:BC:D:EF, D is not locked. Therefore if we also have AF:BCDE the ring is

```
A B:C D E:F        A—B—C
A:B C:D:E F        |     |
F A:B C D E        F————E
```

Notice that D does not find new partners in the second variation.

Because of the way we locate rings of this kind, we shall locate the same ring repeatedly. Therefore we attach the serial numbers of the variations to the rings, and when we sort the rings we discard the duplicates. A ring is not a duplicate of another unless it has the same elements in the same order and has been made up from the same variations. For the same ring may result from different variations, and the same variations may result in more than one ring. This last circumstance we must now illustrate.

The same variations can result in more than one ring in two ways. One way is illustrated by the variations AB:CD:EF:GH and AC:BD: EH:FG:

```
A B:C D:E F:G:H      A—B        F—G
C A:B   D:  F G:H E  |  |       |  |
                     C—D        E—H
```

Here there are two failures to line up, not one. The variations fall into two separate parts, as shown by the fact that some of the colons can be lined up, and each part has a ring sequence. The other way in which the same variation can result in more than one ring is illustrated by the variations ABC:DEF and AD:BE:CF. Here there are three failures to line up, not one:

```
    A B C:D E F              B C A:D E F              C A B:D E F
    D A:B      E             E B:C       F            F C:A    D
```

What has happened is that having written two of the groups in the complex variation more or less under the simple, we cannot write the third at all. In the middle example, for instance, if we write in the group AD we split up the group CF; in the others we would have to split up the remaining group to write it in and we should then split up one of the other groups as well. Each failure to line up gives a different ring, none having all the sigla in its elements:

```
    A—B              B—C              C—A
    |  |             |  |             |  |
    D—E              E—F              F—D
```

As we identify each ring, we may at once, if we have already made our pair counts, determine the "strength" of its connections. Otherwise, we can write in the strengths for all rings as a separate third operation. The strength of a connection is the largest pair count among the connected sigla. For example, suppose we have the variations and occurrences C:ABDE (1), AB:CDE (2), AE:BCD (3), and A:B:C:DE (2). We then have a ring and pair counts as follows:

```
        A B:C D E             AB 3
        E A:B C D             AC 0   BC 3
            A————B            AD 1   BD 4   CD 5
            |    |            AE 4   BE 1   CE 2   DE 5
            E——— CD
```

The strength of the A—B connection is 3, the strength of the A—E connection is 4. The strength of the B—CD connection is the larger of the BC and BD pair-counts, or 4. The strength of the CD—E connection is the larger of the CE and DE pair counts, or 5. If we had a connection AB—CD, its strength would be the largest of the four pair counts AC, AD, BC, and BD. And so on.

The next operation is to sort the rings in descending order of the weakest connection in each, that is, strongest weakest connection first, weakest weakest connection last.

The next operation is to break the rings and rewrite the variations causing them, as necessary. We break the rings at the weakest connections, dividing the elements in the variations as necessary, and putting an asterisk in front of the rewritten variations to mark them as synthetic. Thus, in our example just above, where the A—B connection has a strength of 3, the A—E and B—CD connections have strengths of 4, and the CD—E connection has a strength of 5, we break the A—B connection, which means dividing A from B in the variation AB:CDE. We therefore rewrite this variation as *A:B:CDE and temporarily keep the original form and the rewritten form together.

If a ring has more than one equally weak weakest connection, we break them all. We show an example of this below.

Having broken one ring, we have broken as well any other in which the states now separated are in different elements and comprise all of at least one of the elements. Therefore, before breaking a ring, we examine the variations causing it to see if it has already been broken as a result of breaking a previous ring (the break may not come at the weakest link of the new ring, but that is no matter). For example, suppose that in addition to the ring just broken we have another in the same problem caused by the variation and occurrence AD:BE:C (1). This would give us pair counts of 2 for AD and BE instead of 1 as above, and two more rings:

$$
\begin{array}{ll}
\text{A B:E D C} & \text{A—B} \\
\text{D A:B E \ \ :C} & \text{|\ \ \ |} \\
& \text{D—E}
\end{array}
$$

$$
\begin{array}{ll}
& \text{A—D} \\
\text{E A:D B C} & \text{|\ \ \ |} \\
\text{B E:A D \ \ :C} & \text{E—B}
\end{array}
$$

Now under other circumstances we should break the first of these two rings at the A—D and B—E connections because they are the weakest and are equally weak, the strength of each being 2, but as we see from the synthetic variation *A:B:CDE we have divided A from B in the variation AB:CDE, so that the ring is already broken at the A—B connection. In the second of the two rings the A—D and B—E connections are again the weakest and equally weak, but neither of the other two has been broken. We therefore rewrite the complex variation as *A:B:C:D:E.

But if we had had two examples of AD:BE:C instead of one, so that the AD and BE pair counts were 3 instead of 2, then the A—D and B—E connections in the last two rings would have been just as strong as the A—B connection in the first ring. In that event we should have made all the breaks indicated in all the rings, no matter which we happened to come upon first. There is no priority among equally strong connections, whether in the same ring or in different rings.

We should also notice that the elements to be divided may not comprise all the states in the group that is to be rewritten. In that case we divide the elements from themselves and from the other states in the group. Thus if we have variations AC:BDE and AB:CD:E giving a ring in which E is not an element and if the pair counts show that the B—D link is to be divided, we rewrite the simple variation as *AC:B:D:E.

Finally we should notice that a group may have to be divided more than once. For example, if we have a group ABCD: . . . that one ring shows ought to be divided *AB:CD: and that another ring shows ought to be divided *AC:BD: we have to make both divisions. The first division separates A and B from C and D, the second separates A from B and C from D (A being already separated from D and B from C). The result is four synthetic groups, *A:B:C:D: . . . .

Suppose we have variations AB:CDEF, ABCF:DE, and ACE:BDF. The first and third form a ring, and so do the second and third, but the first and second do not. Suppose we break the ring formed by the second and third variations at the AC—BF connection, rewriting the second variation as *AC:BF:DE. Now the first and second variations form a ring. Therefore, when we have broken the rings indicated by the original variations we test for rings with the rewritten variations. If we find new rings, we break them as before, except that we use the original pair counts, and test again, until no new rings are found.

When all variations have been rewritten as much as necessary, the final rewritings replace the originals in the rest of the steps.

To a bibliographer rings indicate conflation. If he breaks them in the same way as a textual analyst, he will have worked out the primary ancestry of his records. When a bibliographer must recognize conflation, he may reasonably supplement the methods of textual analysis in resolving it because some textual agreements may be owing to emendation or to chance rather than to conflation and can therefore if they can be identified be set aside as not the result of copying. Chance agreements should be few and scattered. Emendation should spring from obvious and easily correctible errors. Also, bibliographers may determine the weakest connection in a conflation ring differently from textual analysts; for them, the weakest connection may be the one across which have passed the most readings likely to have resulted from conflation or emendation. Since errors invite correction, the correcter readings are those most likely to be the result of conflation, unless the correcter readings somehow invite miscopying.

Breaking rings can be enormously tedious and in large problems effectively impossible to do by the calculus illustrated. Ten manuscripts and ten printed editions of Dryden's *Heroick Stanzas*, 114 lines, provide about four hundred rings; eleven manuscripts and two printed editions of his *Mac Flecknoe*, 214 lines, provide about two thousand. Such problems are best solved by computer. If one does not use a mechanical help that is powerful enough to reduce significantly the time he must spend over the rings in his problem, he will inevitably be tempted to take shortcuts. His attention is then likely to focus on the smaller groups in his variations, because they are easier to remember and so seem to call attention to themselves. As a result, he is likely to feel that when he finds variations like AB:CDE and AE:BCD the choice is between separating A from B or from E. This is not correct. Suppose all five states are terminal. Then, to look ahead a little, if we think of the choice as lying between separating A from B or from E we think of the choice as lying between the two following as bits of the preliminary diagram

But in fact, we have also the possibility that CD should be separated from B or E. In other words, we have also to think of the following possibilities:

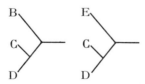

Ironically, the more experienced textual analyst is more likely to be seduced by the smaller groups because he will be able to see farther into the solution of the problem and will be tentatively grouping his states in his mind as they seem to group themselves in the variations. Strict adherence to an algorithm is all the more necessary for him.

4. Finding terminal groups not in simple variations

We are now ready to determine whether any groups of states are terminal which are not in simple variations. We work first with groups found in complex variations, which we process in order of increasing size, starting with singleton groups.

We could examine the complex groups for singleton groups, and, when we found one, look to see if it were a singleton group in a type-1 variation. But it is more efficient to go down the list of type-1 variations and, when we find a state that is not a singleton group, look to see if it is a singleton group in a complex variation. If it is not, we continue to search the list of type-1 variations. Otherwise we write the state and under it the variation in which the state is a singleton group, rewriting the variation as necessary to put the singleton at the left end.

Suppose we have the variations B:ACD, AB:CD, and A:BC:D. We notice that A:BCD is missing from the type-1 variations, and that A is a singleton group in the complex variation. Therefore we write:

A
A:B C:D

We now line up the type-2 and other complex variations, if any, under the first variation, one at a time. We can rewrite the variations as long as we keep the state we are testing at the left end. In the present example we write:

A
A:B C:D
A B:C D

We then draw a line, as in addition, copy the states in their columns, and insert colons as follows: (1) wherever the first variation has a colon to the left of the leftmost colon in the second variation; and (2) wherever both variations have a colon. In our example we write:

A
A:B C:D
A B:C D
─────────
A:B C D

If the result is a simple variation, we put an asterisk in front to mark it as synthetic and insert it in the list of variations. In our example, we shall insert *A:BCD before B:ACD.

The next state not a singleton among the type-1 variations is C. It is not a singleton in the complex variation, so we return to the type-1 variations, where we find that D is not a singleton. We then proceed as before:

$$
\begin{array}{l}
\text{D} \\
\text{D: C B:A} \\
\underline{\text{D C:B A}} \\
\text{D: C B A}
\end{array}
$$

We rewrite the synthetic simple variation in standard form, *D:ABC, and insert it after B:ACD in the list of variations.

When we have finished testing for singleton groups we go down the separate list of true groups of type-4 variations. First we look to see if the group is also found among the type-2 groups, and if it is we cross it off the list of type-4 groups. We also look to see if it "overlaps" one of the type-2 groups, that is, if type-4 and type-2 groups have at least one siglum in common and each has at least one siglum not in the other. For example, the type-4 group BC and the type-2 group AB overlap. If we find such an overlap we go to the next type-4 group. Otherwise we proceed very much as with the singleton groups. One difference is that we can rewrite the group if it will help us to line up the variations. Another difference is that we may not be able to line up the variations no matter how we rewrite them. If this happens, we go at once to the next type-4 group. A third difference is that when variations have colons that come between the sigla of the test group, we ignore the variations if they are simple, and if they are complex we ignore the colons (except as explained below).

Suppose we have variations and groups as follows:

1 E:AB CD	AB–3
2 A:B C:DE	B C–2
3 AB: CD:E	CD–3
	DE–2

The numbers to the right of the type-4 groups are not occurrence counts but the serial numbers of the variations in which they occur (their "parent" variations). Using the serial numbers to help us find the parent variations, we write:

$$
\begin{array}{l}
\text{A B} \\
\text{A B: C D:E} \\
\underline{\text{A:B C:D E}} \\
\text{*A B: C D E}
\end{array}
$$

We insert the resulting synthetic simple variation in the list and cross the test group off the list of type-4 variations.

The type-4 group BC overlaps the group AB in our new synthetic simple variation, so we will not process it. When we come to the type-4 group CD, we find that the variations will not line up. Even rewriting the group does not help.

C D   D C

C D:E:A B   D C:B A:E

B C:D E:A   E D:C B:A

We therefore leave CD in the list of type-4 variations. When we come to the group DE we ignore the simple variation because its colon comes between the sigla of the test group. When we use the two complex variations to test the group DE, however, we find no overlap and get results similar to those for AB:

E D

E D: C B:A

E:D C:B A

————————

*E D: C B A

We then rewrite the synthetic simple variation in normal order, *DE: ABC, and insert it in the list of variations. We cross the test group off the list of type-4 variations.

A fourth and again an important difference from testing singleton groups is a limitation on variations that "divide off and divide up" the test group. The following are examples:

A B   B C E

A:B: C D E:F   B:C E:A D F:G H

These variations can only be used in the tests if other variations have already locked the sigla of the test group into a sequence and the new variation extends this sequence away from the test group. The members of the test group themselves need not be locked in sequence, but they must be included in such a sequence. The following are examples:

A B   A B

A B: C D:E:F   A B: C D:E:F

A:B C:D E:F   A B C:D E:F

In the first example, all the sigla from A through E are locked in sequence. In the second example the sigla in the test group could be reversed but they are locked in sequence with respect to C, and this

sequence also extends through E. In either event, a variation A:B:
CD:EF, even though it divides off and divides up AB, extends the
sequence away from AB, and therefore can be used with the results
of the first tests:

A B	A B
A B: C D:E: F	A B: C D:E: F
A:B C:D E:F	A B C:D E:F
*A B: C D E:F	*A B: C D E:F
A:B: C D:E F	A:B: C D:E F
*A B: C D E F	*A B: C D E F

When it appears that the only way to obtain a synthetic simple
variation is to use one or more variations that divide off and divide
up the test group, it may be necessary to try several combinations of
earlier variations to obtain the necessary sequence. We proceed in this
case exactly as we did when looking for sequences that might form
rings, since this will guarantee our testing every sequence.

When we have identified all the complex groups that are terminal,
we are ready to see if groups of states not in any variations are terminal. These will be made up of groups found in the variations that
have, taken two by two, at least one siglum in common and at least
one siglum not in the other group. We search first for overlaps of a
type-4 group with one or more simple groups. For example, suppose
we have variations and groups as follows:

1 AB: CD:EF	AB–1	CD–1	EF–1
2 A:B C:DE: F	B C–2	DE–2	

By the processes already described we shall obtain from these

*A:B CDEF	B C–2
*F:AB CDE	CD–1
*AB: CDEF	DE–2
*EF:AB CD	
1 AB: CD:EF	
2 A:B C:DE: F	

As before, we go down the list of the type-4 groups, which is now
somewhat shorter than it was, some of the groups having been crossed
off. We see that BC overlaps the groups in *AB:CDEF, giving *ABC
and *BCDEF. We mark overlaps with asterisks as they also are synthetic. We see that *BCDEF is the same as a group in *A:BCDEF,
so we ignore it and proceed with *ABC.

Testing proceeds very much as with the type-4 groups. We look first to see if the overlap is the same as one of the groups in the type-2 variations, and if it is we go to another overlap. We do not, however, check the overlap for overlap with the type-2 groups. The type-4 group in each overlap is crucial. We must keep its sigla together when we write or rewrite the overlap. We start the test with its parent variation. A variation divides off and divides up the overlap only if in the process it divides up the sigla in the type-4 group. And if testing produces a synthetic simple variation we cross the type-4 group from the list. For these reasons we put a bar over the sigla from the type-4 variation in each overlap. In the result, we always put a colon after the test overlap.

$$*\text{A } \overline{\text{B C}}$$
$$\text{A:B C:D E:F}$$
$$\underline{\text{A B:C D:E F}}$$
$$*\text{A B C:D E F}$$

We insert the new simple variation in the list of variations and delete BC from the list of type-4 variations.

The group CD now overlaps the groups in *ABC:DEF, giving *ABCD and *CDEF. Since both of these are the same as groups in the simple variations (it makes no difference that they are synthetic simple variations), we ignore both.

The group DE overlaps the groups in *EF:ABCD, giving *DEF and *ABCDE. Once more we see that both are the same as groups in the simple variations and ignore both.

One last and very important difference from the operation with type-4 groups is this. If we have added a new synthetic variation to the list of variations, we go back through the list of type-4 groups and look for new overlaps with the new synthetic groups. In our present example, since no groups remain in the type-4 list, the testing is complete.

It may happen that a type-4 group will overlap groups from more than one type-2 variation. To make all possible overlaps we must try all possible combinations of first and second type-2 groups with each type-4 group, except groups from the same type-2 variation and groups that have sigla in common. The rest must be tested one at a time, starting with the usual search of the type-2 variations to see if the overlaps are the same as one of the groups there.

With AB:CDEFG, CDE:ABFG, and A:BC:DE:FG, for example, we see that the type-4 group BC is overlapped by groups in both the simple variations. The possible combinations of simple groups are AB and CDE (first groups in both variations), AB and ABFG (first group in first variation and second in second), CDE and CDEFG (first group in second variation and second in first), and CDEFG and ABFG (second groups in both variations). We add BC to the first pair to obtain the overlap *ABCDE and test it in the usual way. The other pairs have sigla in common, so we pass them by.

When we have tested all the overlaps of individual type-4 groups with groups from the simple variations, we test any type-4 groups remaining for overlap with one another. Here we radically alter the calculus. In the first place we cannot proceed unless there remain at least two type-4 groups from each of at least two parent variations. Finding such variations, we choose two groups from one. Then we must find another such variation with groups that separately overlap both the type-4 starting groups. If the two overlaps do not include all the sigla, we must now search for a pair that will extend both the locked sequences established by the first four groups. These two groups can come from either of the first two variations or from any other such variation. When we cannot extend the two overlaps any more and they still do not include all the texts, we can try to extend them one at a time by groups from the type-2 variations. Any such type-2 group must include only one or all but one of the elements in the overlaps formed by the type-4 groups. If by this process we manage to include all the states, we can make up a synthetic simple variation in which each group has the same states as one of the overlaps. For example, suppose we have variations A:BC:D:EF and AB:C:DE:F. Our list of type-4 groups will then have two groups from each parent variation. We may start with BC and EF:

$$
\begin{array}{l}
\text{B C:F E} \\
\text{A:B C:F E:D} \\
\underline{\text{A B:C:F:E D}} \\
\text{*A B C:F E D}
\end{array}
$$

If there are more possible starting groups, we must try each possible pair. For example, if we had AB, CD, and EF from a parent variation AB:CD:EF, we should have to treat AB and CD, AB and EF, and CD and EF.

Lastly, we may note that under certain circumstances the following is possible:

A B
A B: C D:E: F
A B: C:D:E F
*A B: C D:E F

We see that the test group excludes and is excluded by other true groups in turn, but only by one in each variation. We need not insert a colon where both variations have one, if the groups when divided, for example, C:D and E:F are divided at least into their immediate subgroups and these are all terminal, that is, in the illustration, if C, D, E, and F are all terminal.

5. CONNECTING THE TERMINAL GROUPS (PRODUCING THE PRELIMINARY DIAGRAM)

A preliminary diagram as opposed to a final diagram does not have anything that can be called a top because it is made without consideration for any directionality in the variations. We can avoid getting a sense that it has a top by drawing it so that no state is at the top, or at least not at the top center.

Let us suppose we have A:BCD, B:ACD, AB:CD and A:BD:C. From the type-2 and the type-3 variations we derive *C:ABD. We now work only with the groups in the simple variations, including the synthetic, starting with the smallest and including those with half the states. If there is an odd number of states, we necessarily include only the groups with the nearest whole number to exactly half the states, that is, if there are five states in all, we include only groups with one and two states.

From all the singleton groups in the type-1 variations, we draw a line:

A—   B—   C—

In the larger groups, if all the states already have lines drawn from them, we connect the lines and draw another line from the connection. We may have to do a certain amount of redrawing to get the results to come out neatly, though legibility rather than neatness can be our only criterion at this point:

If one of the states in the group does not have a line drawn from it, we connect to it the lines from those that do and draw a line from it:

C—D—

When the process has been repeated as often as possible we run the tag-end lines together if there are only two:

If there are more than two tag ends and some member has no line drawn from it, we connect the lines to this member. Thus if we had only A:BCD, B:ACD, and C:ABD, we should draw lines from A, B, and C, and connect them to D:

Otherwise we connect the tag ends together at a single intersection. Thus if we had only A:BC, B:AC, and C:AB, we should draw lines from each siglum and connect them as follows:

The examples are minimal, but the same procedures hold for any number of states.

It may be that a group will be found that has no terminal states. Suppose we have AB:CDE but no A:BCDE or B:ACDE. In that case, we treat the group as if it were a terminal state:

$$AB—$$

It may be that a group will have more than one state from which no lines have as yet been drawn. Suppose we have ABC:DEF and A: BCDEF, but no B:ACDEF, C:ABDEF, or BC:ADEF. In that case we treat the several states with no lines yet drawn as if they were one:

$$A—B\,C—$$

When we must place more than one state at the same place in the diagram, we shall discover either that we have been treating duplicate records as if they were states or that we have what we may call effective duplicates. A bibliographer, working with records only, would accept the duplicates, but a state by definition differs from every other state. Effective duplicates differ in the complex variations, which we do not use in constructing the preliminary diagram. An example is given below.

We need to inspect the complex variations anyway, as we may find among them what we may call anomalous variations. An anomalous variation indicates that the preliminary diagram does not have enough intermediaries, but does not tell us where they belong. There are two kinds of anomalous variation. One shows that a simple group ought to have subgroups but fails to identify the subgroups. The simplest example is of the following sort. Suppose we have the variations A:BCDE, B:ACDE, C:ABDE, D:ABCE, E:ABCD, and AB:CD:E. Since neither of the true groups in the type-4 variation is terminal, the preliminary diagram is:

Yet the type-4 variation indicates that A and B must have a different intermediary than C and D in order for the readings to flow between them without interruption. It does not, however, tell us which of the following is correct:

The second kind of anomalous variation indicates that an extant intermediary is in the wrong place but does not indicate whether it should merely be moved or made terminal as well. The simplest example is of the following sort. Suppose we have the variations A:BCD, B:ACD, C:ABD, and AB:C:D. Since the groups AB and D in the type-3 variation are not terminal, the preliminary diagram is:

Yet the type-3 variation indicates that there must be an uninterrupted connection between A and B. It does not, however, tell us which of the following is correct:

Our normal practice is to treat a state as intermediary if it is not terminal and to hold the intermediaries to a minimum, two procedures that are mutually exclusive in anomalies of the second kind.

A similar but not strictly anomalous situation arises in cases like the following, which is the simplest example. Suppose we have variations A:BCDE, E:ABCD, and AB:C:DE. Since none of the groups in the type-4 variation is terminal, the preliminary diagram is:

$$A—BCD—E$$

The type-4 variation shows that B, C, and D are effective duplicates, but if we were to interpret it instead as indicating that A and B, D and E must have connections uninterrupted by each other or by C, then we could not tell which of the following to prefer:

$$A—B—C—D—E \qquad \begin{array}{c} A—B—D—E \\ | \\ C \end{array} \qquad \begin{array}{c} A—B—D—E \\ | \\ C \end{array}$$

Preliminary diagrams with anomalous variations can be annotated, or the alternates can be worked out and presented together.

6. LOCATING THE ARCHETYPE (PRODUCING THE TREE)

There are four preliminaries to locating the archetype. First, we must assign sigla to the inferential intermediaries in the preliminary diagram. Next we must reexamine the partially directional variations to see if they have the effect of fully directional variations. If a group from which an arrow points in the variation is terminal in the diagram, and no state in the diagram comes between it and the group to which the arrow points, we normally rewrite the variation by putting all but the first group into one. Thus if we have a preliminary diagram

$$A—B—C$$

and a partially directional variation A→B—C, we rewrite the latter as *A→BC. But if the group from which the arrow points has more than one state, all these states must be grouped together in the preliminary diagram; if they have been split up to avoid a ring, the variation cannot be rewritten.

If a group to which an arrow points in the variation is terminal in the diagram, and no state in the diagram comes between it and the group from which the arrow points, we normally rewrite the variation by putting all but the first group into one. Thus if we have a preliminary diagram as before and a partially directional variation A—B→C, we rewrite the latter as *AB→C. But if the group to which the arrow points has been split up to avoid a ring, we need to write instead separate synthetic variations in which each part of the group has an arrow pointing to it from a group made up of all the other states, including those originally in the group itself.

The rules may apply more than once to the same variation. Suppose we have a preliminary diagram

$$A—B—C—D$$

and a variation A→B:C→D. Then we write synthetic variations *A→ BCD and *ABC→D.

The rules do not apply if the results would suggest rings in the diagram when taken with either an original or another synthetic variation (in the latter case we write neither synthetic variation).

Finally we take the fully directional variations, whether original or synthetic, and drop off the arrows and the groups to which they point. To the other groups we add the inferential intermediaries between their extant states in the preliminary diagram. For example, if we have a preliminary diagram with an inferential intermediary to which we have assigned the siglum x:

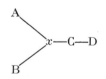

and directional variations A←BCD, B←ACD, and AB→CD, we drop off A and the arrow from the first, B and the arrow from the second, CD and the arrow from the third, and add x to the remainder in each case: BCDx, ACDx, ABx.

If any state occurs in all the groups that we obtain in this manner, it is the archetype. In the example, the archetype is x, and the tree indicated is:

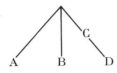

If more than one state occurs in all the groups we obtain from the directional variations, any one of those so occurring can be the archetype, and alternate trees are equally acceptable. If no state occurs in all the groups, we look to see whether any two groups have all the states with no duplication, and, if so, we look to see if every other group is either the same as or wholly includes one of the two. If so, the archetype lies between the two groups. Otherwise the directional variations indicate a ring or rings in the tree. Suppose we have the same preliminary diagram and directional variations as before, except that we also have A→BCD. When we reduce this to A we see that no state is found in all the groups, but that A and BCDx together include all the states with no duplication. We also see that both the other groups wholly include A. The tree indicated, therefore, is

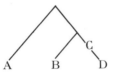

If the directional variations indicate a ring or rings in the tree, we include the archetype in the variations and begin the analysis anew. The archetype has all the earliest readings in the fully directional variations. In the other variations it forms a singleton state, as this does not imply any particular genealogical relationship. It can be given any convenient siglum.

It will sometimes happen that partially directional variations will not fit with the fully directional. They indicate rings only if their groups conflict in the same way as in fully directional variations that indicate rings. Otherwise they only show that some additional states are terminal, or that we must relocate the archetype, or both. If, in our preceding example, we also had a directional variation AB←D:C, the archetype and the immediate ancestor of C and D would have the same reading as D, from which the other readings would have descended:

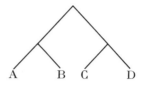

If the archetype is not one of the extant states, we reconstruct it as much as possible. It must agree with any two states independently descended from it, when they agree and we have not split them to avoid a ring. When none agree, the archetype must have the more original reading if the variation is directional. Otherwise, the reading of the archetype is indeterminate. It is reasonable in the latter instance to suppose that the archetype will agree with the state it agrees with most often elsewhere, but some critics take the trouble to warn the reader by underlining in the apparatus readings rejected as non-archetypal on this ground alone.

The textual analyst who has to reconstruct an archetype and who must print a text may decide to normalize spelling, punctuation, and so on. Otherwise he chooses a record called a copy-text and introduces into it as necessary the substantive and quasi-substantive readings of the archetype. Normally the copy-text will be chosen on the basis of its closeness to the author's practice in accidentals; but critics differ as to how to determine this closeness. For example, one manuscript of Dryden's *Indian Emperour* antedates the first edition but is not its ancestor. In estimating which of the two preserved more of Dryden's spellings and therefore ought to be the copy-text, Fredson Bowers gave more weight to some spellings than to others, giving in fact no weight at all to many; I gave equal weight to all spellings and chose another copy-text.[53] More will be said about copy-texts in chapter 5.

7. EMENDING THE ARCHETYPE

We have now passed beyond the realm of textual analysis proper and have come to a consideration of what to do with its results. I used to believe that critics working with texts in English had all followed the lead of Samuel Johnson in his edition of Shakespeare: "As I practised conjecture more, I learned to trust it less; and after I had printed

---

[53] *Four Tragedies*, p. 33; John Dryden, *Works*, ed. H. T. Swedenberg, Jr., *et al.* (Berkeley, 1956——), IX, 382. See also Vinton A. Dearing, "Concepts of Copy-Text Old and New," *The Library*, 5th series, XXVIII (1973), 281-293.

a few plays, resolved to insert none of my own readings in the text. Upon this caution I now congratulate myself, for every day encreases my doubt of my emendations."[54] James Thorpe's examples of modern practice[55] have disabused me of my former notion, however, and I apologize to critics working with the Bible for having thought less of them than they deserve by comparison. I still believe that Johnson was right.

Actually, Johnson did not stop making emendations; he merely kept them to his notes: "Since I have confined my imagination to the margin, it must not be considered as very reprehensible, if I have suffered it to play some freaks in its own dominion. There is no danger in conjecture, if it be proposed as conjecture; and while the text remains uninjured, those changes may be safely offered, which are not considered even by him that offers them as necessary or safe."

Conservative practice in emending today demands that emendation be first necessary and second possible, and emendation is defined as impossible not only when no emendation suggests itself but also when more than one equally likely emendation suggests itself. The first rule was also Johnson's: "It has been my settled principle, that the reading of the ancient books is probably true, and therefore is not to be disturbed for the sake of elegance, perspicuity, or mere improvement of the sense. For though much credit is not due to the fidelity, nor any to the judgement of the first publishers, yet they who had the copy before their eyes were more likely to read it right, than we who only read it by imagination." As a result, Johnson, who was not the first to emend Shakespeare, was able to say, "I have rescued many lines from the violations of temerity, and secured many scenes from the inroads of correction." And it is because critics have continued, in Johnson's words, "to turn the old text on every side, and try if there be any interstice, through which light can find its way" that some have concluded that "a Table of greene fields" in Mistress Quickly's description of Falstaff's death needs no emendation, because "table" can mean "picture."

The second modern rule Johnson followed less rigorously: "where any passage appeared inextricably perplexed, [I] have endeavoured to dis-

[54] Samuel Johnson, *Selected Prose and Poetry*, ed. Bertrand H. Bronson (New York, 1952); this and subsequent quotations are from pp. 281-283.

[55] Thorpe, *op. cit.*, pp. 3-49.

cover how it may be recalled to sense, with least violence." A more rigorous rule he would have regarded as timidity: "It is evident that [the first publishers] have often made strange mistakes by ignorance or negligence, and that therefore something may be properly attempted by criticism, keeping the middle way between presumption and timidity." In addition, he gave himself more freedom in small matters than in large: "In restoring the authour's works to their integrity, I have considered the punctuation as wholly in my power; for what could be their care of colons and commas, who corrupted words and sentences . . . . The same liberty has been taken with a few particles, or other words of slight effect." Modern textual critics tend not to agree with Johnson here, and to his argument that "the first publishers . . . had the copy before their eyes" add the argument that even if the first publishers or transcribers did not follow copy consciously in detail, they probably, if they were contemporaries of the author, used a similar system of punctuation, spelling, capitalization, italicization, and so on, and are likely to have been reasonably accurate on this ground alone, or at least to have produced results of which he would have approved.

Those who follow this rule of emendation with some rigor insist on what is called "transcriptional probability," that is, they say that the proposed emendation must be one that would be likely to be corrupted into the archetypal reading by one of the more mechanical processes we have already observed in discussing directional variations. This is why those who feel Mistress Quickly's speech needs emending may not be satisfied that "babl'd" is any better than "talk'd": the two words are so similar in one of the handwritings of the period (secretary hand) that "table" could be a mistranscription of either.

When there are lacunae in the text, however, we need not always leave a gap when we cannot determine how to fill it by the probabilities of mechanical transcription. An author has a style with probabilities of its own, and we may appeal to these to restore what is lost. Of course, this is the kind of emendation that Housman prided himself upon being able to make even when there were no lacunae. One may justifiably cast a cold if not fishy eye on Housman's pretensions, because they rest ultimately on a theory that denies an author the right of using synonymous expressions or of falling below himself, the same theory that is behind the work of textual disintegrators among the higher critics. Every author has unique expressions; no author never nods. Critics like Housman are aestheticians. Even if their emendations are found subsequently in early manuscripts, the result is no more than one of the weaker sorts of directional variation, not a triumphant proof. But when a text has a lacuna, either an actual hole, illegibility, or erasure, or else an apparent omission, we can attempt to fill it on the basis of the text that remains.[56] We are still making the author more consistent than he probably was, but we are not affirming some of the evidence at the expense of the rest.

I close this section and chapter with one more quotation from Johnson, the wisest and best textual critic that English literature has produced: "The greater part of readers . . . will wonder that on mere trifles so much labour is expended, with such importance of debate, and such solemnity of diction. To these I answer with confidence, that they are judging of an art which they do not understand; yet cannot much reproach them with their ignorance, nor promise that they would become in general, by learning criticism, more useful, happier, or wiser." I can only add that textual analysis, having absolute rules, is not an art, and that practicing it means exercising qualities of mind that can indeed make us more useful, happier, and wiser.

[56] Paul Tasman has reported successful restoration of lacunae of up to five words artificially introduced into texts from the Dead Sea Scrolls ("Literary Data Processing," IBM *Journal of Research*, July, 1957). This reference is the earliest one I know to the use of computers for this work, and computers are surely the tools to use for it in these days.

III

The Formal Theory of Textual Analysis

It is not necessary to read this chapter in order to carry out textual analysis correctly, and those who have no interest in why textual analysis is correct can safely pass it by. I here present the axiom system of textual analysis and demonstrate its inevitability as well as its correctness. I shall continue to use the term "reading," although a more abstract term such as "characteristic" would better point up the generality of the axioms. In the examples, however, I shall not give sample readings but use lower-case letters of the alphabet similar to the variables of symbolic logic. As in logic, if the reader is in doubt about the truth of the manipulation of the variables he may substitute constants for them, that is, readings of his own, until he gets an intuitive sense of the correctness of the reasoning.

I shall also continue to use the capital letters A, B, and so on, to represent states of a text, and A—B, and so on, to represent states of a text which have their common readings because one is a descendant of the other or both are descendants of an inferential intermediary. Since a state by definition differs from all other states, we cannot use the notation A—B if both A and B have the same readings, for they are then the same state, and we shall have to use either of the letters alone.

Most of what follows can also be taken as the formal theory of genealogical bibliography merely by replacing "state" by "record" and enlarging the definition of "reading" to include all characteristics, such as those of format, which provide genealogical evidence to the bibliographer.

We disallow the possibility that any reading found in both A and B has occurred spontaneously in both. This is a fundamental axiom of textual analysis, the importance of which can be seen from its larger applications. Thus if we have A—C—B, a reading w found in A and B must also be found in C. If C were to have nothing, or a reading x, instead of w, then to allow A—C—B would be to say that any genealogical arrangement is a good as any other, and no further reasoning would be possible.

It is important to remember that textual analysis is a logic of results, not a logic of causes. Causally speaking, we know that two states may agree occasionally by chance or emendation. The *result*, however, is the same as if there were a genealogical connection, so we accept it as such. The first axiom of textual analysis is therefore:

1. *A state* A *that has a reading* w *which another state* B *also has must be connected to* B *by a line uninterrupted by any state that has no such reading, or that has a reading* x *instead of* w.

This exclusion rule allows that any state may interrupt the genealogical connection between any two other states as long as they do not both have a reading that it lacks.

It follows from the axiom that if A:BCD occurs, then A is not to interrupt the connections between B, C, or D. Similarly, if we have AB:CD, neither A nor B is to interrupt the connection between C and D, and vice versa. Therefore, if we have ABC:D as well, we can connect the states as follows: A—B—C—D. If we say that A:BCD represents the alternation of the readings u and v, AB:CD represents the alternation of w and x, and ABC:D of y and z, and if we represent the states by their readings, we obtain $uwy—vwy—vxy—vxz$, and we see that the conditions underlying the axiom have been met.

We can also meet these conditions by connecting the states in the following and a number of similar ways:

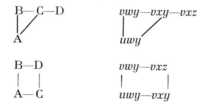

It will be seen that the sequence of the members can be different if we allow rings, so that once again it becomes impossible to say that one genealogical arrangement is better than another, and reasoning comes to a halt. We obtain both a single diagram and a single sequence, however, if we outlaw rings. Therefore, the first corollary to the axiom is as follows:

a. *States must not be connected in a ring.*

When we cannot connect the states in the kind of series just illustrated, we can often connect them through a state we infer from the others and give the required readings. Thus if we have B:ACD in addition to A:BCD, AB:CD, and ABC:D, so that B cannot interrupt the connections between A, C, or D, we cannot manage a connection between them that has no rings—unless we infer a state (E) and give it the readings shared by A and B, as well as those shared by A and the rest and by B and the rest. If we say that B:ACD represents the alternation of the readings *s* and *t*, then (E) will have the readings *tvwy*:

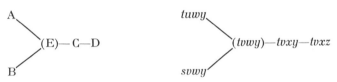

On the other hand, we should not infer (E) if B:ACD did not occur, for in that case, (E) would have the readings *vwy*, which would be the same as those of B; in other words, B and (E) would be the same state. A bibliographer, who accepts records as both distinct and duplicates, would still not infer (E), for if he allows free inference of duplicate records it once again becomes impossible to say that one genealogical relationship is better than another, and reasoning comes to a halt.

From all this follows the second corollary to the axiom:

b. *States are to be inferred with readings as necessary to provide the connections.*

The comparable corollary for a bibliographer would be: Additional records are to be inferred as necessary to make the connections, but no more records than necessary.

There will be many instances when the second corollary will not meet the requirements of the first. For example, if we have A:BCD, AB:CD, and two examples of AC:BD, representing respectively *u:v*, *w:x*, *o:p*, and *q:r*, then the only way to connect the members according to their readings is in a ring:

$$\begin{array}{cc}
\text{A---B} & \quad oquw\text{---}prvw \\
| \quad | & \quad | \qquad\qquad | \\
\text{C---D} & \quad oqvx\text{---}prvx
\end{array}$$

We shall continue to work with this very simple ring, but we ought to note parenthetically that it is unusual in being the only possible ring under the circumstances. Once we add direction to a ring, one element will be at the bottom, with one (above it and) connected to it on each side. Any of these three elements can be groups in simple variations without requiring any change in the ring. When any other element is a group in a simple variation, however, one of the elements must be replaced by an inferential intermediary to which the displaced element must be connected, or there must be an additional connection that bypasses the element, making a ring within a ring. Since it is normal for elements to be groups in simple variations also, in general there is no way to decide whether to increase the number of rings or to replace an element of the ring with an intermediary and, in the latter case, which element to replace. It therefore becomes for the most part just as impossible to reason genealogically about rings when it would seem that they must occur as it would be if we allowed them into the diagram when there was no need for them at all.

The only way we can continue to reason when a ring seems to be forced upon us is to break it at some logical point. Returning, then, to our sample ring above we notice that the only reading transmitted between A and B is w, whereas two are transmitted between A and C and between C and D, oq and vx respectively, and three between B and D, to wit, prv. In textual analysis we say that a connection representing the transmission of one reading is weaker than a connection representing the transmission of two readings, and so on. Then the weakest connection in the example is that between A and B. We can break this connection by treating A and B as though the reading had occurred independently in both, which is, in effect, to treat the reading w as though it were two different readings. If the readings in A and B were different we should write A:B:CD instead of AB:CD. If we decide, then, to treat the reading w as two we can rewrite AB:CD as *A:B:CD, using the asterisk to indicate that A:B:CD does not in fact occur.

Then we recognize that as B cannot come between C and D (*A:B:CD) or between A and C (AC:BD) it cannot interrupt the connections between A, C, and D, a fact that we can record by writing *B:ACD, for B:ACD if it had occurred would similarly have prevented B from interrupting the connections between A, C, and D.

From A:BCD, AC:BD, and *B:ACD we can connect the members as follows: A—C—D—B. *A:B:CD, which may be said to represent $*w^1{:}w^2{:}x$, fits this connection: $oquw^1$—$oqvx$—$prvx$—$prvw^2$.

We cannot, of course, break rings freely at any connection, since that would mean again that any genealogical relationship was as good as any other, and reasoning would come to a halt. Breaking the weakest instead of some other standard connection reflects the principle of parsimony. The fewest possible readings are treated as something different from what they really are. This happens also to maximize the readings the states will have in common in the ringless diagram.

It will be seen that in diagrams naturally without rings as well is in those with rings the states share more readings with those nearest to them in the diagram than with those farther off, and that the number of common readings decreases (except that it cannot be less than zero) as the intermediaries between states increase. This condition survives when we break a ring. Working right from A, in our example A—C—D—B, A and C share o and q, A and D share nothing, and A and B also share nothing, now that we have divided w into w^1 and w^2. Working left from C, A and C share o and q; working right, C and D share v and x, C and B share v. Working left from D, D and C share v and x, D and A share nothing; working right, D and B share p, r, and v. Working left from B, B and D share p, r, and v, B and C share v, and B and A share nothing, now that we have divided w into w^1 and w^2. The condition holds true even if the diagram, after breaking the ring, has inferential intermediaries. If in addition to the foregoing variations we also had ABC:D, representing the alternation of the readings y and z, we should have the same ring and break it at the same connection:

A—B   *oquwy*—*prvwy*
| | | |
C—D   *oqvxy* — *prvxz*

But we should have to infer an intermediary (E) with readings *prvxy* between B and D and the rest:

We should then see that the nearest states, including the inferential intermediary, once more have the most readings in common, and that the number of common readings decreases as the intermediaries between states increase:

A and C	*oqy*	C and A	*oqy*	D and (E)	*prvx*	B and (E)	*prvy*
A and (E)	*y*	C and (E)	*vxy*	D and B	*prv*	B and D	*prv*
A and D	none	C and D	*vx*	D and C	*vx*	B and C	*vy*
A and B	*y*	C and B	*vy*	D and A	none	B and A	*y*

From all this follows the third corollary to rule 2:

c. *In instances where it is impossible to avoid a ring by inferring states, the weakest connection making up the ring is to be set aside.*

A bibliographer following this process is determining the principal relationships of his records, and so may define "weakest" differently than a textual analyst. Because he concerns himself with cause rather than effect, he must consider chance and emendation as causes for agreement. He may therefore give less weight to agreements that he feels may reflect these causes and more weight to striking errors and to peculiarities in the manufacture of the records. "Weakest" for him then would mean "having the least weight of agreements" rather than having the least number.

It will be seen that the foregoing axiom and its corollaries operate without regard to the direction of transmission of the readings from state to state. If A has a reading *w* that has in some way given rise to the alternate reading *x* in B, then the direction of transmission is from A to B. To say the opposite would be to deny that the connection between A and B was genealogical. If instead of the foregoing B has a reading *y* that has in some way given rise to the reading *z* in A, then the direction of transmission is from B to A. If both the foregoing occur, then the direction of transmission is to A and B independently from an inferential intermediary (C) with readings *yw*:

Here the textual analyst may seem to be dealing with causes, like the bibliographer, but in fact he is not. Causally speaking, a corruption may give rise to an emendation, but if the emendation is successful the *result* is the same as if the emendation had given rise to the corruption, and the textual analyst accepts it as having done so.

But an objection may still remain. Is not descent purely physical and are not states of a text purely mental? How can a concrete physical process be equated with an abstract mental relationship? In short, when we take the step from a preliminary diagram to a tree, have we not involved ourselves in a contradiction? I believe that the objection arises out of too biological a sense of genealogy. In biological genealogy the ancestors are themselves the creators of their descendants. In bibliographical genealogy, however, a manuscript ancestor does not create a manuscript descendant, a scribe creates the descendant after a model provided by the ancestor. The same is true of textual genealogy. Once a text is in existence, whether we think of it as a manuscript or as a message, no other state or record of the text can come into existence except through the activities of an agent using a model—unless we suppose that the likenesses we observe between the two can have occurred spontaneously, and that we are unwilling to do. If, then, we are to deny the concept of descent to states of a text we must deny it also to records, for there is no difference in the way in which they come into being. In fact, we can have a purely abstract relationship among states of a text only if we assume that they can occur spontaneously. Note, too, that the creator of the new state is not an idea. We can therefore without contradiction draw upon evidence of his physical activities to distinguish between his model and his creation, that is, to pass from the preliminary diagram to the tree.

As we have seen, a real or apparent omission of a characteristic may cause it to be supplied, and a really or apparently superfluous characteristic may cause itself to be omitted. Let us agree that these situations are forms of substituting the characteristic x for w in which w or x is in fact the absence of the other characteristic. With this understanding the second axiom of textual analysis and its first corollary are:

2. *When a reading w can be recognized as having given rise to a reading x some state having w must stand above all states having x in the textual tree.*

a. *If necessary a state having the reading w is to be inferred.*

A reading w may give rise to a reading x, and x may then give rise to y, and so on. Then some state having w must stand above all states having x, some state having x must stand above all states having y, and so on. So much is obvious. If w gives rise to x and also to y, then some state having w must stand above all states having x and above all states having y. On the other hand, when we cannot determine whether w has given rise to x or x to w, a state A having w need not stand above a state B having x unless A also has a reading y that has given rise to a reading z found in B. Therefore the second corollary to rule 3 is as follows:

b. *The archetype must not have a reading x when a state having a reading w must stand above all states having x.*

Such are the very simple rules of textual analysis. To give a final example, if we have A:BCD, B:ACD, C:ABD, D:ABC, and AB:CD, we connect the four members by inferring two more as follows:

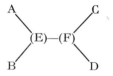

If A:BCD represents $u{:}v$, AB:CD represents $w{:}x$, D:ACB represents $z{:}y$, C:ABD represents $n{:}m$, and B:ACD represents $t{:}s$, then (E) and (F) have the characteristics shown:

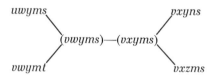

If in addition v has given rise to u, w to x, and s to t, then (E) has all the characteristics that have given rise to others and is the archetype.

As we have seen, it is not necessary to represent the inferential states by anything more than junctures in the lines. The foregoing tree then reduces to

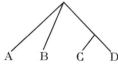

The first axiom and its second corollary act like the centrifugal and centripetal forces in the solar system to determine the form of the genealogical system, making some members and groups necessarily terminal and others necessarily intermediary. For example, if we have

A:BCD, representing *y:z*, B:ACD, representing *w:x*, C:ABD, representing *u:v*, and D:ABC, representing *s:t*, we need an inferential intermediary to make the connections:

Thus the groups A, B, C, and D are necessarily terminal, and so are the groups BCD(E), ACD(E), ABC(E), and ABD(E), though it may take a moment's thought to recognize the terminality of the true groups.

Then if we also have such variations as A:B:CD, representing *m:n:o*, and AB:C:D, representing *p:q:r*, we still need only the same single inferential intermediary:

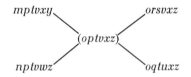

Thus the group AB(E) is necessarily intermediary between C and D and the group CD(E) necessarily intermediary between A and B.

In what follows the inferential intermediaries will not be overtly specified, but the reader must be aware that they exist.

When a variation with two true groups has both groups overlapped by two groups in a second variation in such a way that one of the two in each overlaps both in the other, a connection results that makes the doubly overlapped groups intermediary between the remaining states in the other groups. Thus if we have the variations A:BC:DE, and AB:CD:E, representing *x:y:z* and *u:v:w*, the groups BC and CD must be intermediary:

A—B—C—D—E   *ux—uy—vy—vz—wz*

Even if we have variations B:ACDE and C:ABDE, representing *q:r* and *s:t*, the group BC is still intermediary:

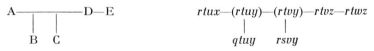

And the same would be true for the group CD if D were also terminal.

If we were to make BC as well as B and C terminal, we should have to accept the characteristic *u* in A and B or the characteristic *v* in C and D as the result not of transmission but of spontaneous appearance:

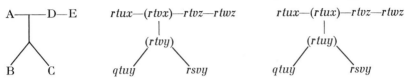

And similarly if we were to make CD terminal. Therefore we make these groups intermediary.

Intermediacy will extend to more than two groups if there are enough overlapping groups in the two variations, as in AB:CD:EF and A:BC: DE:F, which make BC, CD, and DE intermediary, or if there are suitable groups in another variation, as in AB:CD:E:F, A:BC:DE:F, and A:B: CD:EF, which also make BC, CD, and DE intermediary, or AB:CD: E:F:G:H, A:BC:DE:FG:H, and A:B:C:D:EF:GH, which make BC, CD, DE, EF, and FG intermediary. Notice that the order of the intermediary groups is also fixed: CD is necessarily intermediary between BC and DE, a fact that is important in the derivation of synthetic simple variations.

Notice that with AB:CD:E:F, A:BC:DE:F, and A:B:CD:EF, the first and last variations have the same group, CD, which is overlapped by the groups BC and DE in the second variation. With AB:CD:E:F:G:H, A:BC:DE:FG:H, and A:B:C:D:EF:GH, no group in the first variation is the same as a group in the last variation, but both have a group that overlaps the group DE in the second variation. Either type of sequence extends the overlaps between the first and second variations into the overlaps between the second and third variations.

Notice that each of the groups making up the overlap is divided into two elements in the overlap sequence, for example, AB in the original examples above becomes A—B, BC becomes B—C. An intermediate element in a sequence is a state or a number of states that have different states grouped with them in different variations that make the sequence.

When two variations have groups that make an overlap sequence and one of these has a group with states from both end elements of the sequence, we have a ring. For example, if we have a variation AB:CDE:FG, representing *x:y:z*, and a variation AG:BCD:EF, representing *u:v:w*, we will have, if we start our thinking with the group

AB, a sequence A—B—CD—E—F—G that the group AG makes into a ring:

$$
\begin{array}{ll}
\text{A—B—CD} & ux—vx—vy \\
\text{|\ \ \ \ \ |} & |\ \ \ \ \ \ \ \ | \\
\text{G—F—E} & uz—wz—wy
\end{array}
$$

Or two or more variations may establish a sequence that another variation will make into a ring. For example, if we have variations A:BC:DE, representing *r:s:t*, and AB:CD:E, representing *o:p:q*, we have a sequence A—B—C—D—E that the variation AE:BCD, representing *m:n*, makes into a ring:

$$
\begin{array}{ll}
\text{A—B—C} & mor—nos—nps \\
\text{|\ \ \ \ \ |} & |\ \ \ \ \ \ \ \ \ \ \ \ | \\
\text{E———D} & mqt————npt
\end{array}
$$

A requirement in all ring-closing variations is that they have in addition to the ring-closing group another group with states from at least two elements in the ring, at least one of which is different from the elements in the ring-closing group. The requirement is met automatically when the ring is made from only two variations, but not otherwise. In the event that the requirement is not met, the sequence is not in fact closed; instead we have evidence of terminality or we have identified part of another ring, or both. Suppose we have the variations ABC:DE:FG, representing *x:y:z*, and AB:CD:EFG, representing *u:v:w*, which together give an overlap sequence AB—C—D—E—FG. Suppose we also have a variation AG:BF:C:D:E, representing *p:q:r:s:t*. This variation does not make a ring of the whole sequence, for each of the intermediate elements of the sequence can be terminal, leaving the connections for *p* and *q* uninterrupted except by each other:

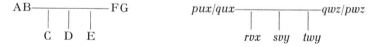

If the third variation had two or more of the last three states in a true group, it would make a ring of the sequence. Suppose it were AG:BF:CD:E, representing *p:q:r:s*. Then C would have *rvx* as before, but D would have *rvy*, and there would have to be a connection between them for *r* which would not be interrupted by nor interrupt the connections for *p* and *q*. In short, there would be a ring. Returning to the variation AG:BF:C:D:E we see that it does make a ring with each of the first two variations separately. The elements in each ring are the same, but the readings in question are different:

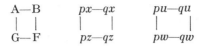

A ring is a closed sequence in which all elements are intermediary. We notice that the ring made up by the first and third variations results from groups ABC, FG, AG, and BF, and that C, having rx, is not an element. Suppose that other evidence leads us to break the ring at the A—B connection. What do we do with C? There is nothing in the readings to indicate whether C should be kept with A or with B. We solve the problem by separating the elements from each other and from any other states in their group. Thus we should rewrite the first variation *A:B:C:DE:FG. In this way we imply nothing as to the relationship of C to A and to B, but leave the matter to be decided by the evidence of other variations. The situation is the same with E in the ring made up by the second and third variations. In the same way, AB:CDE:FG and AG:BC:D:EF form a ring in which D is not an element, even though states in the group CDE make up the ring. Finally, if we have variations AB:CD:EF and ABC:DE:F, making a sequence AB—C—D—E—F, and a ring-closing variation AF:B:CDE, B is not an element in the ring. In each instance we see that the nonelement fails to conform to the definition of an element, namely, a state that has different states grouped with it in the different variations that make the sequence.

The other problems in breaking rings we solve by returning to the principle of parsimony, which in one application means never rewriting two variations when rewriting one will serve. In the first place, if an elements consists of more than one state, so that we can break the ring by dividing the element, we still do not do so because it would mean rewriting two variations. For example, suppose we have a ring formed by AB:CDE:FG and AG:BCD:EF:

```
A—B—CD
|   |    |
G—F——E
```

If we were to break the ring by dividing C from D we should have to rewrite both of the groups CDE and BCD.

In the second place, when we extend an overlap with a new variation, we let the preceding variations determine the elements in the part of the overlap they establish. Thus if we have AB:CD:EF:GH, A:BC: DEF:GH, and AB:CDE:FG:H we do not concern ourselves with the fact that we get different sequences depending upon whether we start with the first and second and extend with the second and third or start with the first and third and extend with the second and third:

$$A—B—C—D—EF—G—H$$
$$H—G—F—E—CD—B—A$$

Instead, we make both sequences and break any rings of which they may be a part according to the elements in each and the variations that determine the elements. If the first sequence made a ring with a fourth variation that was to be broken between C and D, we should rewrite only the first variation, not the third as well.

In the third place, we do not divide an element in a sequence when the ring-closing variation has groups that would divide it. For example, if we have A:BCD:EF and AB:CDE:F we have a sequence A—B—CD—E—F that a variation AF:BC:DE makes into a ring. But the ring has five elements, not six,

even though the ring-closing variation would make a sequence with either of the others in which C and D were separate elements. If we made a six-element ring

$$
\begin{array}{ccc}
A—B—C \\
| \quad\quad | \\
F—E—D
\end{array}
$$

and then found the C—D connection was the one to break, we should have to rewrite two groups, BCD and CDE, instead of only one.

And in the fourth place, when the ring-closing group in a variation includes more than the end elements of a sequence established by other variations, we ignore all but the elements in the ring-closing group which are closest together in the sequence. This procedure makes the ring as small as possible and keeps us from having to rewrite more than one variation. For example, if we have variations AB:CD:EF and A:BC:DE:F, giving a sequence A—B—C—D—E—F, and a ring-closing variation ABF:CDE, the ring indicated does not include A:

We see that if we included A in the ring and decided that the A—B connection was the one to break we should have to rewrite two groups, AB and ABF.

With the pencil and paper calculus in chapter 2 we must determine the smallest ring by inspection because we determine a whole sequence at once; with the calculi in the appendixes we build the sequences group by group and test for rings each time we add a group.

A final application of the principle of parsimony in breaking rings means never rewriting two groups in a variation if one would serve. Suppose we have variations A:BC:DEF, AB:C:DEF, and AF:BE:CD. The first and third form a ring, and so do the second and third, in both of which B—E is a connection. Therefore we can break both rings by breaking the one connection, provided, of course, that it is the weakest connection in at least one of the rings, and provided also that we break the rings in decreasing order of the strengths of their weakest connections. If our rule were to break the rings in the opposite order, and the A—F connection were the weakest in one ring and the B—E in the other, we should break both rings separately and divide two groups in AF:BE:CD.

The rule of breaking the strongest weakest connection first may seem to involve us in difficulties with variations such as AB:CDEF, ABCF: DE, and ACE:BDF, where the first and third and the second and third form rings. If we had to break the second of these rings before the first, and we had to do so by rewriting the second variation as *AC: BF:DE, we should produce a ring between the first and second variations. Might we not avoid this new ring if we could break the rings in the reverse order? No, the new ring would be produced even if the third variation had been rewritten: neither *A:CE:BDF nor *ACE:B:DF will form a ring with the second variation that can be broken by dividing the group ABCF into *AB:CF or into groups of three states and a singleton. We could introduce additional rules to take care of such problems, but because the rules we have will take care of the problems if we apply them repeatedly, we simply start the ring testing again after we have broken all the rings disclosed by the preceding series of tests. We use the original pair counts when we need to reiterate the ring-breaking process, because they reflect the original variations, and because any reiteration is still solving problems posed by the original variations, even if not recognized before.

The discovery of another state may introduce rings or alter our solution of rings. Thus A:BCD and AB:CD do not indicate a ring, but AE:BCD and AB:CDE do. This possibility is of more concern to a bibliographer, who is attempting to discover the principal ancestries of his records, than to a textual analyst. The textual analyst is giving a genealogical ordering to the known states of his text. If a new state becomes known, he does not feel that it invalidates his earlier work any more than T. S. Eliot felt that because a wholly new work of art alters the relationships between previous works, the previous relationships between those works were invalid.

In textual analysis we say that if a state A of a text has *u* where B and C have *v*, B has *w* where A and C have *x*, and C has *y* where A and B have *z*, giving the readings *uxz* in A, *vwz* in B, and *vxy* in C, we infer a state (D) with readings *vxz* intermediary between the other three:

But in bibliography we cannot always say that a record A with readings *uxz*, B with *vwz*, and C with *vxy* implies a record (D) with *vxz*. Under normal circumstances we infer the existence of such a record in the past or overlooked by us, but if we somehow know that no such intermediary ever existed, we obviously cannot infer it. As a result, if we find variations A:BC, B:AC, and C:AB, and no inferential intermediary is possible, we must conclude that one of the three records is conflated:

Many bibliographers, however, leap too quickly to the conclusion that they are in possession of all the records. It is strictly impossible to assert that one has every manuscript of a work, for every manuscript is an individual, and thus too easily lost or left unrecorded. Therefore while it is certainly possible for a copyist to combine the readings of two independent ancestors, it is more probable that the readings were first found together in a lost intermediary between the three extant manuscripts (a little thought will show that the intermediary need not be the ancestor of the other records):

Even if a variation A:B:C, representing *r:s:t*, could be interpreted as a reading in one manuscript which was a corruption of both the alternate readings, it is still possible that the readings existed in the lost intermediary and were corrupted together from there (a little more thought will show that once again the intermediary need not be the ancestor of the other records):

Printed records have less chance of disappearing, but the corrected copy of an edition sent for reprinting is as unique as a manuscript and as likely to disappear. Therefore even if A, B, and C in the former examples were editions of many copies each, it might be that none was conflated, but that two were set in type from a corrected copy of the third or even that all were set from the same manuscript.

By the first axiom, every group in a variation excludes the rest of the members from being intermediary between its members. If in turn all its members are excluded from being intermediary between any of the other members, the group is terminal. The groups in a simple variation are terminal because each includes all the members not included in the other. A group in a complex variation may be intermediary between other groups in the variation. If, however a complex group excludes and is excluded by AB in one variation and by BC in another, it obviously excludes and is excluded from being intermediary between any of the overlap *ABC. We cannot say that it could be intermediary between A and C, because that would introduce a ring. And if *ABC includes all the other states of the text, the group and the overlap must also be terminal. Thus it is possible to identify complex groups and overlaps of groups as terminal and to record the fact in synthetic simple variations in which the terminal overlaps appear as groups.

For example, the variations AB:CD:EF, representing *t:u:v,* and A:BC:DE:F, representing *w:x:y:z,* indicate a sequence:

A—B—C—D—E—F   *tw—tx—ux—uy—vy—vz*

Here we see that the group A and the overlap *BCDEF, resulting from BC, CD, DE, and EF, are terminal, a fact that we can record by writing the synthetic simple variation *A:BCDEF. For similar reasons we can write *F:ABCDE, *AB:CDEF, and *EF:ABCD. Finally we see that the two overlaps *ABC and *DEF are terminal, a fact that we can record by writing the synthetic simple variation *ABC:DEF.

If a group in a simple variation overlaps a complex group, the complex group is intermediary; if a group in a simple variation wholly includes a single complex group the complex group is terminal; but if a group in a simple variation wholly includes more than one complex group or is wholly included in a complex group no information is given about terminality or intermediacy. For example, variations EF:ABCD, representing *v:w*, and ABC:DE:F, representing *x:y:z*, give a sequence

ABC—D—E—F   *wx—wy—vy—vz*

from which we see that DE is intermediary and ABC and F terminal. On the other hand the variations AB:CDEF, representing *t:u*, and ABC:DE:F, representing *x:y:z*, do not make any of the complex groups either terminal or intermediary, since any of the following sequences is possible:

DE—C—F   *uy—ux—uz*
   | |
 AB   *tx*

AB—C—DE—F   *tx—ux—uy—uz*

AB—C—F—DE   *tx—ux—uz—uy*

Often enough, more than two variations are required to establish a unique sequence. For example, the variations A:BC:DE, representing *x:y:z*, and AB:C:DE, representing *u:v:w*, allow three sequences:

A—B—C—DE   *ux—uy—vy—wz*

C—B—A—DE   *vy—uy—ux—wz*

A—B—DE   *ux—uy—wz*
 | |
 C   *vy*

These sequences are enough to show that the group DE and the overlap *ABC are terminal, but they tell us nothing more. The variation AB:CD:E, representing *r:s:t*, however, gives a unique sequence:

A—B—C—D—E   *rux—ruy—svy—swz—twz*

From this sequence we see that A, E, AB and DE are terminal, and BC, CD and BCD intermediary. With no other variations, B, C, and D will be intermediary by default, but other variations may show that they also are terminal, as for instance ABE:C:D, representing *o:p:q*, makes C and D terminal:

A—B————— E   *orux—oruy—(osvy)—(oswz)—olwz*
      | |
      C D   *psvy   qswz*

The left-hand inferential intermediary could have *u, w,* nothing, or some other reading, instead of *v*, since no two of the states between which it is intermediary agree here. Notice that even though both states of the group CD are terminal, the group is still intermediary. This is possible only with groups in complex variations; groups in simple variations are always terminal.

Sometimes we cannot use a variation that divides off and divides up a group as proof that the group is terminal. For example, if we have A:BCDE, representing *y:z*, B:ACDE, representing *w:x*, AB:C:DE, representing *t:u:v*, and A:B:CD:E, representing *p:q:r:s*, the group AB has no more need to be terminal than C or DE, even though the overlap of CD and DE excludes both A and B.

C————————D—E   *ruxz—(rtxz)—rvxz—svxz*
   / \
  A   B   *ptxy   qtwz*

Nor is the exclusion more necessary if the test group includes a non-terminal text that might be the intermediary of the group. This text has no more need to be intermediary than an inferential intermediary, as we can see by deleting A:BCDE, representing *y:z*, from the foregoing.

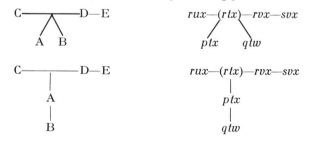

In the second of the alternates the inferential intermediary might have *u, v,* nothing, or some other reading instead of *t*, since no two of the states between which it is intermediary agree here. Both the foregoing diagrams conform equally well to the axioms of textual analysis. Together they are an example of an ambiguity that we shall have more to say about when we discuss building the preliminary diagram from the simple variations.

On the other hand, A:BCDEF, representing *y:z*, B:ACDEF, representing *w:x*, AB:CD:E:F, representing *s:t:u:v*, A:BC:DE:F, representing *o:p:q:r*, and A:B:CD:EF, representing *k:l:m:n*, make the group AB terminal, even if we assign its inferential intermediary the characteristic *m* instead of *k* or *l*.

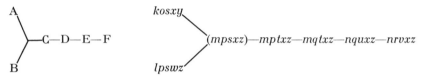

We cannot put the intermediary between C and D because they have *t* where A and B have *s*; if we were to do so and gave the intermediary the reading *s* we would interrupt the connection between C and D, which the first axiom will not allow, and if we gave it the reading *t* we would interrupt the connection between A and B. Similarly, if we were to put it between D and E we would either interrupt the connection between them or between B and C (which have *p* where they have *q*), and if we were to put it between E and F we would still interrupt the connection between B and C. All this would be true even if C, D, E, and F were terminal, so that other inferential intermediaries were required.

What has happened here is that the overlap of the groups AB and CD in the third variation with the groups BC and DE in the fourth has set up a sequence A—B—C—D—E that the overlap of CD and EF in the fifth variation with BC and DE in the fourth has extended in a direction away from A and B. Hence the question of whether AB is divided in the fifth variation is immaterial.

Let us use the term "prime intermediary" for an intermediary in a group that is not also an intermediary in a subgroup of the group. To take the diagram just above, the inferential intermediary is the prime intermediary of the group AB, C is the prime intermediary of the group ABC, E is the prime intermediary of the group EF, D is the prime intermediary of the group DEF. The same state can be the prime intermediary of a group of less than half the states and of one or more groups of more than half the states. Thus D is also the prime intermediary of the group ABCD, and the inferential intermediary is also the prime intermediary of the groups ACDEF and BCDEF.

If an overlap of a complex and one or more simple groups proves to be a terminal group, its prime intermediary will be found among or between the members of the complex group, for the overlapping simple group or groups already have their own prime intermediaries. Therefore a variation in which the test overlap is divided and in which its complex group is also divided cannot be used in establishing a complementary overlap unless the variation extends the complementary overlap away from the test overlap. The reason is the same as for ignoring a variation that simply divides a test group and does not extend the complementary overlap away from the test group: unless there is other evidence to the contrary, there will always be a way to make the test overlap intermediary.

The limitation on the number of intermediaries allows us to recognize terminality in two special cases, which can be recognized, however, only when the complex groups and overlaps of individual complex with simple groups have all been analyzed.

The first case is when two overlaps of complex groups with complex groups, each overlap perhaps overlapping simple groups, include all the states of the text. For example, if we have A:BC:D:EF, representing *w:x:y:z*, and AB:C:DE:F, representing *s:t:u:v*, the overlaps *ABC and *DEF are terminal. The following diagram assumes that all the states are terminal as well, but does not show the readings that would indicate it.

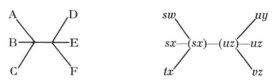

Such overlaps can be extended by overlap with groups from type-2 variations as long as these include only one or all but one of the elements previously established. Thus if we have AB:C:DE:F:G, representing *v:w:x:y:z*, and A:BC:D:EF:G, representing *q:r:s:t:u*, we have an overlap like the foregoing in which G is not an element. A variation FG:ABCDE, representing *o:p*, will extend the overlap to include G:

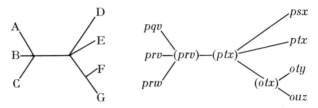

The right-hand inferential intermediary could have y, z, nothing, or some other reading, instead of x. But a variation EFG:ABCD, representing $m{:}n$, allows either of the following:

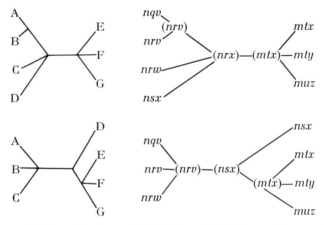

In the second alternate the middle inferential intermediary could have r, t, nothing, or some other reading instead of s.

The second special case is when a complex group excludes and is excluded by other complex groups in turn, but only one in each variation, the immediate subgroups of which are terminal. For example, if we have AB:C:D:EF, representing $s{:}t{:}u{:}v$, and AB:CD:E:F, representing $w{:}x{:}y{:}z$, and C, D, E, and F are terminal (the readings requiring this not being shown), the following diagram is required by the limitation on the number of intermediaries:

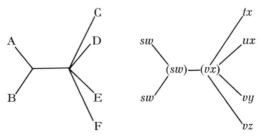

But if one or more of C, D, E, or F can be intermediary, then the group AB need not be terminal:

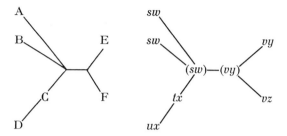

The second reading of the inferential intermediary on the right is not defined, it could be *w*, *z*, nothing, or something else, but it is clear that we have no more added intermediaries than before, whereas if C had been terminal we should have had to infer a third intermediary with the first reading undefined and the second *x* before we could make CD terminal and AB intermediary.

Let us suppose we have A:BCD, representing *y:z*, B:ACD, representing *w:x*, AB:CD, representing *u:v*, and *C:ABD, derived from the foregoing, and A:BD:C, representing *r:s:t*. We draw a line from each singleton group in the type-1 variations: we connect the lines from A and B and draw a line from the connection. We connect the line from C to D and draw a line from D. Finally we run the tag end lines together. When we substitute the readings for the states in the resulting diagram, we see it is correct, and that our procedure is therefore correct:

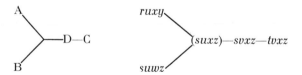

If we have A:BCD, representing *y:z*, B:ACD, representing *w:x*, and C:ABD, representing *u:v*, we connect the lines from A, B, and C at D:

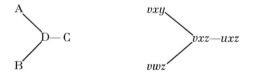

And if we have the foregoing and D:ABC, representing *s:t*, we connect the lines from the four members together.

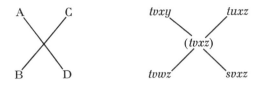

If a terminal group consists wholly of states that are not terminal, we may have duplicate records, rather than states, or they may be equally substitutable for one another in the resulting diagram, in which case we have effective duplicates. For example, if we have A:BCD, representing *y:z*, B:ACD, representing *w:x*, and AB:CD, representing *u:v*, C and D, both having *vxz*, are records of the same state. If in addition to the foregoing we have AB:C:D, representing *r:s:t*, C has *svxz* and D has *tvxz*, but this complex variation will not yield synthetic simple variations, so the resulting diagram is necessarily as follows:

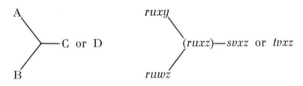

In the same way, if two states can equally well be the prime intermediaries for their group they are either one state in duplicate records or effective duplicates. One state in duplicate records may be an effective duplicate of a second state, three states may be effective duplicates, and so on.

We come now to anomalous variations. If all the states are terminal and we have AB:CDEF, representing *y:z*, and AB:CD:EF, representing *v:w:x*, we should diagram as follows because the complex variation does not yield synthetic simple variations:

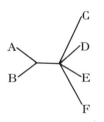

Yet it is clear that one of the following must be true instead (the readings making the individual members terminal are not shown):

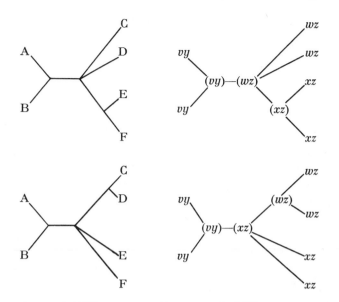

If we have A:BCD, representing y:z, B:ACD, representing w:x, C:ABD, representing u:v, and AB:C:D, representing r:s:t, we should diagram as follows because the complex variation does not yield synthetic simple variations:

Yet it is clear that one of the following must be true instead:

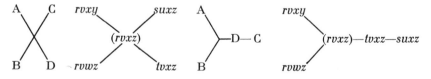

Before we leave this subject we may notice one other phenomenon. If we have A:BCD:E, representing x:y:z, and AB:C:DE, representing u:v:w, we shall obtain from them the synthetic variations *A:BCDE and *E:ABCD, and from these the diagram

A—B or C or D—E ux—uy or vy or wy—wz

We could expand this diagram in three ways:

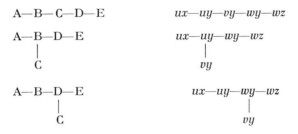

But to choose any one of these diagram is to go against our required practice elsewhere, which on the one hand makes intermediaries of states not necessarily terminal, and on the other holds the number of intermediaries to a minimum.

If A:B represents $y\cdot z$, and the reading y has somehow given rise to z, we write A→B and we say that y is the most (or more) original reading. If A:B:C represents $x\,y{:}z$, and (1) x has given rise to y and y to z, or (2) other variations show that A is terminal, and B is contiguous to A in the preliminary diagram, and x has given rise to y, we write A→B→C, and we say that x is the most original reading. In either case the variation indicates a tree of the following form:

$$
\begin{array}{ccc}
\text{A} & x & x \\
| & \downarrow & \downarrow \\
\text{B} & y \quad\text{or}\quad & y \\
| & \downarrow & | \\
\text{C} & z & z
\end{array}
$$

The only way, in the right-hand instance, to make C earlier than the other states would be to introduce a ring, making C an ancestor of B.

If A:B:C represents $x{:}y{:}z$, and y has given rise to x and to z, we write A←B→C. Here the variation indicates a tree of the following form:

If A:B:C represents $x{:}y{:}z$, other variations show that C is contiguous to B in the preliminary diagram and that y has given rise to z, we cannot decide between the two foregoing trees. We can indicate this uncertainty by writting a synthetic simple variation *AB→C, which will fit both trees.

It may seem that if we have two examples of A:B:C, representing $u{:}v{:}w$ and $x{:}y{:}z$, and u has given rise to v and y to z, the two variations indicate a tree of the following form:

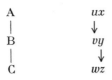

In fact, however, the following are equally possible:

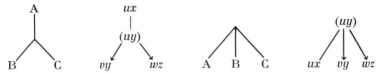

Other suggestive combinations of partially directional variations may occur to the reader but all must be rejected for similar reasons.

Finally, A:B:C may appear to represent $x:y:z$ where both x and z give rise to y, but it is impossible for two readings to give rise to a third. Instead the apparent third will be found to be a double reading, and we shall write A→B:C, representing x in A, y^1 in B, and no alternate in C, A:B←C representing z in C, y^2 in B, and no alternate in A. The two variations indicate a ring, as we shall see below.

We use the same reasoning with more than three states. For instance, if the preliminary diagram is

$$A—B—C—D$$

and we have A:B:C:D, representing $w:x:y:z$, and x has given rise to y, we write *AB→CD. If the preliminary diagram is

the inferential intermediary is contiguous to A, B, and C, and agrees with any two that agree. Consequently variations AB:C:D may include examples of AB→C:D, AB←C→D, *AB←CD, and so on; variations A:BC:D may include examples of A→BC:D, A←BC→D, *A←BCD *D←ABC, and so on; and similarly with AC:B:D.

But in the event that the states are not contiguous, the only kind of complex variation that is fully directional is that in which all characteristics are identifiable as more or less original. Thus, if A, B, and C are connected through an inferential intermediary, a variation A:B:C does not indicate the reading of the inferential intermediary. Therefore, if it represents *x:y:z* and if all we can say is that *x* has given rise to *y*, the inferential intermediary may also have *x*, and we cannot decide between the trees:

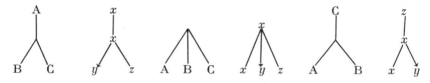

Synthetic complex variations that result from resolving conflations offer no problems if the groups that were divided do not have the most original readings. If AB→CD is resolved into *AB:C:D, no problems arise. The resultant variation with arrows is *C←AB→D. Otherwise the variations are not directional. If AB→CD is resolved into *A:B:CD, we cannot tell whether the reading in A or in B gave rise to that in CD. We might think that we could then write A→CD←B, but the arrows would then indicate that A and B were independent ancestors of CD, and this is not what the variation indicates.

From all the foregoing we see that it is only after we have worked out the preliminary diagram that we can finally decide which variations among the complex are fully directional.

Normally, some combination of directional variations defines a tree. Sometimes there will not be enough evidence for definition; sometimes the evidence will point to conflation that was not previously recognized. The reasoning is as follows. By the second corollary of the second axiom, an archetype has all the most original readings in the fully directional variations. Suppose we have the following preliminary diagram:

If the directional variations are at a minimum AB←CD, representing *y*←*z*, and D←ABC, representing *w*←*x*, with perhaps also A←BCD, representing *u*←*v*, and B←ACD, representing *s*←*t*, we locate the archetype at C:

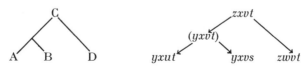

If the directional variations are as before but with AB→CD, representing $q→r$, instead of AB←CD, we locate the archetype at the inferential intermediary:

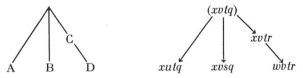

If several states have all the most original readings, any one can be the archetype. If the preliminary diagram is as before, but the only directional variations are B←ACD and AB→CD, the following are equally possible:

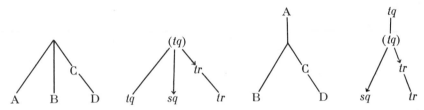

If no state has all the most original readings, then we must infer one that does. We can locate this final inferential intermediary among the other members only under the following conditions: (1) there are two directional variations in one of which the group having the most original reading has all the states not in the group having the most original reading in the other variation; (2) in any other directional variations the groups having the most original readings are either the same as one of the former groups or wholly include one of them. In this case the archetype belongs between the first two groups. Thus if we had AB→CD and AB←CD at a minimum, and perhaps A←BCD, and so on, we should locate the archetype between C and the inferential intermediary between it and A and B:

If we had D←ABC and D→ABC, representing $o→p$, at a minimum, we should locate the archetype between C and D:

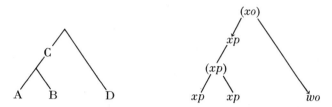

If the foregoing conditions are not met, the archetype does not lie in the preliminary diagram; some states in the diagram have their readings through a ring. Such a situation would be indicated, in our example, if we had AB→CD and D→ABC, for instance, or both AB→CD and AB←CD and D→ABC as well. In such cases we must add the archetype into the variations and begin the analysis anew. It must agree with any state or states having a more original reading. In other instances, its readings are unknown, so it must be written as a singleton. Thus if we have AB→CD we write *AB(A):CD, but if we have AB:CD, we write *AB:CD:(A).

If a partially directional variation will not fit in a tree established by the fully directional variations, we do not have a ring in the tree unless the arrows conflict in the same way as in fully directional variations that indicate rings. Otherwise they show only that some additional state or states are terminal, or that we must relocate the archetype, or both. Suppose we have AB:C←D, representing $l{:}m{\leftarrow}n$, and the evidence of the fully directional variations indicates that the tree is

Then we see that C must be terminal and that we must relocate the archetype:

If we have had to break rings in order to establish a tree, we may be tempted to try to indicate the nature of the rings in the tree itself. We shall then discover that it is impossible to decide on the form of the tree if there are more than four states in it, including inferential intermediaries. For example, suppose that we have variations CE:ABD and DE:ABC, the former of which we have resolved into the synthetic complex variation *AB:CE:D, from which we have with DE:ABC derived *AB:CDE and *D:ABCE, and that we have A:BCDE, B:ACDE, C:ABDE, and E:ABCD. Suppose also that directional variations indicate a tree as follows:

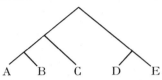

If we wish to make a connection between D and AB as shown in CE: ABD, the following are all equally logical, if we put D at the bottom of the ring, and we have a similar range of choices if we put A or B or the intermediary between them at the bottom of the ring. Note also that other states that were before terminal can now be intermediary:

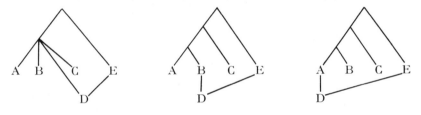

IV

Probabilistic Methods in Textual Criticism

Textual analysis has been referred to more than once by textual critics as a mathematical method. Some counting may be involved in breaking rings, but it should be clear by now to the reader that textual analysis is a logical, not a mathematical, method. I shall now proceed to muddy the waters once more by suggesting that the methods of mathematical probability may have a place in it. The idea is not new, of course, and I shall preface my own view of the matter by pointing out what I regard as the logical errors of others who have proposed different probabilistic methods.

Antonin Hruby has proposed to determine independent descent by the rules of mathematical probability for independent events.[1] Suppose we have three states of a text with variations A:BC, B:AC, C:AB, and A:B:C occurring several times each, some occurrences being fully directional variations with arrows pointing to each of the sigla, for example AC→B and A←B→C. Textual analysis says the tree indicated is

If it were not for the variations A:B:C the textual analyst would have no other choice, for the archetype would be the only other state. The

---

[1] "Statistical Methods in Textual Criticism," *General Linguistics*, V, no. 3, suppl. (1962), 75-138; a simpler treatment in "A Quantitative Solution of the Ambiguity of Three Texts," *Studies in Bibliography*, XVIII (1965), 147-182.

possibility exists, hoever, that when none of the states agree, two of them might have an immediate ancestor with a different reading than the archetype. A bibliographer could consider the possibility that the archetypal state was also recorded in an immediate common ancestor of two of the other records. But in either case, the principle of parsimony requires accepting the tree above, which has the fewest intermediaries required to explain the variations. Professor Hruby, however, says that this can only be a correct analysis if the agreements and disagreements with the archetype in the other three states are independent events. If they are not independent events, he says, then one of the following must be the correct tree:

Professor Hruby says that the laws of probability will indicate which of the alternates is the correct one in any particular instance, but we need not investigate these much more complex matters if we can see that he is wrong in the simpler instance.

What is an independent event?[2] When you toss a coin and it falls heads, that is an event. When it falls tails, that is an event. Experiment has proved that in the long run coins tend to fall heads as often as tails on the average. Alternate probabilities are conventionally represented as fractions with a total value of 1. The two alternatives H (heads) and T (tails), having equal probabilities of occurring, are said to have a probability of $1/2$ each. The events H and T are not independent if we toss a coin only once, but they are if we toss the coin twice, or two coins once each. If the result of the first toss is H, the result of the second can be H or T, or if the result of the first toss is T, the result of the second can be H or T. Since H or T is equally likely on each toss, the four possible outcomes HH, HT, TH, and TT are also

---

[2] All the probabilistic definitions and methods in this chapter except the method of "growing" family trees and the problem of whether statistical inference applies to the past can be found in Frederick Mosteller, Robert E. K. Rourke, and George B. Thomas, Jr., *Probability and Statistics* (Reading, Mass., 1961), and in almost any other elementary text; for the philosophical question see the section "Has 'Probability' One or Many Meanings?" in the article "Probability" in the *Encyclopedia Britannica* [c1961].

equally likely. We can arrange the outcomes in what is called a sample space:

$$\{HH,\ HT,\ TH,\ TT\}$$

In more complex problems, as we shall see, sample spaces help us to calculate the relative probabilities of the outcomes, but in this simple example it is easy enough to see, even without setting up a sample space, that the probability of each outcome is 1/4.

We also see that each outcome consists of the cooccurrence of two events whose probabilities of occurrence multiplied together are the same as the probability of the outcome: $1/2 \times 1/2 = 1/4$. Under these circumstances, H and T are independent events. The definition of independent events, in other words, is that the probability of the events occurring together is the product of their probabilities of occurring at all. Any number of events can be independent, and the events do not need to be of equal probability, but if they are to be accepted as independent they must meet the multiplication test.

The following is a simple example of events that are not independent. It is clear that the probability of having the same result on two tosses of a coin, viz., HH and TT, is the same as the probability of having different results on both tosses, viz., HT and TH, so that the probability that both tosses will have the same result is 1/2. But when we test the events "heads on first toss," "heads on second toss," and "same results on both tosses," we see that they are not independent, for $1/2 \times 1/2 \times 1/2 = 1/8$, but the probability that all the events will occur together, that is, the probability of HH, is 1/4.

The reader may feel that there must be more to independency or the lack of it than meeting or failing to meet the multiplication text. Of course there is. The test would not have been set up unless it reflected a notion of independency. But once set up, it is no longer necessary to inquire in individual cases what the notion behind the test may be, any more than it is necessary to reason out why $1/2 \times 1/2 = 1/4$ or $5/7 \times 2/3 = 10/21$ once one has learned that common fractions are multiplied by multiplying numerators and denominators separately. And in any case we do not need to go beyond the definition to understand how Professor Hruby has used it.

The events Professor Hruby is concerned with are the correct or incorrect copying of the words of a text. If he found, for example, that there were no variations in half the words of a text extant in three states, then he could suppose as an initial estimate, before examining the variations, that state A was correct in nine words in ten, state B in eight words in ten, and state C in seven words in ten and that these instances of correctness were independent events, because .9 × .8 × .7 = .504, or one-half. A half is less than .504, but probability is so iffy in the first place that small differences can be ignored. For example, if one tossed a coin a thousand times and got heads 504 times, he could conclude that he had a fair coin.

If Professor Hruby also found that variations AB:C occurred in one-fifth of the words, his supposition would be strengthened. A variation is a combination of correct and incorrect copying. If C is correct seven times in ten, it is incorrect three times in ten. When we multiply .9, .8, and .3, we get .216, so these instances of correctness and uncorrectness are independent events. And if all the variations occurred in proportions corresponding to the corresponding multiples, then his supposition of the relative accuracy of the three states would meet the definition of independency in all their individual instances of correct and incorrect copying of the text.

But does the fact that all these individual instances of correct and incorrect copying were by definition independent events mean that they resulted from independent descent, and do other events not by definition all independent mean that they have resulted from some other kind of descent? The answer is no. To say that events are independent is quite another thing from explaining how they came to be independent. It is not how we toss a coin nor the fact that we toss a coin instead of something else that makes the outcomes of two tosses independent events; it is the probabilities of the various outcomes separately and in combination. So it is not the descent of the states that makes their individual instances of correctness and incorrectness independent; it is the correctness of their readings separately and in combination.

To put the matter another way, we can imagine any number of situations where independent descent will not result in independent events, and situations where another kind of descent will result in independent events. To take the latter point first, the alternatives to independent descent with three states of a text are of the pattern

All we have to suppose is that A is correct nine times in ten, B, eight times in ten, C, seven times in ten, and the immediate ancestor of B and C almost always, to get close enough to .504 for no variations, .216 for A:BC, and so on, to satisfy the multiplication rule for independent descent. The closer the value for the ancestor approaches 1, the closer the results will be to .504 and so on, because multiplying any value by 1 leaves it unaltered. And if we think, as Professor Hruby does, of records instead of states, then the ancestor of B and C may record the same state as the archetype, in which case its proportion of accuracy is exactly 1.

And on the other side of the coin, there is nothing in the nature of independent descent that forces us to suppose any particular standard of accuracy in the descendants. It is perfectly possible that all the states would be equally accurate. Here we must realize that while equal accuracy must be rare, so must the combination of relative accuracies of .9, .8, and .7 be rare. We tend to *notice* certain occurrences as rare; for example, when the total at the cash register comes to exactly a dollar. If we kept records we should find that it was equally rare for the cash register total to come to exactly ninety-nine cents, or a dollar and a quarter. We lump all the instances of more-or-less-than-a-dollar against the instances of exactly-a-dollar, and think of the latter as rarer. Equal accuracy in all the states is like exactly-a-dollar; we tend to lump against it all the instances of unequal accuracy. Any combination of relative accuracies is possible in independent descent, because there is nothing in the descent itself that makes the descendants more or less accurate. Their accuracy is determined by the accuracy of those who recorded them, at a minimum, and possibly also by the amount of damage suffered by the records from which they were taken and by the accuracy of those who made those records over longer or shorter chains of copying. And similarly, any combination of accuracy is possible in the descendants when the descent is not independent. Professor Hruby is aware of these facts. but he does not see that they prevent us from concluding anything about the descent of states of a text from the independency or lack of independency of their individual readings.

David Vieth has also appealed to the probabilities of independent events to decide whether an archetypal record is more likely to be a manuscript or a printed book. If there are a thousand copies of a printed book, the probability that a person making a manuscript copy of the book will have in his hands any particular one of the thousand is 1/1,000.

A second person making a manuscript copy of the printed book also has a probability of 1/1,000 of holding any particular one of the thousand. If we take the two copyists having books in their hands to be independent events, the probability that the two will have the same book is one in a million, for 1/1,000 $\times$ 1/1,000 = 1/1,000,000. Professor Vieth's conclusion from this is that "when two or more manuscript versions of a work agree in some of their readings against a printed text, they almost certainly do not derive from it."[3]

We observe first of all that if two or more manuscripts agree in some of their readings against a printed text, they can be accepted as deriving from the same copy of the book, if they derive from it at all, because their agreement against the printed text indicates that they have a common intermediary between them and it, and the intermediary can be accepted as deriving from a single copy of the book. But what is the probability that the manuscripts derive from the printed book at all? Let us go back to the two people who made manuscript copies of the printed book. Suppose the second of these lets two other people make copies of his manuscript. From which copy of the printed book are the third and fourth manuscripts derived? Clearly, from the same copy as the second manuscript, which is their common intermediary between them and the printed copy. There is not room enough for a sample space that will show all the possibilities with a thousand printed copies, so let us assume only two. The result will be the same in any case. What are the probabilities that the four manuscripts derive from the same one of two printed copies? If the first manuscript derives from the first printed copy, the second, third, and fourth may all derive from that copy, or all from the other, that is, we may have 1111 or 1222. If the first manuscript derives from the second printed copy, the second, third, and fourth manuscripts may all derive from that copy or all from the other, that is, we may have 2222 or 2111. There are no other possibilities, because the second, third, and fourth manuscripts all derive from the same printed copy, whichever it is. Our sample space is, then,

$$\{1111, \ 1222, \ 2111, \ 2222\}$$

The four possible outcomes are equally likely, just as with the coin tosses, and just as with the coin tosses, the probability of each is 1/4.

[3] *Attribution in Restoration Poetry* (New Haven, 1963), p. 47.

There being only two copies of the printed text, each manuscript has a probability of 1/2 of deriving from either. If the descent of the manuscripts is to be judged by the probabilities of independent events, the probability that all four derive from the same copy, for example, the probability of 1111, ought to be $1/2 \times 1/2 \times 1/2 \times 1/2 = 1/16$ instead of 1/4. To test the manuscripts in pairs we can make reduced sample spaces. Let us take the first two manuscripts. The reduced sample space for these is

$$\{11, \ 12, \ 21, \ 22\}$$

As before the probability of each outcome is 1/4, and $1/2 \times 1/2 = 1/4$. The descent of the first two manuscripts can then be judged by the probability of independent events. Let us, however, take any two of the last three manuscripts, since they alone correspond to Professor Vieth's manuscripts that agree in some of their readings against a printed text. The reduced sample space for these is

$$\{11, \ 11, \ 22, \ 22\}$$

The probability of each outcome is 2/4. But $1/2 \times 1/2 = 1/4$, so the descent of these two manuscripts cannot be judged by the probabilities of independent events. The result does not mean that such manuscripts must derive from a printed book; it merely means that one cannot estimate the probability that they do or do not by assuming that they could have descended from different copies, or by analogy with the probability that manuscripts differently descended could have.

Biblical scholars have sought over the years to classify their texts in various ways, and to this endeavor Ernest C. Colwell has contributed a technique for quantitative representation of the differences between manuscripts.[4] His method is statistical rather than probabilistic, but probability and statistics are so commonly associated that I have undertaken to discuss it here. If it is thought of as an attempt to make the Lachmannian method work every time, then like the Lachmannian method it runs afoul of Greg's discovery that different family trees will explain the same variations.

Suppose we have two occurrences of AB:CDE and one of DE:ABC. The pairwise agreements of the states are

---

[4] *Studies in Methodology in Textual Criticism of the New Testament* (Grand Rapids, 1969), pp. 56-62.

AB 3
AC 1 BC 1
AD 0 BD 0 CD 2
AE 0 BE 0 CE 2 DE 3

According to President Colwell, states with larger pairwise agreements are "closer kin" those than with smaller. Supposing all five states are terminal, the following is a possible tree:

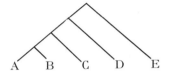

Are D and E more closely akin than C and D? Are C and D more closely akin than B and C? If President Colwell's method is interpreted genealogically, it gives the same tree as Lachmann's would:

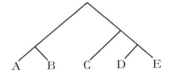

but if this is not the only possible tree, we cannot use the method to decide between the possibilities.

Is the situation any better when the variations indicate rings in the diagram, which is the particular problem President Colwell's method is designed to alleviate? Suppose we have in addition to the foregoing variations an example of AE:BCD. Then the pairwise agreements are

AB 3
AC 1 BC 2
AD 0 BD 1 CD 3
AE 1 BE 0 CE 2 DE 3

It seems to me that the situation has worsened, for now, not only is a different choice of archetype still possible, but we have covered over the evidence in the variations that DE is a separate group.

We have seen that textual analysis uses pairwise agreements to break rings, but that procedure has quite different results.

The Claremont profile method of Paul R. McReynolds and Frederik Wisse groups manuscripts with greater precision than President Colwell's method, but its groupings are not necessarily genealogical either, and for the same reason, namely, that relative likeness of states to one another is not a function of their genealogical relationships alone.[5]

Archibald Hill has proposed that we can decide among the various trees we could construct from the same preliminary diagram by weighting their lines of descent and choosing the tree which has the smallest total weight.[6] Lines leading to or from an inferential intermediary in a possible tree are weighted 2; the rest of the lines in the tree are weighted 1. As a result, when the directional variations limit the choice to accepting an extant manuscript as archetype or to inferring an archetype between this manuscript and the rest, for example, to

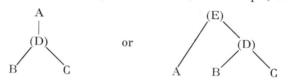

the former choice is automatic, because the former tree always scores one less than the latter (i.e., an inferred archetype is not counted as an inferential intermediary). On the other hand when the directional variations allow that an inferential intermediary may also be the archetype, for example, when in addition to the former trees

is possible, then the last choice is automatic, because this last tree always scores less than the first (three less in our example). Professor Hill remarks that his weighting is arbitrary, but that he has not found it distorts the facts, which is as much as to say that the weights probably result in correct choices.

Unfortunately, this reasoning is circular. Bibliographical and textual analysis result in genealogical trees based on certain evidence, but the trees cannot then be cited as proofs that other trees based on similar evidence are correct. The trees are not facts, they are deductions from facts. Congruent deductions do not prove one another true.

[5] Paul McReynolds, "The Value and Limitations of the Claremont Profile Method," *Society of Biblical Literature One Hundred Eighth Annual Meeting Book of Seminar Papers* (1972), I, 1-7, and references there.

[6] "Some Postulates for Distributional Study of Texts," *Studies in Bibliography*, III (1950-1951), 63-95.

Nevertheless, there may be a way to appeal to facts, using a different statistical model from Professor Hruby. Before applying the laws of probability in this instance, however, there are two fundamental questions to be answered. The first and more fundamental is whether we can calculate the probabilities of past events at all. No one doubts that the statistics of past events give us some idea of the probability that similar events will occur in the future. But do the statistics of present events give us any idea of the probability that similar events occurred in the past? I shall not attempt to resolve the problem, upon which opinion is divided, but a bibliographer who does not believe that the probabilities of past events can be calculated will find nothing more of interest in this chapter until he changes his opinion. On the other hand the textual analyst cannot strictly use the methods of probability, for they apply to records. At best he can decide that when his methods fail to determine between alternate possible trees for the states of a text he may adopt the most probable family tree for their records. A textual analyst who does not wish to accept this solution will not find the rest of this chapter of interest until he undertakes a bibliographical problem.

The second question is whether a methodology that will apply to a machine turning out screws will apply to a copyist turning out words. My answer is that the laws of probability have been found to apply to groups of humans producing other humans, and that I see no reason to deny their applicability to groups of humans producing manuscripts taken as wholes (I am not concerned with individual readings). The elements of choice and opportunity seem to be entirely similar in both activities, and both result in family trees of the same sort—indeed if we equate the copyist with the wife, his exemplar with the husband, secondary exemplars resulting in conflated manuscripts with adoptive fathers, and the resulting manuscripts with children, the trees are perfectly similar. If I am wrong, or if I am right but have chosen the wrong statistical model, then what follows is valueless. It should also be emphasized that the method does not apply when directional variations will solve the problem. A bibliographer working with printed books alone or together with manuscripts will also have to decide whether the elements of choice and opportunity are the same as with manuscripts alone.

Since there is no known law for the development of family trees of manuscripts, they must be said to grow at random. One might predict that a manuscript of a particular class in a particular place at a particular time—say a pulpit Bible in a Greek monastery in the tenth century—would tend to be copied more or less often than another manuscript under other circumstances—say a private copy of the Scriptures brought to Italy by a refugee from Constantinople—but one could hardly predict what their textual relationship would be, or even that they would necessarily exist. Too many variables affect the copying of manuscripts for this kind of prediction to be possible.

Now if the growth of such a tree is a random process, it is easy to simulate. The second manuscript in a real tree must be a copy of the first (allowing that writing from memory is a copying process), but the third may be a copy of either (allowing that if it owes something to both, one is the primary ancestor), and there is no way to predict which. In simulating the growth of a tree, then, the ancestor of the third manuscript may be chosen by tossing a coin. The fourth manuscript in a real tree may be a copy of any of the first three; there is no way to predict which. In simulating the growth of a tree, then, the ancestor of the fourth manuscript may be chosen by tossing a coin twice, or by casting a die one or more times. And so on with more manuscripts. The following are three trees grown by casting a die. Each tree began with manuscript 1 the ancestor of 2. The ancestry of 3 was determined in each instance by casting the die until a 1 or a 2 came up, the ancestry of 4 by casting until 1, 2, or 3 came up, and so on.

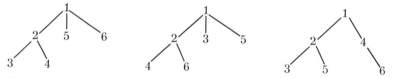

Random loss of manuscripts is as easily simulated. The following trees are the results of random elimination of all but three manuscripts from the foregoing trees by casting a die. In the first example, 1, 2, and 3 were eliminated in that order, in the second they were eliminated in a different order.

In these examples it happens that manuscript 1 is always the archetype, whether it survives or not, but this is not necessarily the case. Had, for example, 2, 3, and 5 survived in the last tree, 2 would be the archetype. The archetype is the latest common ancestor of the surviving manuscripts, or if it survives itself it is the earliest surviving common ancestor of the other survivors; it is not the earliest ancestor of all the manuscripts, surviving or not. It is important to keep this in mind in the ensuing discussion.

In these examples, also, no manuscripts were lost while the tree was growing, but of course simulation of loss during growth is equally easy: if a manuscript has been chosen as lost, then if it is subsequently chosen as an ancestor the latter choice is void and another choice is made. It is thus perfectly easy to simulate the conditions of growth and loss for particular classes of manuscripts when these are generally known. The sample trees just given might simulate those of minor Restoration political poems, which ought to have gained what currency they had before there was much loss, and to have sustained most of their losses after the fad of collecting this kind of verse disapperaed in the eighteenth century. A different mixture of growth and loss would be required to simulate the tree for the manuscripts of the *Iliad* (in fact, unless we agreed to treat the oral versions like the manuscripts, we should have to consider growing several trees). Here there was comparatively little growth before loss began to occur; for long periods loss balanced growth; growth was stimulated from time to time by such events as Alexander's conquests, and loss was stimulated from time to time by such events as the barbarian invasions; there was a brief period of growth in the Renaissance cut off by the spread of printing. But even the most complex pattern of growth and loss that our knowledge of history allows us to rough out can still be simulated easily, for only three situations can occur and only one at a time: growth exceeding loss, loss exceeding growth, or loss and growth balanced.

Finally, we can vary the pattern of the simulation within reasonable bounds and so determine what effect possible error in our historical reconstruction will have on the validity of our conclusions. Thus we can obtain a measure of the probable accuracy of the conclusions.

To say that this simulation is easy is not to say that it can be done easily by casting a die, or even a handful of dice. The mechanism to use in generating the random numbers is a computer, using a program like that described in Appendix B, below.[7]

---

[7] See also J. F. Raskin, "Tutorial on Random Number Generation," *Computers and the Humanities*, IV (1970), 307-311. For the difficulty in defining randomness see "Probability" article cited in n. 2 above.

I began my experiments in simulation without any preconceptions as to the mechanism of textual transmission, but it soon became clear that the number of manuscripts in the tree was the most important factor. Apparently the only way to offset this factor is for the tree to wither away to a single manuscript before beginning to grow again—which is the equivalent of beginning a new tree.

Experiment indicates that when only two manuscripts have survived the probability that one is the ancestor of the other will almost always be less than half if more than eight were lost and continues to decrease as the number of lost manuscripts increases. Once the results are in, the reason becomes obvious enough: the trees tend to branch; the more texts the more branches; the more branches the more likelihood that two residual manuscripts will be in different branches. Experiment shows also, as might be expected, that the faster a tree grows (i.e., the smaller the admixture of loss during periods when gain exceeds loss) the less chance there is that one of two remaining manuscripts will be the ancestor of the other.

When only two manuscripts have survived, the determination of their relationship is a binary problem—one or neither is an ancestor of the other—and the number of experiments (that is, the number of simulated trees) can be kept to a minimum. The foregoing discussion is based, for example, on only 105,000 simulated manuscripts. With more surviving manuscripts, the number of experiments must be markedly increased to obtain enough examples of all possible relationships for the results to approximate the long-run average. The remainder of the discussion rests on sets of three and four thousand experiments, a total of 1,043,000 simulated manuscripts, and even these are only preliminary explorations.

With more than two manuscripts we are seldom interested in the probabilities of all possible trees, since the variations normally limit our chances. Thus, with three manuscripts, there are two large classes of interest, that in which one of the extant manuscripts is intermediary and that in which all are terminal. And within each class are subclasses, depending upon which of the extant texts might be the archetype. The first large class has the general diagram A—B—C in which B, if it is not the intermediary itself, may be a duplicate of the intermediary. Here, if neither B nor C can be the archetype, we are concerned only with which is more probable,

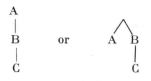

or

not with the probabilities of these relative to the probabilities of

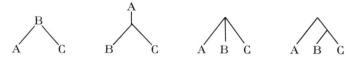

and so on. On the other hand, if we have the same general diagram, but both A and B can be the archetype, we are interested in four probabilities:

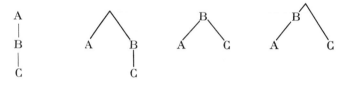

And so on.

With three surviving manuscripts, experiment indicates that when seven are lost the probability that one of the manuscripts is intermediary between the others is always a good deal better than the probability that all are terminal, and that this probability roughly reverses itself when more than forty are lost. Within the first class, in which one manuscript is intermediary, there is a similar change in the probabilities that an extant text which might be the archetype will in fact be so, though they are not so high with fewer lost manuscripts and lower with more.

In the second class, in which all manuscripts are terminal, experiment indicates that with seven lost manuscripts the most probable situation is that the extant manuscripts have a single intermediary that is the archetype; the next most probable is that one of the extant manuscripts is the archetype and the next that there are two intermediaries, the archetype and intermediary between it and the two latest in date of the extant manuscripts. With seventeen lost manuscripts, the third possibility is about as probable as the first, but the second has fallen to the least likely of all the possibilities; and these proportions seem to hold for larger numbers of lost texts as well.

There was no point in the foregoing survey in introducing exact results, but of course when one has a particular problem to solve he will not depend upon these generalizations but work with the values the computer provides him. In so doing one must remember that more than one historical circumstance may result in the same tree. For example, if A, B, and C are datable in that order,

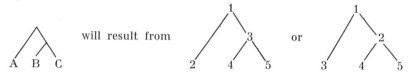

The probability of such a tree is the sum of the probabilities of the historical circumstances that may have produced it. On the other hand, for another example, if A and B are earlier than C but we cannot tell whether A is earlier or later than B, we cannot tell whether

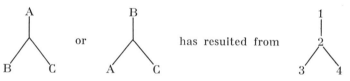

In such cases, each possible tree has the same probability as the historical circumstance that may have produced it. Obviously a combination of the preceding types of cases may occur.

Unfortunately, even with a computer, the kind of experimentation described is limited by the enormous increase in the number of possible trees as the number of extant manuscripts increases. Two manuscripts may be arranged in two ways, three in eleven, four in more than a hundred, six in more than twenty thousand. The greater the number of possible trees, the greater the number of experiments required to produce a representative number of each. Normally we can see that the archetype must be located in a part of the tree that we could define with fewer than the full set of extant texts. For example, if only the following are possible

we do not need both C and D, which have the same relationship in each tree, to locate the archetype. If we assign the siglum x to the immediate common ancestor of C and D, the following have the same archetypes respectively as the foregoing:

From this fact it would appear that there might be some way to extrapolate from probabilities based on a selection of the extant manuscripts to those for the whole set. The difficulty is that the trees on which the probabilities are based are always whole trees, never parts. Therefore if we substitute x for C and D some of the probabilities will be based on trees in which the state corresponding to x has only one or no line of descent from it, whereas we know that x has two. If, however, one feels that the probabilities will not be badly distorted, he may wish to extrapolate from them in this way.

It would appear that printed records may always be simulated along with manuscripts as long as, if there is more than one, they are set from different manuscripts. Printed records, because of the number of duplicates, have essentially no chance of loss, but then neither do manuscripts of great value. The printed record, in this way of looking at it, is the equivalent of a very well-known and easily accessible manuscript. Just as we cannot predict the place of such manuscripts in a tree, so we cannot predict the place of random printed records. When records are printed from one another, however, their occurence will no longer be random if their publishers tend to keep the work in print by sending a copy of the most recent printing to be reprinted and to sell off or otherwise dispose of the rest of the old before selling the new. Such a tendency is generally observable, at least in English printing. Because the resulting trees do not grow at random, their growth cannot be simulated by the methods just described.

Lastly we may note that while there is no way to test the validity of the theory that random generation of manuscript trees provides a guide to locating archetypes, experience does confirm that these trees have many branches. Direct descent even of two manuscripts in a large set is very rare.

Let us next examine the question of whether a manuscript should be accepted as an archetype when it has all the better readings, or should be deemed a descendant of an archetype from which it has

happened to inherit all the better readings. The following are examples
of the types of textual trees in question:

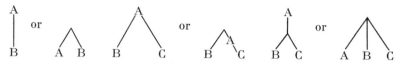

Answering this question is an exercise in conditional probability, in
which there are three matters that require investigation: first, the probability that an extant manuscript will be an archetype, a matter we
have already discussed; second, the probability that an extant manuscript will have all the better readings; and third, the effect when one
probability is conditional upon another. For example, let us suppose
that we have two manuscripts, A and B, of which A has the only two
readings that can be identified as better. Let us also suppose that
without considering the directional variations the probability that one
will be the ancestor of the other is only 1/3. We might then be inclined
to adopt the diagram

But let us suppose that given this diagram the probability that A will
have both the better readings is only 1/4. We might then be inclined
to adopt the diagram

A
|
B

We should be justified in this particular case in following our second
inclination, but how do we know?

In answering this question we shall use "better reading" to mean a
better reading that is traceable to the archetype. As we have seen,
with the tree

and a variation A:B:C where B has a better reading than C but the
quality of the reading in A is indeterminate, the archetype may agree
with A, with B, or with neither. We exclude better readings of this
sort from our discussion.

When a surviving manuscript is the archetype it obviously has all the better readings, since this is part of the definition of an archetype. When no surviving manuscript is the archetype, the probability that one will have all the better readings is conditional on the nature of the variants, their number, the number of independent descendants both of the archetype and of any ancestors intermediate between it and the manuscript in question, and the number of these ancestors. We cannot, however, reduce the foregoing abstract statement of the situation to practical terms unless we limit ourselves to surviving ancestors and to inferential intermediaries, and to readings that are identifiable as better without reference to the family tree. As there is no way to predict which scribe will be inaccurate at a point and in a way that will allow the better reading to be thus identified, the probability of each scribe's so doing may be said to be equal. That is not to say that all manuscripts tend to have the same number of errors or that all scribes probably have the same error rate, which is of course false. All we are saying is that if there is a worse reading, we cannot predict which manuscript it will occur in. Let us then examine some of the simpler family trees from this point of view.

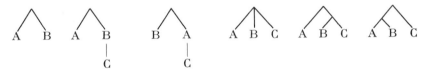

To simplify the discussion we shall concern ourselves only with manuscript A.

In the first three situations, the archetype has two independent descendants, one of which is A. With only two independent descendants, there are two equally likely possibilities for any one variation: A better, other worse; A worse, other better. Therefore the probability of a better reading in A is 1/2 for any single variation.

In the fourth situation, by the rules of textual analysis, any two manuscripts that agree preserve the reading of the archetype. But if all three disagree the equally likely possibilities are A better, B worse, C worse; A worse, B better, C worse; A worse, B worse, C better. In this situation, therefore, the probability that A will have the better reading is 1/3.

In the last two situations, the archetype has two independent descendants, one of which is a lost common ancestor of two of the surviving manuscripts. By the rules of textual analysis, agreement between these two manuscripts merely gives the reading of their common ancestor. We have, then, three sets of probabilities, according to the nature of the variations.

In the fifth situation, if B and C agree against A, the equally likely possibilities are: A better, B and C worse; A worse, B and C better. Therefore the probability that A will have the better reading when the others agree against it is $1/2$. If, however, A and B or A and C agree, A must have the better reading by the rules of textual analysis, because it has the archetypal reading. If all three disagree, the readings of the lost manuscripts are not determined by those in the others, but the probability that A has the better reading is once again $1/2$.

In the sixth situation, if B and C agree against A, A cannot have the better reading, whereas if A and C agree against B, A must have the better reading. If A and B agree against C, the equally likely possibilities are: A and B better, C worse; A and B worse, C better. Therefore the possibility that A will have the better reading when it agrees with B against C is $1/2$. If all three manuscripts disagree, the readings of the lost manuscripts are not determined by those in the others, but the probability that the lost common ancestor of A and B will have the better reading is $1/2$ and the probability that A will have the reading of that ancestor is $1/2$, so that the probability that A has the better reading is $1/2 \times 1/2 = 1/4$.

The third and sixth situations have alternates obtainable by interchanging B and C. The discussion of the sixth situation can be adjusted to fit the alternate situation by interchanging B and C in the discussion.

We must now come to a clear understanding of what happens to the probabilities when more than one reading is identifiable as better. Working our way through a manuscript and observing that it has better readings consistently, we may predict that we shall find better readings in it to the end, but we want here to know the probability that a carefully copied manuscript will occur at all. From this point of view, a better reading at one place does not affect the probability of a better reading at another.

Construction of a sample space will help us visualize the problem and understand its solution. Let us assume the last family tree above. Let us also assume that there are two readings identifiable as better, the first shared by A and B, the second found only in A, and at a point where all three manuscripts disagree.

We concern ourselves now with A. As we have seen, the probability that A will have the better reading is 1/2 when it agrees with B and 1/4 when all three disagree. If A had these better (*b*) or worse (*w*) readings repeatedly, then, when the first reading was *b* the second would be *b* one out of four times: which we may represent by *bb, bw, bw, bw*. And similarly when the first reading was *w: wb, ww, ww, ww*. Putting these all together gives us the sample space

{ *bb, bw, bw, bw, wb, ww, ww, ww* }

We see that *bb* occurs only once, so that the probability that A will have both better readings is 1/8. This fraction is the product of the probabilities that A will have the better readings in each place, 1/2 × 1/4 = 1/8, that is, the probability that A will have all the better readings is the product of the probabilities that it will have each of them. This relationship holds in all similar cases. It follows that the probability that any manuscript will have all the better readings falls rapidly as the number of identifiable better readings increases.

What is the effect when one probability is conditional upon another? For our example, let us return to the problem with which we began: shall we choose

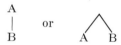

assuming that the second tree will probably occur twice as often as the first on the average in the long run under similar historical circumstances, and that A has the better readings in the only two instances where better readings can be identified?

Let us use P(*a*) for the probability that a text will be the archetype in its set, and P(*ā*) for the alternate probability that it will not be the archetype (the bar over the *a* means "not"). In our example, P(*a*) for A is 1/3 and the alternate P(*ā*) is 1 – P(*a*), or 2/3. Let us use P(*b*|*ā*) for the probability that a text will have all the better readings when it is not the archetype, and P(*b̄*|*ā*) for the alternate probability that a text will not have all the better readings when it is not the archetype (the vertical stroke means "given"). In our example, P(*b*|*ā*) for A is 1/4, because each of the two better readings has a probability of 1/2 of occurring in A if it is not the archetype, and the alternate P(*b̄*|*ā*) is 1 – P(*b*|*ā*), or 3/4.

If A could occur repeatedly, then when it was not the archetype it would have the better readings one out of four times, which we may represent by $\bar{a}b$, $\bar{a}\bar{b}$, $\bar{a}\bar{b}$, $\bar{a}\bar{b}$. When it was the archetype it would always have the better readings. It would not be the archetype twice as often as it would be. Putting all these ratios together we obtain the following sample space for A:

$$\{\ \bar{a}b,\ \bar{a}\bar{b},\ \bar{a}\bar{b},\ \bar{a}\bar{b},\ \bar{a}\bar{b},\ \bar{a}\bar{b},\ \bar{a}\bar{b},\ \bar{a}\bar{b},\ ab,\ ab,\ ab,\ ab\ \}$$

Since A does have the better readings in our example, we determine the probabilities for the two trees from the reduced sample space that includes all the examples of b:

$$\{\ \bar{a}b,\ \bar{a}b,\ ab,\ ab,\ ab,\ ab\ \}$$

$P(a|b)$ for A, the probability of

when A has the better readings, is the proportion of a in the reduced sample space, 4/6, or 2/3. $P(\bar{a}|b)$ for A, the probability of

when A has the better readings, is the proportion of $\bar{a}$ in the reduced sample space, 2/6, or 1/3. From this we see that the former tree is twice as likely to have occurred as the latter under the circumstances assumed, and is therefore the one to choose.

Construction of sample spaces is obviously cumbersome. Happily, we can obtain the same results by using some simple formulas. The probabilities $P(a \cap b)$ and $P(\bar{a} \cap b)$ in these formulas correspond to the proportions of ab and $\bar{a}b$ in a full sample space (the $\cap$ means "cooccurs with"). By experiment we determine the probabilities of the alternate family trees. For each tree we determine the probability that the text which might be the archetype if we did not infer an archetype will have the better readings it has. In other words, we determine $P(a)$, $P(\bar{a})$, $P(b|a)$, which is always 1, and $P(b|\bar{a})$ for each text. We then find its $P(a|b)$ and $P(\bar{a}|b)$ as follows (values at the right are for A in our problem, and can be checked by reference to the sample spaces above):

$$P(a \cap b) = P(b \mid a) \cdot P(a) \qquad 1/3 = 1 \cdot 1/3$$
$$P(\bar{a} \cap b) = P(b \mid \bar{a}) \cdot P(\bar{a}) \qquad 1/6 = 1{,}4 \cdot 2/3$$
$$P(b) = P(a \cap b) + P(\bar{a} \cap b) \qquad 1/2 = 1/3 + 1/6$$
$$P(a \mid b) = P(a \cap b) / P(b) \qquad 2/3 = (1/3) / (1/2)$$
$$P(\bar{a} \mid b) = 1 - P(a \mid b) \qquad 1/3 = 1 - 2/3$$

In our example there was only one candidate for archetype in the set, and the question was only whether to accept it as such or to infer an archetype. How do we proceed when we have more than one candidate? If both A and (D) have all the better readings, how do we decide among

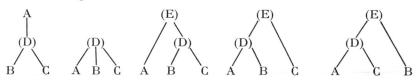

The question is still whether to infer an archetype, as in the last three trees, or not, as in the first two. Experiment will show which of the first two trees is more likely and which of the last three is most likely. We eliminate the others from consideration and decide between the remaining two just as before. Thus, if the choice is between

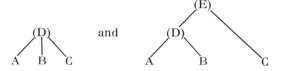

and $P(a \mid b)$ for (D) is less than 1/2 we shall choose the latter tree.

V

Editing Texts and Documents

In this chapter the word "text" is used in its common meanings, which embrace both "record" and "state."

The editor of a document that exists in a single manuscript is concerned with little more than transcribing, emending, and normalizing his text, but others may have tasks of sufficient magnitude to warrant use of the critical-path method of analyzing and carrying them out. Those who employ the critical-path method analyze their tasks into components; they determine which parts of the work may be pursued simultaneously and which must wait upon the completion of other parts. The longest sequence of components, that is, the one that will take the longest to work through, determines the minimum time that must be allotted to the task and progress through it is critical. Progress along any parallel paths needs watching but calls for special effort only when it has fallen so far behind as to hold up work in the critical path. This method is entirely applicable to any tasks where ease and dispatch bring comfort or reward and has therefore been understandably popular wherever foresight will replace pressure and confusion with preparedness and order.

Following is a critical-path diagram for textual editing:

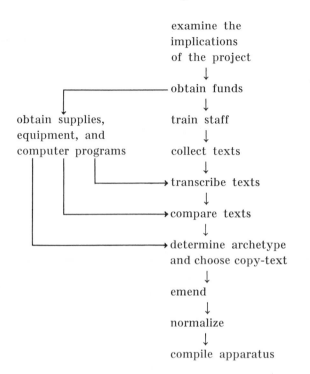

Obtaining funds may be a continuing process, in which case it may prove to be the most critical path of all. Otherwise, if the editor wishes to use computers but does not wish to use the programs described in Appendix B, the most critical path will probably run through obtaining the computer programs.

Exploring the implications of the project is not so simple a matter as it may seem, and if one conscientiously examines other projects and seeks the advice of others, he may spend a month or two before he is ready to go ahead. Many questions must be answered. First, is the end in view to reproduce a text already accepted as standard or one that owing to wide circulation and influence has its own historical importance, or is the goal to embody in a new text the author's best conception of his work? In the latter event, what text-critical method is to be employed? Next, should contemporary spelling be reproduced, or should it be "discreetly modernized," as the cover blurb on the Viking Portable Milton discreetly puts it? What variations are to be recorded? How much of the task can be automated? Having determined so much, one must ask, like Burr in *The Wild Gallant*, "Where's the money for this, dear heart?" Will there be generous funds for research and publication, so that one may have satisfaction in the work itself and in its product? And satisfaction is not dependent merely upon adequate funds. Is the textual editor alone to determine every detail of the text and the form and extent of the textual annotations? If not, what freedom will the other editors have to choose readings and make emendations? What share will they and the officials of the press have in the design of the text and notes? Even if the textual editor is not to bestride his narrow world like a Colossus, he should be satisfied with the working arrangement he negotiates.

Equally important is investigating whether the edition will ever appear. Textual editing is a long, exacting, and often monotonous task, whose sole monument, almost, will be the finished edition. What guarantees can the textual editor receive here, and what guarantees can he give? Can he complete his part of the edition in reasonable time? Is he willing to share his task with others if necessary to speed the work? If he should decide to withdraw from the project, would he expect his successor to do the work over, or would he expect the next man to have free use of the materials already collected? These questions answered, what evidence is there that all the associates in the project will answer these questions similarly? If there are any doubts here, it is surely wiser that text and commentary appear in separate volumes; and, if the work has already begun on some other plan, one ought not to enter it.

Finally, if one is to have continuing satisfaction in the project he will need to believe and continue to believe that the project is worth the effort he will be expending on it. Here he must make the most serious examination into his reasons for undertaking the task and into the firmness of his literary tastes. The importance of exploring the implications of the project cannot be overestimated.

Now for collecting the texts. If an editor is to reproduce a standard or received form of a work, he may yet wish to discover any differences in the texts that have been accepted as equivalents. If he is producing a new text, he will wish to identify all the changes that have been introduced into the work, with a view to separating out any that were not intended by the author, and commonly also with a view to establishing the genealogy of the texts, at least during the author's lifetime. If one does not care to establish the genealogy of the texts after it has ceased to cast light on the author's intentions, he can normally save time and effort.

There are, therefore, two questions to be answered: How many texts are to be examined, and how many copies of each? The editors of the California Dryden examine (1) all printings and manuscripts they can locate, down to the author's death; (2) all manuscripts down to the first printing of posthumous works; and (3) the earliest eighteenth-century collected editions, in the event that they may prove to have drawn upon manuscript material now lost. The editors also examine the major scholarly editions preceding their own, but there they are looking for useful emendations. The reader will recognize that un-examined printings and manuscripts may trace back to the author's holographs independently of those examined, but the risk was felt to be slight.

The other question—how many copies of a printed text ought to be compared—is an extremely interesting and complex problem for the editor who wishes to sort out any changes not introduced by the author. One's goal is the identification of copies that preserve the text as it was before it was tampered with. Unauthorized changes may be intro-duced at the same time as authorial revisions are introduced, and they may be introduced at more than one stage in the run of the press. Of course, changes may be introduced independently on each side of the printed sheet.

Now, how many copies must one examine to locate all the possible changes? To simplify the calculations, let us say that "success" is locating at least one copy of every sheet in the state of that sheet which had the fewest copies produced. By this definition of success, the search becomes a binary experiment in probability, and there are tables from which one can answer the question. Supposing an edition size of 1,500 to 2,000 copies, that the copies coming to hand are a representative or random sample, and that within each copy all the sheets were printed about the same place in each run—that is, if its sheet A was nearly the last of all the sheets A to be printed, its sheet B is also nearly the last, and so on—one must examine 100 copies to be 99 44/100 percent sure that he has located all the changes found in 5 percent or more of the copies, and to have about two chances out of three of having located all changes found in 1 percent or more of the copies.

These figures pose the problem of whether the expense of such an examination is justified by the results. Surely it will be seldom that one can answer yes. Most editors would have doubts about the ex-pense of comparing ten copies. What is the probability that a sample of ten copies will include an example of the state found in the least number of copies? It is 98 percent certain to include an example if that state was common to one-third of the copies produced, and it has three chances in four of including an example if that state was common to at least one-eighth of the copies produced. If the order of the sheets as printed has been mixed in the process of drying them or in any of the other moves from the press to the bindery, the probability will be less in proportion to the length of the volume and amount of mixing. For example, if one assumes that no change would be peculiar to less than one-eighth of the run in printing each side of the sheet, then by comparing ten copies of a book of ten sheets (a play, for instance) that suffered some mixing of the order of those sheets after printing, one might have something like a fifty-fifty chance of having located all the changes.

Under the circumstances, there appear to be three ways of approaching the problem of expense. The first is not to compare multiple copies except in editions printed from independent manuscripts or evidently revised by the author, and so to compare more than would otherwise be possible. The second is to take a random sample of passages from the text in the editions examined, and so to compare more copies than would be possible if each were compared throughout. The third, sugested to me by Professor James Jackson, is to search for passages that either seem to have been corrected or seem to need correction and to examine these passages in a large number of copies.

Since the foregoing paragraphs were written, David Shaw has provided us with special formulas and tables to guide our calculations more surely.[1] The textual editor is like the boy who found nothing at the end of the foggy alley where he expected to find the omnibus of the Surbiton and Celestial Road Car Company. "'Give the bus every chance,' he thought cynically, and returned into the alley. But the omnibus was there." Certainty about variants is the textual editor's celestial omnibus, and if he can only determine what constitutes giving it "every chance" he will find it. The editors of the California Dryden normally examine five copies of every edition likely to reflect the author's intentions, three copies of other contemporary editions, and one only of the rest. Professor Bowers normally compares many more.

---

[1] David Shaw, "A Sampling Theory for Bibliographical Research," *The Library*, 5th ser., XXVII (1972), 310-319.

But only Charlton Hinman and Harris Fletcher in their work with Shakespeare and Milton can be said to have found their omnibus by examining really large numbers of copies.

If many texts are to be collected, two years is a normal minimum for the work. One year will be devoted to searching published lists and to securing grants for microfilm and for travel to distant libraries. Since the textual editor can argue that microfilm may not reproduce important characteristics of manuscripts and printed books—Professor William Jackson and others have written and spoken eloquently on this subject, and may be cited in his support—and since there is little likelihood that grant-making will be automated, it may be that two years will remain a normal minimum. But the time spent in going through printed lists will be significantly reduced as book-finding is automated.

What is the present situation with printed texts? If a Jackson has preceded one with a Pforzheimer catalog or a Greg or a Bowers with bibliographies and checklists based on minute examination of many copies, one has little more to do. Some of the other published catalogs of the great private collections of the recent past or present give fairly full descriptions of many books, and there are briefer but still distinctive descriptions in many other published library catalogs and in book-sellers' and auctioneers' catalogs. Workers in the neoclassical period have also an immensely valuable first-line index to poems in miscellany volumes, compiled by Richard C. Boys and Arthur Mizener and as yet unpublished. Editors of Dryden are particularly fortunate, for they have Hugh Macdonald's descriptive bibliography of Dryden and James Osborn's report on discoveries made by a group of scholars who at his request compared Macdonald's descriptions with the holdings of major libraries in this country; they have Gertrude L. Woodward's and James G. McManaway's *Check List of English Plays 1660-1700*, and Fredson Bowers's *Supplement* to it. Even so, they occasionnally turn up something new. If one is the first to survey his field, he is quite likely to find something new in the catalogue of every library he visits.

It is harder with manuscripts. New Testament scholars are uniquely fortunate in having all their texts except the most recent discoveries listed in Kurt Aland's *Kurzgefasste Liste der griechischen Handschriften des Neuen Testaments,* and in being able to write to Professor Aland for the reports of late discoveries which are transmitted to him as a matter of routine by all scholars who make new finds.[2] Texts in English are harder to locate, and those in any other language harder still. All manuscripts known to contain Anglo-Saxon and almost all those known to contain Middle English verse have been catalogued, but the only extensive guides to other British manuscripts in public collections are the catalogs of the British Museum, of the college and university libraries at Oxford and Cambridge—particularly, of course, the Bodleian—and of the Folger Shakespeare Library. The Public Archives of Canada has published a Union List of Manuscripts in Canadian Repositories and now publishes a series, *General Inventory. Manuscripts.* The National Library of Scotland and a few others have published catalogs of most of their holdings. *The National Union Catalogue of Manuscript Collections* will in due course provide an adequate guide for the United States. My feeling is that manuscript material in any volume ceases to flow to public collections well within a century of the death of the author in question; therefore workers in the more hallowed fields of English literature need not be particularly concerned that catalogs of recent acquisitions, especially by the Bodleian, have not yet been published. Major acquisitions appear in annual reports and bulletins published by the libraries.

The British Museum has a relatively complete first- and last-line index to the manuscript poems in its collections, of which Yale and the Bodleian have copies on microfilm. Margaret Crum has edited the *First-Line Index of English Poetry 1500-1800 in Manuscripts of the Bodleian Library.* The British Museum has a consolidated subject index in volumes, the Bodleian has a consolidated author, title, and subject index on cards. I did not find, myself, that subject indexing provided many leads I did not pick up elsewhere more easily, but I hesitate to set this up as a general rule. The *Aslib Directory* gives some idea of the holdings of other libraries, and their librarians will answer queries. The editors of the *Poems on Affairs of State* wrote to libraries to inquire if they had any likely holdings and were good enough to share what they had learned with the editors of the California Dryden. But manuscript cataloging at present is incomplete enough in most libraries to warrant a visit by the textual editor to any whose holdings sound promising. In searching for manuscripts of Dryden's works, my greatest propor-

---

[2] Supplement in *Materialen zur Neutestamentlichen Handschriftenkunde* (Berlin, 1969), pp. 1-53.

tion of plums to pudding came during a morning at the University of Nottingham among the manuscript miscellanies in the Portland Papers.

Workers in American literature now have the Modern Language Association's *American Literary Manuscripts: A Checklist of Holdings in Academic, Historical, and Public Libraries in the United States*, Phillip N. Hamer's *Guide to Archives and Manuscripts in the United States*, and Bernard R. Crick's and Miriam Alman's *Guide to Manuscripts Relating to America in Great Britain and Ireland*. Before these appeared, they had to rely almost solely upon the bulletins and annual reports of the various libraries. Until the advent of automation there will be no other way of bringing these publications up to date, except by making inquiries among friends. Of course, the milk of human kindness flows freely in the scholarly world, and nothing is more pleasant than to review the letters that accumulate during a textual investigation.

For locating manuscripts in booksellers' and private hands, James M. Osborn's article in the *English Institute Annual* for 1939 is surely the best guide. It is in some ways the counsel of perfection, but all the more useful for being so, and it reflects the experience not only of a scholar but of one of the foremost private collectors of our time.

Whether one is searching for books or manuscripts, he must not forget that music will often include literary texts and that in many libraries music and books are cataloged separately.

Finally, where his texts are monumental inscriptions, the editor should get in touch with a local historian or the local historical society. The Gloucestershire County archivist told me by return mail that I should find in Haresfield Church the original of Dryden's epitaph headed in the printed editions "On young Mr. Rogers of Gloucestershire." Wyndham Ketton-Cremer similarly located for me the epitaph "On Mrs. Margaret Paston of Barningham in Norfolk," a member of the famous Paston family about which Ketton-Cremer has written so well and who is not buried at Barningham. A bank of pews now covers most of this inscription, which is on the floor of the parish church at Blofield, Norfolk, but the rector sent me a copy made by the father of one of his parishioners before the pews were installed.

Having collected his texts the editor must assign sigla to any that do not already have them. Simply because they are repeated so often, sigla should be as brief as possible. Perhaps ideally they ought also to indicate something of the manuscript or of the state of the text it records, although when there are very many this may not be practical. Thus the Greek minuscule manuscripts of the New Testament are now identified simply by a serial Arabic numeral. Hermann von Soden, however, numbered these manuscripts according to a system of classification he devised. Classification is a science in itself, and its complications daunt the average scholar, who is usually content to adopt sigla already established or to establish his own by some simpler method. The following examples of current practice are drawn partly from widely accepted systems and partly from those set up for the nonce by various scholars. Sigla may reflect the provenance of the manuscript:

A   Codex Alexandrinus of the Bible, whose earliest certainly traceable owner was the Patriarchal cell of Alexandria.

B   The Bannatyne Manuscript of Scottish poetry, copied out by George Bannatyne.

P   Codex Pithoeanus of the *Pervigilium Veneris*, once owned by Pierre Pithou, who first published the poem in modern times.

The present resting place of the manuscript:

W   Codex Washingtonianus of the Gospels, in the Freer Gallery of Art, Washington, D.C.

L   The manuscript of Dryden's *Mac Flecknoe* now bound in Lambeth Palace MS 711.

L   Laurentian MS 37.9 of Persius.

The catalog number of the manuscript:

A   Chaucer's *Lak of Stedfastnesse* in British Museum Add. MS. 22139.

Co   An eighteenth-century transcript of the copy of the *Lak of Stedfastnesse* in Cotton Otho A. XVIII, which was burned in 1731.

The format of the book:

Fl   The first folio of Shakespeare's *Comedies, Histories, & Tragedies*.

Q0   A fragment of an early quarto of his *1 Henry IV*, discovered after the series Q1-Q8 was established.

The language:

Syr^{Sin} The Sinaitic Syriac manuscript of the Gospels, found in the library of the Monastery of St. Catherine at the foot of Mount Sinai.

D and *d*   Codex Bezae, the former the Greek, the latter the Latin, found in parallel columns in the manuscript.

The editor or edition:

   ς   The Textus Receptus of the Greek New Testmant, from Henri Estienne (Stephanus), editor, printer, and publisher of the first editions.

   J   The edition of Cicero's *Letters to Atticus* printed by Jenson, Venice, 1470.

   S.-S.   The Scott-Saintsbury edition of Dryden's *Works*, Sir Walter Scott's notes revised by George Saintsbury.

The date of the edition:

   1734   Pope's *Epistle to Dr. Arbuthnot*, first edition, 1734.

   12   *The Examiners for the Year 1711*, first collected edition, 1712.

The order of printing:

   1, 2, 3, 4, 5   The first five editions of Swift's *Tale of a Tub*.

   1714a, 1714b, 1714c   The first three separate editions of Pope's *Rape of the Lock*.

   A, B, C   The first three editions of Nashe's *Pierce Penilesse*.

The script or material of the manuscript:

   E and 1   Codex Basileensis in each case, but the former an uncial, the latter a minuscule, manuscript of the Gospels.

   p^{45} One of the Chester Beatty Biblical papyri.

The evaluation set on the state of the text:

   א   Codex Sinaiticus of the Bible, an uncial manuscript which from the lateness of its discovery would normally have been assigned a Roman or Greek capital far down in the alphabet and which its discoverer (Tischendorf) rated as at least equal in importance to those assigned the sigla A and B.

   C and c   Codex Gudianus and Codex Laurentianus 66.39 of Suetonius, the latter regarded as inferior to the former by the editor (Preud'homme) using these sigla.

It will be seen that the same manuscript may have different sigla assigned to different parts of its contents. Occasionally also two or more closely related manuscripts are assigned the same siglum (D of the Gospels and Acts is Codex Bezae, D of the Pauline Epistles is Codex Claromontanus). When the different manuscripts have to be cited in the same context, they are identified by added numerals or by superscript abbreviations in most cases, although one may not be so identified by common agreement (Syr^{Cu}, Syr^{Sin}; D, D^{Paul}). Sigla indicative of editors may have added to them a number, usually in superscript

Arabic numerals, marking a specific edition referred to (Rowe[1], Rowe[2], or Rowe i, Rowe ii). Sigla indicative of format are regularly followed by a serial number, which will indicate the chronological order of the edition within the format if that is determinable.

Compounded sigla are often devised, as Ff for the four Shakespeare folios, Pope+ for Pope and for a specified list of subsequent editors of Shakespeare, $\mathfrak{H}$ for a group of uncials recording the ecclesiastical text of Mark, fam[13] for the so-called Ferrar group of manuscripts, usually found in agreement. One such siglum may include another, as ω is used for the whole group of inferior manuscripts of Juvenal, φ for the seven of these cited by Housman in his edition. Exceptions to the usual agreements are then indicated in parenthesis, as $\mathfrak{H}$ (–K), or in some other convenient way.

Since sigla have normally been assigned to the manuscripts rather than to the states of the text recorded, editors have devised methods of indicating different states in the same manuscript. An asterisk following a siglum indicates the original reading of a manuscript. It will be used when the manuscript has been corrected by only one hand or by hands that cannot be distinguished, but it can always be used when it will make the context clearer. When several correcting hands are identifiable, it is customary to assign them superscript letters indicating their chronological order, as $\aleph^b$ for the second corrector of Codex Sinaiticus. The various correctors of Codex Pithoeanus (P) of Juvenal, however, have been lumped together as p. The original readings and the corrections in Codex Mediceus 49.18, Cicero's *Letters to Atticus*, have been identified as M^1 and M^2. Scholars working with texts in early printed books, where any one copy may have any combination of corrected and uncorrected forms, must also devise methods of idenfying the various states of proof correction.

The variations listed in the apparatus criticus may give a variety of information useful to others but that will not be used by the textual editor. MacEdward Leach has said that editions of Middle English texts should include a record of every possible difference among the manuscripts because we still have much to learn about such things as the orthography of the period.[3] When texts are compared by computer it is easier to record every difference than not, but humans usually have

---

[3] "Some Problems in Editing Middle English Manuscripts," *English Institute Annual, 1939* (New York, 1940), pp. 145-157.

some notion of what variations will be at least comparatively uninteresting. The critic should define the interesting variations as precisely as possible so as to be consistent and accurate himself and to facilitate consistency and accuracy in the work of his staff or associates. Doubtful variations discovered after work has begun will have to be excluded or the task will have to be begun again.

A number of the possible comparison processes require transcription of at least one text, and the text finally printed will be a transcription. Transcription of manuscripts should follow the rules for diplomatic texts (i.e., facsimile transcripts or reprints), as they are commonly understood in the editor's discipline. Historians, classicists, and literary medievalists follow slightly different systems, with individual differences among editors. Workers in more modern literatures can usually devise simpler systems of their own. The main purpose of these rules is to attain consistency, which besides an aesthetic appeal and a usefulness in preventing readers from seeing differences where none in fact exist is especially valuable if texts are to be compared by computer. It is generally uneconomical to program a computer to ignore or normalize inconsistencies.

Very early in the process of comparing the texts one must decide which will be the base with which the others will be compared. Ideally, this will be the text upon which the edition will principally be based, because then there will be a minimum of rewriting the notes that set forth the variations, notes that are always keyed to the text printed with them. If you open the heart of a textual editor you will find written there, "Beware of the leaven of the scribes," and he is under no illusions as to the difficulties of avoiding scribal error in rewriting his textual notes. But he cannot decide on his copy-text until he has completed his comparison. If he does not make his comparisons against some standard form of the text, he may guess that the first apparently authorized edition or the earliest "good" manuscript will turn out to be his copy-text and proceed accordingly.

One part of the comparison work could begin while the editor is visiting libraries, that is, the comparison of copies printed from the same or nearly the same setting of type, which is most conveniently done with Hinman collating machines. These machines can only be used with the books themselves or with carefully made photographic copies of them, and only a few libraries have enough books that may be compared to make it worthwhile for them to purchase a machine. The only other reason why it might be more efficient to begin comparison before collecting all the texts would be that the editor was doing the work himself at intervals in a life largely given to other things. If he employs students at an hourly rate, and they are not much concerned about a steady income, he can do the same. But if he pays weekly or monthly wages to his assistants, and especially if he rents machines, he will do well to put off the comparison until he can work men and machines without interruption, perhaps even on double shifts, until the work is done.

Ideally, the texts themselves should be examined. Reproductions are subject to all sorts of unexpected failures to perform their function. If a reproduction is used, it ought first to be checked with its original, strictly speaking with the same care as if it were itself an original.

George Guffey has described how to order microfilm that will produce Xerox copies almost exactly to true size so that they may be compared with the Hinman machine.[4] When films of different magnification must be compared it is possible to speed the work with two slide projectors adapted for unperforated roll film and with a shutter or shutters for alternately interrupting the images they project.[5] The more sophisticated one can make the devices to interrupt the images and to turn, tilt, elevate, and advance or draw back the projectors, the better. Even with very crude equipment and with having given no special instructions to the microfilm photographer, one can normally make the images from the projectors coincide more or less perfectly over an area of a third to half a page, but the cruder the device the slower the work. If the films are very different in size it may be necessary to insert an auxiliary magnifying lens in the barrel of one of the projectors; a cheap magnifying glass will do. Having the images superimposed, one starts to interrupt them alternately. Any difference in the images will result in a jumping about or a blinking on and off of the letters and punctuation marks, just as with a Hinman machine. With microfilm, however, there will be more or less adventitious jumping about in those parts of the page where the images do not coincide perfectly.

---

[4] "Standardization of Photographic Reproductions for Mechanical Collation," *Papers of the Bibliographical Society of America (PBSA)*, LXII (1968), 237-240.

[5] Vinton A. Dearing, "The Poor Man's Mark IV or Ersatz Hinman Collator," *PBSA*, LX (1966), 149-158; Gerald A. Smith, "Collating Machine, Poor Man's Mark VII," *ibid.*, LXI (1967), 110-113; Richard Levin, "A Poor Man's Collating Machine," *Research Opportunities in Renaissance Drama*, IX (1966), 25-26.

I should warn anyone who wishes to try such a device that, in its cruder forms, the adjustments may become tiresome when no variants appear. One should at least provide screws for tilting one projector and elevating the other, a fixed track for fore and aft movement of one projector, and a fixed pivot for the other; and he should start his work with pages where he already knows there are variants, for the thrill of seeing them pop out as the type jumps about will hearten him for the much larger number of pages where he will merely be proving that no variants exist.

There are at least five other methods of comparing texts. The first is to take an available printed text, correct it to agree with the base text, and note any variations in other texts in its margins; it is the best way in the world to have one's slips show. Any failure to correct the text used will allow a late variant to creep into the text printed. Montague Summers, for example, obviously sent to the press a copy of the 1701 folio of Dryden's plays with which he had compared the earlier editions.

The editors of the California Dryden have used both typescripts and Xerox copies of their copy-texts. Typescripts are more satisfactory when the text must be altered a good deal by the editor, but Xerox copies are cheaper and more accurate—although they must still be proofread. Typescripts and Xerox copies on flexible paper allow the editor to juxtapose his texts when comparing them so that he does not need to depend on his memory as he must when he moves his eye from one to the other. He rolls his paper over his index fingers, holding the turned back portion with his other fingers and the rest with his thumbs, and brings the lines one by one even with his index fingers. He rests his index fingers on the text with which he is comparing his paper so that he can see just above the first visible line on his paper the corresponding line in the text with which he is making his comparison. He can then see both lines at once. He must still watch carefully for additions in the other texts that might fall between the last line on one typed sheet or Xerox copy and the first line on the next, and, when the texts are prose, additions that fall between the last word on one typed or Xerox copy line and the first word on the next line.

I once entered the variants I found by this method between the lines of the typescript. Only a few texts had to be compared, but even so it became hard to read between the lines, so to speak, in many places, and this resulted in more rechecking than would otherwise have been necessary.

Another way of recording variants is to enter them in columns on separate sheets, one set of sheets for each edition, the readings of the base text on the left, the variants therefrom on the right. The sheets must then be consolidated in a master set, which not only takes extra time in itself but introduces the possibility of error in transcription. The comparisons for the first volume of the poems in the California Dryden were prepared in this way, but as the work was done carefully, and rechecked by a number of people, the results seem to have been accurate. Robert Chamberlin introduced in place of the separate sets of sheets the use of multicolumned ledger sheets on which the readings of the base text are entered in the left column and the variants in series in their proper columns to the right. One must estimate how many blank lines to leave between variants, since others will be turning up as the work proceeds, but this objection has not proved to be insuperable. Having always before the eye the variants previously discovered draws one's attention to oversights, should any creep into the work, and this is a definite advantage. With a base text of approximately 70 pages, Dean Chamberlin needed about 125 hours to compare seven other texts in minute detail, that is, even as to capitalization.

When the texts being compared are not juxtaposed as described above, it is helpful to hold a blank card under the line being read in each text. Comparisons may be made visually by one person, or one can read aloud to another or even to several others. No doubt accuracy becomes increasingly hard to obtain as more persons are engaged in the process, although printers' proofreading is regularly done by two persons together because of the considerable saving of time. Fatigue is a constant source of error and must be carefully guarded against. The results of the comparison should be checked at least once, preferably by someone else. According to the so-called laws of chance, a check performed with the same efficiency as the initial comparison should reduce its errors more or less by half; two additional checks will be required to halve the remaining errors, and correspondingly more to halve them again, so that three checks are usually all that are feasible. A better way to insure accuracy is to approach the work with the expectancy of attaining it, to proceed letter by letter and point by point without impatience, and to derive satisfaction from both the perfection and the value of the results. The laws of chance do not necessarily apply, as conscientious typists demonstrate every day.

John M. Manly's and Edith Rickert's method of recording variants not only relieves the memory but has so many other advantages as to make it the most perfect method of comparison, if one has the time to use it.[6] In this method, each line of the base text is typed at the very top of a card, slip, or sheet on which has been printed, dittoed, or mimeographed a list of the texts to be compared. The card is proofread by placing it on the base text so that it covers any lines in that text below the one in question. The eye can then see at once whether the typing is correct; no memory work is involved. The cards are then compared with the other texts in the same way, and any variants noted are written in their proper place below the typed line, together with the sigla of the texts in which they have been found. As each card is compared with each text, the list of texts on it is marked, so that there will be no question as to whether a text has been examined—as there might otherwise be if it did not vary from the base text.

Having completed his collating, the editor can examine his base text on its cards, with all the variants written out beneath the lines in which they occur, decide which variants, if any, he will take into his own text, insert these variants and any other changes he wishes to make in the typed lines, and turn his packet of cards over to a typist. He can read proof on the text the typist produces by positioning his cards as before. The typescript is then ready for submission to the press with a minimum of further change. He can read his printed proof in the same way. During all these proofreadings, his list of variants is always at hand for immediate consultation should doubts arise as to the evidence for any of the readings he has printed. Finally, he can compile his textual apparatus easily and accurately, since all the material for each entry is already gathered together on one sheet.

The method is easiest to use with poetry, because the lining is usually the same in every text. It is not much less advantageous for prose, but memory is involved when the line on the card or typescript is partly on one line of the text being checked and partly on another—additions or omissions at the ends or the beginnings of the lines must be specially watched for. One prime advantage—being able to juxtapose the lines compared—will be lost if the typing is not at the very top of the card, if the texts to be examined are under glass (Manly and Rickert used

---

[6] John M. Manly and Edith Rickert, *The Text of Chaucer's Canterbury Tales* (Chicago, 1940), II, 3-12.

photostats of their manuscripts), or if one is not permitted to touch the texts with the cards.

Manly's and Rickert's cards allow rapid as well as accurate work once they have been prepared. I have compared in detail approximately 600 octavo pages in two months, and manuscripts of 1 John in three or four hours apiece. When one is pressed for time, especially if he already has a typescript of his copy text, he has some difficulty in reconciling himself to making another copy on cards or slips. It is probable, however, that even under these circumstances it would be better to take the time. In preparing the text of the first volume of Dryden's plays, for example, the editors spent so much time in checking and proofreading, time that they would have saved had they used cards or slips, that I believe the additional typing would have been more than justified.

A computer program mentioned in Appendix B produces a listing of the variations similar to that on Manly's and Rickert's cards. The base text is reproduced complete and the others compared with it line by line. Texts that agree exactly in a line are grouped together, and no part of the line in the second and following texts in each group is printed. If the first text in a group differs from the base text, its line is printed out only from the first through the last variant word (a word and following punctuation are treated as a unit), and when the variant does not have the same number of characters as the base reading and does not reach to the end of the line, an additional word is printed out and marked with a left parenthesis immediately following. Texts totally omitting the line are listed after the other variants. Lines added in any texts appear in correct sequence, the variants in these texts being treated as before. Misplaced lines will be located if they fall within a range specified by the user. Texts can be prose or verse. If they are prose, any text chosen by the user provides a model according to which the other texts are relined before being compared. Relined texts are necessarily printed as relined, but their original line numbers are retained.

The texts are best put into machine-readable form (which usually means keypunched) from Xerox copies that have been preedited, so that the workers do not have to keep a long list of rules in their heads. Preediting means putting in the line numbers (for every line), marking the amount of indentation by series of squares or triangles, substituting special codings for symbols like § that are not on the keyboard, and inserting any grammatical or other coding that may later be useful, for example, in compiling a concordance or an index from the texts. The editor or a thoroughly trained helper should do the preediting, as this is the best time for him to examine the texts closely and to note peculiarities that have meaning to the bibliographer. For example, if blots in two places in a manuscript are the same blot showing through a leaf, then at least one occurrence was not intended by the scribe.

It is best to have two persons make copies of each text and to compare the copies by the program mentioned in Appendix B, which will locate all differences between them. Correcting the differences in both copies will provide one for use if the other is lost. The corrector must work with the texts; he cannot assume that the difference that looks right is right. Probably about one line in ten will have to be corrected in one copy or the other. On a task long enough to absorb delays while waiting to use the computer, it should be possible to produce fifty lines of corrected text in both copies per hour.

Comparison of the texts is a matter of only a few seconds or minutes, barring delays while waiting to use the computer. The computer finds every difference, but not all will be worth recording later. Some will be the result of errors that have slipped through the proofreading process, others will be variations in matters that are not to appear in the apparatus. A few variants will need emphasis or they will be overlooked on subsequent quicker readings. How much time will be spent in reading carefully through the printout, marking and clarifying the significant variations, will depend upon the nature of the texts compared. Obviously, manuscripts make slower going than printed texts.

The process of determining the archetype and copy-text will normally wait until the completion of the comparison of the texts. This process is harder to describe than to perform; analyzing the variations found in a thousand lines in a day is not hard with printed texts.

The textual editor must first decide, if he has not already done so, which variations are significant for his present purpose. Then he must determine which variations are directional. Next he must choose, again if he has not already done so, between the eclectic and genealogical methods and in the latter between textual analysis and bibliography. Finally he must decide whether he will use some kind of machine and if so what kind.

In Appendix A are directions for using an abacus in textual analysis and in Appendix B an account of computer programs for producing a family tree according to the principles of textual analysis and for locating an archetype according to one set of principles of textual probability. There are books that explain how to write programs, but I began with courses given gratis at the computing facility on my campus, and this way is certainly the best. It is difficult to find a book or course that deals with literary data processing, but if one is patient and thinks matters through he can learn easily enough from books or courses intended for business students, who are becoming interested in manipulating characters as much as numbers. It took me eight hours in class to learn the elements of FORTAN, and sixteen more to learn most of its refinements, but of course continued practice was necessary for growth toward mastery. It was then comparatively easy to learn COBOL and other languages better suited for processing literary data.

There are three main sources of wasted time in writing programs. The first is not thinking through what one wishes to do before he starts or gets a friend to start on the job. The second is devising a program that will solve a small-scale problem but will not solve a large-scale problem of the same kind without extensive rewriting. And the third is figuring out for oneself what someone else already knows how to do. When in doubt, ask an expert, or be prepared to write off some time as spent in gaining what may prove to be invaluable experience. Even if one avoids waste, however, I think it would be unwise to allow less than an academic year for perfecting a program that breaks new ground, unless one could work at it full time. Even then it may require months to perfect a complex program. The large program described in Appendix B required more than two years.

The editor's choice of a copy-text will depend upon his sense of how closely the scribes and compositors who worked on his texts followed copy. If he concludes that they tended to follow copy even in accidentals, he can, if he has not already done so, make a bibliographical analysis in which he includes accidental variations with the rest of his evidence, and can make the resulting archetype his copy-text. In the event that the resulting archetype is lost and must be reconstructed, its accidentals can also be reconstructed. Therefore, as Professor Bowers first pointed out, any of the extant texts can be the archetype, although, as a matter of convenience, the editor will normally choose the one he must change the least.

Sir Walter Greg maintained in an influential essay[7] that when scribes and compositors did not follow copy in accidentals, the archetype, if extant, or, if the archetype is not extant, then the extant text with the fewest transcriptional intermediaries between it and the archetype, ought to be the copy-text—with exceptions to be noted below. In fact, Greg's rule implies that scribes and compositors tend to follow copy in accidentals. If the evidence is clear that they did not, then any extant text may be the most like the author in the matter of accidentals, and the bibliographical tree does not limit the editor's choice of copy-text.

It may be argued that an author would wish his work to appear in the latest style, but textual editors today generally prefer to reproduce as much as possible the author's style when he wrote the work. If an author approved every detail of a certain edition—as Pope approved the quarto edition of his First Moral Essay—then his wishes are to be respected. Greg also maintained that when an author revised his text the latest revision proofread by the author should be the copy-text, or the latest revision so thorough as to suggest that the printer worked from a new manuscript, or the latest revision so thorough as to make it difficult to distinguish the author's changes from changes introduced without his authority, whether the former were made by the author directly or introduced by a careful editor from a text now lost.

Authorial changes that postdate the copy-text are normally accepted by textual editors as emendations, but such acceptance often requires hard decisions. An author is quite capable of changing from "laugh" to "smile," back to "laugh," and back to "smile" again (Blake's "The Tiger," line 19[8]). And the author as scribe makes the usual scribal mistakes. Even in revising, he may make a change without noticing that he has upset or confused the meaning of a neighboring context, and so on. It would seem that in many cases the only way to decide whether authorial or editorial revision is more likely in a text is to consider the nature of the work. In the manuscripts of Dryden's *Mac Flecknoe*, for example, a variation that might have either cause more probably

---

[7] "The Rationale of Copy-Text," *Studies in Bibliography*, III (1950-51), 19-36. For a full discussion of this article and Fredson Bowers, "Multiple Authority: New Problems and Concepts of Copy-Text," *The Library*, 5th ser., XVII (1972), 81-115, see Vinton A. Dearing, "Concepts of Copy-Text Old and New," *ibid.*, XVIII, (1973), 281-293. See also review by Tom Davis, *ibid*, pp. 351-354.

[8] *Poetical Works*, ed. John Sampson (London, 1914), pp. 85-88.

reflects authorial revision; in the manuscripts of the Greek New Testament it more probably reflects editorial revision.

Even when authorial revision is probable, it is normally hard to prove individual examples on any absolute principle. Many of the rules in common use are comparatively vague and others are in dispute. For example, when one text is known to be earlier than another, it usually seems reasonable to attribute to authorial revision any striking and otherwise inexplicable differences between them, but the more differences there are that may reasonably be attributed to nonauthorial carelessness or tampering, the more striking must be the differences that are to be attributed to the author. This rule is sufficiently vague but one that the textual editor must often resort to. Arthur Friedman, however, has pointed out that even small changes made in standing type are probably authorial (and the same would be true for small changes in plates), whereas changes in styling found in texts or parts of texts where there appear to be no authorial revisions are probably not authorial elsewhere.[9]

Some textual editors refuse to accept changes accepted by an author but proposed, or even only possibly proposed, by someone else, particularly if the changes appear to have been intended to increase the circulation of the work. Great care is necessary here to avoid substituting one's own impulses for the author's, and particularly in these days to avoid seeing sexual imagery everywhere. Refusal to accept a change merely because it damps a possibly sexual overtone is Bowdlerism in reverse.

Even when there are some changes that the textual editor can reasonably call authorial, he has a problem with the so-called indifferent variations, which, if they do not seem particularly authorial, do not seem particularly nonauthorial either. It used to be the practice to accept indifferent variations as authorial revisions. Greg, in the essay mentioned, has swung many textual editors to the opposite practice of rejecting indifferent variations as nonauthorial. Thus Professor Bowers has proposed that facsimile reprints should reproduce uncorrected states of their texts wherever possible.[10] This new distrust of compositor, scribe,

[9] Arthur Friedman, "The Problem of Indifferent Readings in the Eighteenth Century, with a Solution from *The Deserted Village*," *Studies in Bibliography*, XIII (1960), 143-147.

[10] "The Problem of Variant Forme in a Facsimile Edition," *The Library*, 5th ser., VII (1952), 262-272.

and proofreader runs counter to our attitude toward their handling of the other parts of texts: obviously they cannot have consistently deviated from their copy. The best procedure is to count the changes more or less certainly made by the author and those more or less certainly made by the scribe or compositor, and to assign the rest to the cause with the greater total. We cannot divide the rest proportionately to the totals because there is no way to decide which ones to assign to each cause.

In normalizing the text and writing the textual notes, an editor need no longer be rigidly logical and consistent, but some consistency is desirable in both these processes, and in normalizing, at least, it is a real problem to attain a respectable standard. If one sticks to preestablished rules he can work off a thousand lines a day easily enough, but if he changes or develops rules as he goes along he must go through the text again with the new rules.

Unfortunately, there are no universally recognized rules for normalizing. It is obviously simplest to normalize to modern practice. In the admittedly special case of Pepys's diary, which is written in shorthand, William Matthews decided to normalize to Pepys's longhand, but as Pepys himself was inconsistent in his longhand Professor Matthews had to normalize to Pepys's preferrred spellings. In "old spelling" texts, there may be a certain amount of normalizing of this kind in the correction of misspellings, remembering that even when consultation of historical dictionaries and miscellaneous reading in other literature of the time indicates that a spelling is generally avoided by an author's contemporaries, if it is clear that it is his normal spelling, it is not wrong. Hard as these decisions may be for the conscientious editor, he can comfort himself with the thought that he is often transmitting more than a mere "flavor": one reason we can be sure Wordsworth pronounced "notes" as a perfect rhyme with "thoughts" is because he spelled it *noughts*—a detail one would be sorry not to know of. But an editor is always accounted justified in normalizing or modernizing spelling if he is satisfied that his texts do not give a consistent picture of his author's spelling, as they may not, for instance, when they come from a variety of nonauthorial manuscripts.

I myself prefer to do as little normalizing as possible in various adjuncts to the text, if there seems to be no standard in these matters in the copy-texts. The California Dryden normalizes titles and some captions as a matter of book design but does not normalize the speech headings in the plays nor the names of characters whose names are words of variable spelling, such as Sir Timorous. I should have preferred not to normalize any of the names but have bowed to common opinion.

The final process in the critical path is writing the textual notes. Since the notes are to be understood, not wondered at, a reader ought to be able to see at once the variants from the text printed by the editor and the support among the earlier texts for his text and for the variant readings. A variety of styles in recording variants has been used successfully enough by different editors; but within a single work it no doubt helps the reader's immediate comprehension if the style is generally uniform. At the same time there will often be variants that can be more neatly expressed by some deviation from the normal practice. Ease of comprehension is the criterion. Writing the textual notes is relatively mechanical, but it is time consuming because it must be accurate. Five hundred lines of text a day would very likely be a maximum. In all estimates of time, however, and particularly here, the textual editor would not be unwise to double his figures as a safety factor.

As I said at the beginning, the textual editor can have decided long before he comes to this last task how he is to proceed in it. If in addition he has chosen to use Manly's and Rickert's method of comparing texts, or a computer program, he will find it easy to attain accuracy now, where his accuracy will be easiest to criticize. But he cannot write out his notes in the form in which he will send them to the printer until all his other work is complete.

In its fullest form, a variation consists of an identification by which it can be located in the text, such as a line or other subdivision number, a lemma—which is normally the reading from which the rest of the readings are thought of as varying—the texts having this reading, and the other readings, each with the texts in which it occurs. Commonly the lemma is additionally distinguished by a right-hand square bracket or a colon at the end or by boldface type, and the variants are separated by semicolons or by some other mark of punctuation. Sometimes the lemmas are indicated by superscript letters or numbers in the text, and the variants printed like footnotes after the corresponding letters or numbers; if the lemmas are more than one word long, they are marked at the beginning and end.

In a very large apparatus, the variations in each subdivision may have a paragraph to themselves. When there is more than one variation within a subdivision of the text, they may be separated by a vertical rule if periods are not used to conclude all the variations. If the variations involve passages of more than a few words and there are variations within variations, it may be convenient when the collation comes to be printed to indicate the smaller differences in parentheses after the requisite sigla in the series that otherwise agree in the larger difference. Or it may be easier to indicate the smaller differences, together with the requisite sigla, in parentheses in the middle of the citation of the larger variant; the sigla within the parentheses will then appear again following the larger variant reading. Similarly it is often convenient to condense two or three variations into one statement for printing, with ellipses where all texts agree. Summary statements of sigla, such as "al plus," are not sufficiently indicative for textual analysis.

In the inflected languages a lemma is not always strictly necessary, but its regular use much facilitates the computations attendant upon textual analysis. If the variation is an add-omission, it is well to include in lemma and variant readings a word at one extremity which does not vary, although here again it may be convenient simply to use the abbreviations "om." and " $+$." If the same word appears twice in a line, verse, or other subdivision by which the variations are identified, it is often convenient to label the occurrences 1°, 2°, and so on rather than to repeat the preceding word of the context in lemma and variant reading, but to give the preceding word will make the passages more easily identifiable in the manuscript or book having the variant reading. When the variation is in punctuation, the preceding word is always necessary in the lemma; in the variant readings it can be replaced by a wavy dash ($\sim$). Where the variant is omission of punctuation, it will be unmistakably indicated by a caret ($\wedge$).

When there is more than one way to analyze an add-omission, as explained earlier, it is helpful to set out the variation at such length that the different ways will be clear without recourse to the text. Also as explained earlier there may be more than one way to repair an omission by an insertion. It is then helpful to specify when one state has been changed to another by different insertions in different records. Otherwise the reader may suppose that the shorter state is more than one, with different omissions. Similarly, when a longer state can be represented as adding a phrase here to a shorter state or a different phrase there, one should avoid representing the longer state in both ways. Otherwise the reader may suppose the longer state is more than one, with different additions. Finally, it is helpful to indicate when a scribe has corrected a mistake at once, because in these instances the mistake does not result in a different textual state. Only when a state is complete before it is altered does one record transmit more than one state. When a larger apparatus is compiled from several smaller ones, the compiler is in the position of reader and must take care not to be misled himself.

When the critical apparatus is published separately, the lemmas should be the readings of some more or less standard and easily available edition. When the critical apparatus is made part of an edition, of course, the lemmas must represent the readings of the edition text. In either event, the description of the variations may have to be rewritten. Quentin wisely cautions, however, against unnecessarily recopying textual notes, since errors tend to creep in just as they worked their way into the states of the text being analyzed. Imperfect and fragmentary states, especially, must be carefully checked when rewriting variations.

For tabulating variations between normally duplicate copies, Professor Bowers, who first made full records of this sort of variation, provides a method in his edition of Dekker. The California Dryden uses a variant of this method when there is enough material to warrant a table; otherwise it merely calls attention to such variations in the descriptions of the texts compared. In either case, the relevant material appears again in the list of the other variations.

Those who do not read critical editions for pleasure but study the text in conjunction with the notes may like to have all the textual variants, in fact all the commentary, on the same page as the text to which it refers—even if this squeezes the text right off some pages. But most users probably prefer to have the text stand by itself, some because they like the look of the pages better and others because they dislike learned annotations. I have already noted that an edition may have text and notes in separate volumes. The California Dryden provides a list of variants from the copy text at the foot of the page in a modified columnar arrangement and a full list of variants at the end of the volume keyed to the text by page or title references in the running heads.

Some scholars like to argue some of their emendations or refusals to emend. Others leave these matters to the explanatory notes as being sufficient for details and set forth their general principles only in their textual introductions.

The finest textual introduction ever written—I am tempted to say, the finest that ever will be written—is hidden away in the Preface to Samuel Johnson's edition of Shakespeare, where it is seldom read by the only persons who can fully recognize its greatness, his fellow textual editors. I would close this chapter, if I could, by quoting Johnson's discussion in its entirety. He speaks as both the textual editor of and the commentator on his texts, but many editors even in this age of specialization perform both functions, and all can read him with profit, admiration, and the excitement which comes from observing the operations of a superior mind.

VI

Examples

1. Literary Research

Dryden's "Epilogue" to Etherege's *The Man of Mode* was first printed in the first edition of the play, 1676, and reprinted in the second and third editions, 1684 and 1693, during Dryden's lifetime.[1] The third edition was set in type from a copy of the second. The text of the epilogue is the same in all editions, and as all are quartos, Q may stand for all. Three contemporary manuscripts are known: British Museum MS Sloane 203, folio 95^r (M1), in a volume of medical and other collections made by Dr. John Barnes, M.D., and dated 1640-1690; Sloane 1458, folio 23^r (M2), in a miscellany of poetical and other extracts made by Richard Enock and dated on the title page 1677; and Bodleian Library MS Don. b. 8, pages 558-559 (M3), in a large folio miscellany compiled by Sir William Haward. The state of the text given here is that in the first edition, with the use of italics and romans reversed.

The *EPILOGUE by* Mr Dryden.

Most Modern Wits, such monstrous Fools have shown,
They seem'd not of heav'ns making but their own.
Those Nauseous Harlequins in Farce may pass,
But there goes more to a substantial Ass!
Something of man must be expos'd to View,
That, Gallants, they may more resemble you:
Sir *Fopling* is a Fool so nicely writ,
The Ladies wou'd mistake him for a Wit.
And when he sings, talks lowd, and cocks; wou'd cry,
10   I vow methinks he's pretty Company,

---

[1] The following material was collected in preparing the texts found in Vols. I and III of Dryden's *Works*, ed. E. N. Hooker, H. T. Swedenberg, and Earl Miner (Berkeley and Los Angeles, 1956———).

So brisk, so gay, so travail'd, so refin'd!
As he took pains to graff upon his kind.
True Fops help Natures work, and go to school,
To file and finish god-a'mighty's fool.
Yet none Sir *Fopling* him, or him can call;
He's Knight o' th' Shire, and represents ye all.
From each he meets, he culls what e're he can,
Legion's his name, a people in a Man.
His bulky folly gathers as it goes,
20   And, rolling o're you, like a Snow-ball growes.
His various modes from various Fathers follow,
One taught the Toss, and one the new *French* Wallow.
His Sword-knot, this; his Crevat, this design'd,
And this, the yard long Snake he twirls behind.
From one the sacred Perriwig he gain'd,
Which Wind ne're blew, nor touch of Hat prophan'd.
Anothers diving Bow he did adore,
Which with a shog casts all the hair before:
Till he with full Decorum brings it back,
30   And rises with a Water Spaniel shake.
As for his Songs (the Ladies dear delight)
Those sure he took from most of you who Write.
Yet every man is safe from what he fear'd,
For no one fool is hunted from the herd.

Title No title in M1.   title The *EPILOGUE*] Q, M2; Epilogue to
Sir Fopling Flutter, the Play made by Mr Etheridge. M3.   title *by*
Mr Dryden] Q; written by Mr Dryden and spoken by Smith or S^r
ffopling M2.   1 shown,] Q, M3; ~ ∧ M1; ~. M2.   2 seem'd] Q,
M2-3; seem M1.   3 Those] Q; Such M2; These M1, M3.   6 they]
Q, M1; hee M2; it M3.   10 I vow] Q, M1-2; I, now M3.   12 *After*
this line M2 has two others: Labouring to putt in more as Mr Bayes/
Thrums in Additions to his ten yeares playes.   14 file] Q, M1, M3;
fill M2.   14 god-a'mighty's] Q, M1, M3; God Almighty, M2.
14 fool] Q, M1-2; Toole M3.   14 *After this line M3 has two others*:
Labour, to put in more, as Master Bayes/Thrumms in Additions to his
ten-yeares playes.   15-16 *In M2 these lines follow the line here*
numbered 20.   22 taught the] Q, M2-3; taught a M1.   23-24 *In*
M2 these lines follow the line here numbered 30.   24 he] Q, M2-3;
that M1.   25-26 *Omitted from M2.*   26 nor touch of Hat] Q,
M1; nor Hatt M3.   28 a shog] Q, M1; the shog M2; one shogg M3.
30 a] Q, M1; his M2-3.   32 took . . . who] Q, M1; takes . . . that
M2-3.   33 man] Q, M1, M3; one M2.   34 For] Q, M1, M3; And M2.

Note that the variation in line 1 is quasi-substantive and that there are two variations in line 32. Note also that singleton groups resulting from omissions are shown only indirectly. Thus the three variations in the title are a type 0 (the title as a whole, including the absence of a title) within which are nested two agreement-defined variations, a type 1 (*"EPILOGUE"*), and a type 3 (*"by Mr Dryden"*).

Variations classified by type:

a.	type 1:	M1:Q M2 M3	title, 2, 22, 24
b.		M2:Q M1 M3	12, 14, 14, 15-16, 23-24, 25-26, 33, 34
c.		M3:Q M1 M2	10, 14, 14
d.	type 2:	Q M1:M2 M3	added couplet; 30, 32, 32
e.	type 3:	Q:M1 M3:M2	3
f.		Q M1:M2:M3	6, 26, 28
g.		Q M2:M1:M3	title
h.		Q M3:M1:M2	1
i.	type 0:	Q:M1:M2:M3	title

From variations *d* and *e* we obtain a synthetic type 1:

Q
Q:M1 M3:M2   *e.*
Q M1:M3 M2   *d.*
――――――――――
*Q:M1 M3 M2

There are no rings. The simple variations give the following preliminary diagram:

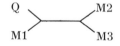

As so often in brief English poems there are not enough directional variations to locate the archetype.

George Thorn-Drury, who first described M3, thought its readings in lines 6 and 10 "worthy of serious consideration,"[2] and H. F. B. Brett-Smith took them into his edition of Etherege's *Dramatic Works.*[3] Brett-Smith also accepted the additional couplet found in M2 and M3 as authoritative but supposed Dryden had rejected it. Willard Thorp, who first described M2, thought that in the order of its lines it was

[2] G. Thorn-Drury, "Some Notes on Dryden," *Review of English Studies,* I (1925), 325-326.

[3] George Etheredge, *Dramatic Works,* ed. H. F. B. Brett-Smith (Oxford, 1927), II, 288, 294.

nearest of all "to what its author originally intended."[4] To me the order of lines in M2 does not seem superior to that in the other states, nor does the reading of M3 in line 6 seem more satisfactory than that of Q and M1 or than that of M2. Neither do they seem inferior. On the other hand, "I vow" in line 10 seems a better reading than "I, now" (aye, now), and it seems easier to suppose that the couplet peculiar to M2 and M3 was not authoritative. Dryden was lampooned in the character of Bayes in Buckingham's *Rehearsal* (1671). Therefore Brett-Smith's conclusion that the lines were a "hit at Buckingham" does not seem so satisfactory as Thorn-Drury's and Thorp's that they were a hit at Dryden. And there seems no reason why Dryden should have seized this opportunity for humorous or sardonic self-reflection. By my reckoning, Q, M1, and their prime intermediary all have all the better readings.

M1 may be earlier than Q. We cannot tell, but it seems unlikely that a copy in a commonplace book would be the ancestor of a copy sent to the printer of an authorized edition. There remain five possible trees:

Considering the nature of the text, it seems likely that there were never many manuscripts and that they were all produced before any had much opportunity to disappear. Assuming that what seems likely was the fact, experiment of the kind described in the last chapter indicates that the third tree is the most probable for the records. Because we do not know the relative dates of any of our four records (the date on the title page of the volume containing M2 is not necessarily the same as the date of M2), the probability of the third tree is the sum of the ten historical circumstances that could have caused it, for instance,

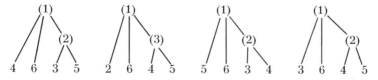

[4] Willard Thorp, "A New Manuscript Version of Dryden's Epilogue to *Sir Fopling Flutter*," *Review of English Studies*, IX (1933), 198-199.

and, as it happens, the probability of each of these is higher than the probabilities of any one of the historical circumstances that could have caused the other trees.

Because Q was printed in authorized editions, it has the most likelihood of representing Dryden's final intentions, and I therefore chose the first edition as the copy-text for the California Dryden. At that time the idea of experiments in probability had not occurred to me, and in addition I felt that the prime intermediary for the manuscripts had probably been copied from the printed text by an interested reader instead of the other way around. Another person might feel that interest in copying the poem would be less, once it was in print. Feeling as I did, I saw no reason to emend Q. One who accepted the tree for the states of the text indicated by the experiments summarized above would have to decide whether Q's reading of "Those" in line 3 was an authorized revision or an error in transcription.

Dryden's song beginning "Go tell Amynta" was first printed in the first edition of *Sylvæ*, 1685 (O1), pages 467-468, and was reprinted in the second edition, 1692 or 1693 (O2), pages 283-284. It was printed with music in *A Collection of Twenty Four Songs*, 1685 (Q), on A4^v, and in *The Theater of Music . . . First Book*, 1685 (F), page 30. The music, which is the same in both, is ascribed to Robert King in F.

The song is found set to music by Purcell in the following manuscripts: British Museum MS Add. 30,382, folios 36^r-37^v (M1), a folio in the hand of Henry Bowman, owned by Katherine Sedley before she became Countess of Dorchester (1686); British Museum R.M.20.h.8, folio 183^{r-v} (M2), "A Score Booke Containing Severall Anthems W.th Sўphonies," a folio in the hand of Henry Purcell and two others (this poem in Purcell's hand); and Folger Dryden MS V.b.197, pages 23-26 (M3), a folio in several seventeenth-century hands, owned by William Penn. Dryden's "Ode on the Death of Mr. Henry Purcell" (1696) appears on the contents leaf of M3 after the entry for "Go tell Amynta." The music is ascribed to Purcell in M1 but not in M2 or M3. The state of the text given here is that of the first edition of *Sylvae*.

SONG.

Go tell *Amynta* gentle Swain,
I wou'd not die nor dare complain,
Thy tuneful Voice with numbers joyn,
Thy words will more prevail than mine;
To Souls opress'd and dumb with grief,

The Gods ordain this kind releif;
That Musick shou'd in sounds convey,
What dying Lovers dare not say.

II.

A Sigh or Tear perhaps she'll give,
10 But love on pitty cannot live.
Tell her that Hearts for Hearts were made,
And love with love is only paid.
Tell her my pains so fast encrease,
That soon they will be past redress;
But ah! the Wretch that speechless lyes,
Attends but Death to close his Eyes.

Texts set to music offer a problem to the collator, for the words are almost always repeated and sometimes repeated often. The solution adopted here is to accept the first appearance of the words, reading left to right, or, if two voices begin a phrase at the same time, top to bottom.

Title SONG.] O1; SONG. BY Mr. *DRYDEN.* O2; *no title* F, Q M1-3.   1 *Amynta*] O1-2, Q, M1-3; *Amyntor* F.   4 words] O1-2; Voyce Q, F, M1-3.   5 To] O1-2; For Q, F, M1-3.   5 dumb] O1-2, Q, M1-3; drown'd F.   6 ordain] O1-2, M1; ordain'd Q, F, M2-3.   9 she'll] O1-2, Q, M1-3; she'd F.   14 they] O1-2, Q, F, M1; it M2-3.   14 redress] O1-2, Q, F, M1-2; address M3.   15 But] O1-2, Q; For F, M1-3.   15 ah! the] O1-2, F; O the Q; the M1-3.

The title gives two variations: O1:O2:F Q M1-3 for the whole title, and O1 O2:F Q M1-3 because O1 and O2 have "SONG." We could simplify the problem by regarding the last two variations as one, *But ah! | For ah! | But O | For,* O1-2:F:Q:M1-3, but they are strictly two, and we treat them as such here.
Variations classified by type:

a.	type 1:	F:O1 O2 Q M1 M2 M3	1, 5, 9
b.		M3:O1 O2 F Q M1 M2	14
c.	type 2:	O1 O2:F Q M1 M2 M3	title, 4, 5
d.		M2 M3:O1 O2 F Q M1	14
e.		O1 O2 Q:F M1 M2 M3	15
f.		O1 O2 M1:F Q M2 M3	6
g.	type 3:	O1:O2:F Q M1 M2 M3	title
h.	type 4:	O1 O2 F:Q:M1 M2 M3	15

Variations *e* and *f* indicate a ring, and so do *f* and *h*:

e/f: O1 O2————Q   *f/h*: O1 O2——F
        | | | |
        M1——F M2 M3   M1——M2 M3

The texts agree as follows:

O1 O2 11
O1 F   3 O2 F   3
O1 Q   6 O2 Q   6 F Q   7
O1 M1   6 O2 M1   6 F M1   7 Q M1 9
O1 M2   4 O2 M2   4 F M2   7 Q M2 9 M1 M2 10
O1 M3   3 O2 M3   3 F M3   6 Q M3 8 M1 M3   9 M2 M3 11

We see that the strongest of the weakest connections are between O1 O2 and Q and between O1 O2 and M1 in the first ring, and that both connections are equally weak. Accordingly, we rewrite *e* as *O1 O2:F M1 M2 M3:Q, and *f* as *O1 O2:F Q M2 M3:M1. The latter change breaks the other ring as well.

We can obtain two synthetic simple variations:

          Q
          *Q:O1 O2:F M1 M2 M3   *e*. (rewritten)
          Q:O1 O2 F:M1 M2 M3   *h*.
          ─────────────────────
          *Q:O1 O2 F M1 M2 M3

          M1
          *M1:M2 M3 Q F:O1 O2   *f*. (rewritten)
          M1 M2 M3:Q:F O1 O2   *h*.
          ─────────────────────
          *M1:M2 M3 Q F O1 O2

O1 and O2 are effective duplicates by the rules of textual analysis, but are of course bibliographically distinct. The preliminary textual diagram indicated by the simple variations, original and synthetic, is:

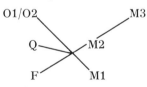

The type-4 variation *h* is anomalous. It indicates that we need an additional intermediary, either for O1/O2 and F or for M1, M2, and M3, but it does not tell us which. Strongly directional variations are lacking, and the better readings, *Amynta* in line 1 and *they* and *redress* in line 14, are found in so many states that we cannot locate the archetype with their aid. There are too many states to permit a solution by experiment. In the California Dryden I set up a bibliographical tree:

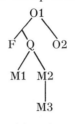

The tree results partly from taking the two variations in line 15 as one, as explained above (this allows Q to be intermediary), partly from considering an accidental variation (O1, O2, and F have a semicolon at the end of line 6, Q a period, M1 and 2 nothing, M3 a comma), and partly from my feeling that the prime intermediary for the musical settings would be taken from the first edition by an interested reader. The last is hardly a necessary conclusion. I took O1 as the copy-text because it appears in a volume Dryden edited and therefore presumably best reflects his wishes. The addition of Dryden's name in the title of O2 is no doubt his revision, but as the titles in the California Dryden have a style of their own I did not have to make a decision.

Dryden's translation of Dr. Archibald Pitcairne's "Epitaphium in Vice-Comitem Dundee" was first published in 1704 in *Poems on Affairs of State*, III, 337 (O1), and in *Poetical Miscellanies: The Fifth Part*, page 76 (O2). It had already circulated widely in manuscript, as may be seen from the number of copies that have been located: Bodleian MS Rawl. poet. 181, folio 28, a very small folio sheet in a seventeenth-century hand (M1); Bodleian MS Firth e.6, a quarto volume of poetry in a single scribal hand of the 1690s, with some prose in an eighteenth-century hand on the last leaves (M2); British Museum MS Add. 21,094, page 180, a folio miscellany of political and satiric prose and verse in various professional and nonprofessional hands of the late seventeenth and early eighteenth centuries (this poem is in the earliest hand), formerly the possession of Basil Feilding, Earl of Denbigh (M3); University of Nottingham MS Portland 116, page 28, a folio of poems in a single scribal hand of 1700 or a little later (M4); University of Nottingham MS Portland 115, page 140, a folio of poems and prose in a single scribal hand of the 1690s, except for the last three (not including this poem) which are in another hand of about the same date (M5);

British Museum MS Lansdowne 852, folio 122ʳ, a folio in various early eighteenth-century hands, with corrections by Edward Harley, second Earl of Oxford (M6); "A Collection of the best Poems, Lampoons, Songs & Satyrs from the Revolucõn 1688. to 1692," Huntington MS EL 8770, pages 25-26 (M7); "A Collection of the most choice and Private Poems, Lampoons &c from the withdrawing of the late King James 1688 to the year 1701 Collected by a Person of Quality," British Museum MS Harley 7315, folio 169ʳ, the second of two folio volumes bound as one, in a single scribal hand (M8); Bodleian MS Eng. poet. c. 18, folio 68ᵛ, a folio volume of prose and verse in various hands, apparently all of the eighteenth century (M9); "A Collection of all the Secret Poems wrote During the Reigne of the late King William," University of Chicago MS 559, page 15 (M10).

The state of the text in O1 follows:

> Epitaphium in Vice-Comitem Dundee
> [Pitcairn's poem here]
> *English'd by Mr.* Dryden
> O Last and best of *Scots*! who didst maintain
> Thy Country's Freedom from a Foreign Reign;
> New People fill the Land now thou art gone,
> New Gods the Temples, and new Kings the Throne.
> *Scotland* and thou did each in other live,
> Thou wouldst not her, not could she thee survive;
> Farewel! who living didst support the State,
> And couldst not fall but with thy Country's Fate.

Title Epitaphium in Vice-Comitum] O1; UPON THE DEATH OF THE EARL OF O2; Upon yᵉ E of M1; On the late Viscᵗ M2; On M3-6, M8-10; On Ld. M7.   *title* English'd by *Mr.* Dryden] O1; By Mr. *DRYDEN*. O2; Said to be writ by Mʳ Dr—n. M2; (by mʳ Dryden.) (1689) M3-5, M9; 1689 By Mʳ Dryden M6, M8; 1689 M7; 1689 by Mʳ B Dryden M10; *omitted* M1.   3 People] O1-2, M2-10; Temples M1.   3 Land] O1-2, M1-2; Earth M3-10.   4 Temples] O1-2, M1, M9; Temple M2-8, M10.   5 thou] O1, M1-10; Thee O2.   5 each in] O1-2, M1; in each M2-9; each M10.   5 live] O1-2, M1-9; Love M10 (*the* o *is dotted*).   6 Thou] O1; Nor O2, M1-10.   6 wouldst] O1-2, M1; cou'd'st M2-10.   6 not] O1; thou O2, M1-10.   6 thee] O1-2, M1-7, M9-10; the M8.   7 living] O1, M1-10; dying O2.   7 didst] O1; did O2, M2-10; couldst M1.   7 the] O1-2, M2-10; a M1.   8 And] O1-2, M2-10; not M1.   8 couldst] O1-2, M1; cou'd M2-10.   8 not . . . with] O1-2, M2-10; Thou . . . by M1.

The title is very complex. Preceding the name *Dundee* we have:

Epitaphium in		Vice-comitem	O1
UPON THE DEATH OF		THE EARL OF	O2
Upon		ye E of	M1
On	the late	Visc^t	M2
On		Ld.	M7
On			M3-6, M8-10

Here the add-omission of *Epitaphium* is variation (1), O1:O2 M1-10. Since the Latin *in* may correspond to either *upon* or *on* it must be separated from both in variation (2), O1:O2 M1:M2-10. The texts that omit the rest of this part of the title form a group, but all the rest differ, giving variation (3), O1:O2:M1:M2:M3-6 M8-10:M7. O2 and M2 agree in having *the* before *death of/late*, giving variation (4), O1:O2 M2:M1: M3-6 M8-10:M7. The varations in Dundee's title, including its omission, give variation (5), O1 M2:O2 M1:M3-6 M8-10:M7.

Dundee is the last word in the title of M1, but the others continue with:

English'd	*by Mr.*	Dryden.	O1	
Said to be writ by M^r		Dr—n.	M2	
1689	By M.^{r}	Dryden	M6,	M8
1689	by M^r B	Dryden	M10	
	(by m.^{r}	Dryden.)	(1689) M3-5,	M9
	By Mr.	*DRYDEN.*	O2	
1689			M7	

The absence of any of these phrases in M1 together with the differences in the others gives variation (6), O1:O2:M1:M2:M3-5 M9:M6 M8:M7:M10. All but M1 and M7 have *by Mr.*, giving variation (7), O1-2 M2-6 M8-10:M1:M7. Because *Dr——n* may be accepted as the equivalent of *Dryden* so long as there is no other candidate with the same initial and final letters, all but M1 and M7 agree in the name, and variation (8) is the same as variation (7). The texts that have a date form a group in a final variation, (9), in which O1, with *English'd*, M2, with *Said to be writ by*, O2 with nothing, and M1 with a larger omission, stand alone, O1:O2:M1:M2:M3-10.

We should also note that the second variation in line 5 is really two, an agreement-defined type-1 variation within a context-defined type-4 variation.

Variations classified by type:

a.	type 1:	O1:O2 M1 M2 M3 M4 M5 M6 M7 M8 M9 M10	title[1], 6, 6
b.		O2:O1 M1 M2 M3 M4 M5 M6 M7 M8 M9 M10	5, 7
c.		M1:O1 O2 M2 M3 M4 M5 M6 M7 M8 M9 M10	3, 7, 8, 8, 8
d.		M8:O1 O2 M1 M2 M3 M4 M5 M6 M7 M9 M10	6
e.		M10:O1 O2 M1 M2 M3 M4 M5 M6 M7 M8 M9	5, 5
f.	type 2:	O1 O2 M1:M2 M3 M4 M5 M6 M7 M8 M9 M10	6, 8
g.		O1 O2 M1 M2:M3 M4 M5 M6 M7 M8 M9 M10	3
h.		O1 O2 M1 M9:M2 M3 M4 M5 M6 M7 M8 M10	4
i.	type 3:	O1:O2:M1:M2:M3 M4 M5 M6 M7 M8 M9 M10	title[9]
j.		O1:O2:M1:M2:M3 M4 M5 M6 M8 M9 M10:M7	title[3]
k.		O1:O2 M2 M3 M4 M5 M6 M7 M8 M9 M10:M1	7
l.		O1 O2 M2 M3 M4 M5 M6 M8 M9 M10:M1:M7	title[7], title[8]
m.	type 4:	O1:O2:M1:M2:M3 M4 M5 M9:M6 M8:M7:M10	title[6]
n.		O1:O2 M1:M2 M3 M4 M5 M6 M7 M8 M9 M10	title[2]
o.		O1:O2 M2:M1:M3 M4 M5 M6 M8 M9 M10:M7	title[4]
p.		O1 M2:O2 M1:M3 M4 M5 M6 M8 M9 M10:M7	title[5]
q.		O1 O2 M1:M2 M3 M4 M5 M6 M7 M8 M9:M10	5

M3-5 are textually duplicate. Variations *g* and *h* indicate a ring, as do *h* and *o*, and *h* and *p*:

g/h: O1 O2 M1———————M2
　　　　|　　　　　　　　　　　　|
　　　M9—M3/5 M6 M7 M8 M10

h/o: O2———————————M2
　　　　|　　　　　　　　　　　　|
　　　M9—M3/5 M6 M8 M10

h/p: O1———————————M9
　　　　|　　　　　　　　　　　　|
　　　M2—M3/5 M6 M8 M10

The states agree as follows:

O1 O2	15					M9 M10	22	M8 M10	22	M7 M10	18
O1 M1	10	O2 M1	12					M8 M9	24	M7 M9	20
O1 M2	13	O2 M2	16	M1 M2	9					M7 M8	20
O1 M3	12	O2 M3	14	M1 M3	8	M2 M3	21				
O1 M6	12	O2 M6	14	M1 M6	8	M2 M6	21	M3 M6	26		
O1 M7	10	O2 M7	12	M1 M7	8	M2 M7	19	M3 M7	21	M6 M7	21
O1 M8	11	O2 M8	13	M1 M8	7	M2 M8	20	M3 M8	25	M6 M8	26
O1 M9	13	O2 M9	15	M1 M9	9	M2 M9	20	M3 M9	26	M6 M9	25
O1 M10	10	O2 M10	12	M1 M10	6	M2 M10	18	M3 M10	23	M6 M10	23

We see then that the weakest connections in the rings are as follows:

　　　g/h: O1 O2 M1—M9 (15)　　　*h/o*: O2—M9 (15)
　　　　　　　h/p: O1—M9 and O1—M2 (13)

Starting with the strongest weakest connections we break the *g/h* ring by separating M9 from O1 O2 M1 in variation *h*:

*O1 O2 M1:M2 M3 M4 M5 M6 M7 M8 M10:M9

This separation breaks the other rings as well.

Examination of the complex variations gives the following synthetic simple variations:

M7	
M7:O1 M2 M3 M4 M5 M6 M8 M9 M10 O2:M1	*l.*
M7:O1 M2:M3 M4 M5 M6 M8 M9 M10:O2 M1	*p.*
*M7:O1 M2 M3 M4 M5 M6 M8 M9 M10 O2 M1	

M9	
*M9:M3 M4 M5 M6 M7 M8 M10 M2:O1 O2 M1	*h.* (rewritten)
M9 M3 M4 M5 M6 M7 M8 M10:M2 O1 O2 M1	*g.*
*M9:M3 M4 M5 M6 M7 M8 M10 M2 O1 O2 M1	

O2 M1	
O2 M1:O1 M2:M3 M4 M5 M6 M8 M9 M10:M7	*p.*
O2 M1 O1:M2 M3 M4 M5 M6 M8 M9 M10 M7	*f.*
*O2 M1:O1 M2 M3 M4 M5 M6 M8 M9 M10 M7	

M6 proves to be an effective duplicate of M3-5, and *l* to be an anomalous variation.

From the simple variations we obtain the following preliminary diagram:

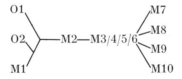

As usual, strongly directional variations are lacking, but we have a number of variants that can be identified as better: "People" and "Land" in line 3, "Temples" in line 4, "each in" or "in each" and "live" in line 5, "didst" in line 7, and "couldst" in line 8. The only state with all these readings is O1, which is therefore the archetype. It is the obvious choice for copy-text. We can see, however, that it is earlier than its record. In a bibliographical tree, then, such as that in the California Dryden, the archetype lies between the first printing and the prime intermediary for the other records. In deriving the tree in the California Dryden, also, I did not analyze the title with the rest of the text, and so accepted M3-7 as simple duplicates and assigned a single intermediary to O1, O2, and M1.

Dryden's "A Song for St. Cecilia's Day" was first printed in 1687 as a broadside (F), and was reprinted without substantive change in *Examen Poeticum*, 1693, pages 242-246 (O). The poem also circulated in manuscript, alone in British Museum MS Add. 27,408, folio 94^{r-v}, a folio leaf in a seventeeth-century hand (M1), and with the music in British Museum MS Royal College of Music 1106, folios 29-74, a folio in two hands, of which that for the "Song" has been identified as that of the composer, John Baptist Draghi (M2); British Museum MS Add. 33,287, folios 221^v-229^v, a very large folio (originally two volumes) in a single late seventeenth-century hand, the "Song" left incomplete (M3), and in British Museum MS Royal College of Music 1097, folios 85-112, a folio in various hands of the late seventeenth and early eighteenth centuries, the "Song" in a hand that may be of either (M4).

The state of the text in F follows:

A Song for St CECILIA's Day, 1687
WRITTEN
By *John Dryden*, Esq; and Compos'd by Mr. *John Baptist Draghi*.

I.
From Harmony, from heav'nly Harmony
This universal Frame began.
When Nature underneath a heap
Of jarring Atomes lay,
And cou'd not heave her Head,
The tuneful Voice was heard from high,
Arise ye more than dead.
Then cold, and hot, and moist, and dry,
In order to their stations leap,
10   And MUSICK's pow'r obey.
From Harmony, from heav'nly Harmony
This universal Frame began:
From Harmony to Harmony
Through all the compass of the Notes it ran,
The Diapason closing full in Man.

II.
What Passion cannot MUSICK raise and quell!
When *Jubal* struck the corded Shell,
His list'ning Brethren stood around

And wond'ring, on their Faces fell
20   To worship that Celestial Sound.
Less than a God they thought there cou'd not dwell
    Within the hollow of that Shell
    That spoke so sweetly and so well.
What Passion cannot MUSICK raise and quell!

III.

The TRUMPETS loud Clangor
    Excites us to Arms
With shrill Notes of Anger
    And mortal Alarms.
The double double double beat
30   Of the thundring DRUM
Cryes, heark the Foes come;
Charge, Charge, 'tis too late to retreat.

IV.

The soft complaining FLUTE
In dying Notes discovers
The Woes of hopeless Lovers,
Whose Dirge is whisper'd by the warbling LUTE.

V.

Sharp VIOLINS proclaim
Their jealous Pangs, and Desperation,
Fury, frantick Indignation,
40   Depth of Pains, and height of Passion,
    For the fair, disdainful Dame.

VI.

But oh! what Art can teach
    What human Voice can reach
The sacred ORGANS praise?
Notes inspiring holy Love,
Notes that wing their heav'nly ways
    To mend the Choires above.

VIII.

Orpheus cou'd lead the savage race;
And Trees unrooted left their place;
50   Sequacious of the Lyre:
But bright *CECILIA* rais'd the wonder high'r;

When to her ORGAN, vocal Breath was giv'n
An Angel heard, and straight appear'd
Mistaking Earth of Heaven.

Grand CHORUS.

As from the pow'r of sacred Lays
 The Spheres began to move,
And sung the great Creator's praise
 To all the bless'd above;
So when the last and dreadful hour
60 *This crumbling Pageant shall devour,*
The TRUMPET *shall be heard on high,*
The Dead shall live, the Living die,
And MUSICK *shall untune the Sky.*

Title omitted M3, M4. *title* A Song for] F, O, M1; Sign.ʳ Baptists Song On M2. *title* WRITTEN By *John Dryden,* Esq; and Compos'd by Mr. *John Baptist Draghi.*] F, O; Performd att Stationers Hall M2; *omitted* M1. 7 Arise] F, O, M1-3; A Rise M4. 8 Then] F, O, M1-3; The M4. 8 hot] F, O, M1-3; heat M4. 10 pow'r] F, O, M1, M3-4; powr's M2. 14 ran] F, O, M1; runs M2 (*subsequently* run); run M3-4. 16 quell!] F, O; ∼? M1 ∼∧ M2-4. 19 their] F, O, M1-2, M4; there M3. 22 of that] F, O, M1; of the M2-4. 24 quell!] F, O; ∼? M1; ∼∧ M2-3; ∼. M4. 26 Excites] F, O, M1, M4; excite M2-3. 27 shrill Notes] F, O, M1; Shrills full M2-4 (*M2 in the margin the first time, correcting the text* "shri full"). 28 Alarms] F, O, M1, M3; alarm M2; alarm's M4. 29 double double double] F, O, M1-3; double beat the double M4. 31-63 *omitted* from M3. 32 too late] F, O, M1-2; to late M4. 35 hopeless] F, O, M2-4; hapless M1. 36 whisper'd . . . warbling] F, O, M1-2; warbl'd . . . whispring M4. 40 Pains] F, O, M1-2; pain M4. 52 ORGAN,] F, O, M1; ORGAN's M2; Organs M4. 57 sung] F, O, M1-2; sing M4. 57 the] F, O, M1; their M2, M4. 57 Creator's] F, O, M4; Creators M1-2. *subscription* Sig.ʳ Baptist Draghi Composed by M.ʳ Bapti[st] M2; *omitted* F, O, M1, M3-4.

Here we see the problem of interpreting punctuation and other accidental variations when past practice is different from present. Writers and even printers in Dryden's time made little distinction between exclamation points and question marks. The following analysis therefore treats the variants in punctuation in lines 16 and 24 as wholly accidental, which is to say that they are ignored. The use of apostrophes at the time was also erratic in the extreme: plurals may have them, singular possessives may not have them, and if they appear at all in plural possessives ending in *s* they come before the *s*. The following analysis therefore disregards *Creator's/Creators* in line 57 (both accepted as possessive), and it treats both *Alarms* and *alarm's* in line 28 and both *Organ's* and *Organs* in line 52 as plurals, the term "a pair of organs" (i.e., two manuals) being in common use at the time.

Variations classified by type:

a.	type 1:	M2:F O M1 M3 M4	10, 28
b.		M3:F O M1 M2 M4	19, 31-subscription
c.		M4:F O M1 M2 M3	7, 8, 8, 29
d.	type 2:	M2 M3:F O M1 M4	26
e.		F O M1:M2 M3 M4	22, 27
f.		F O M1 M2:M3 M4	title
g.	type 3:	F O M1 M2:M3:M4	32, 36, 36, 40, 57
h.		F O M1 M4:M2:M3	subscription
i.		F O M2 M4:M1:M3	35
j.	type 4:	F O:M1:M2:M3 M4	title
k.		F O M1:M2:M3 M4	title, title, 14
l.		F O M1:M2 M4:M3	52, 57

F and O are textually duplicate. Variations *d* and *f* indicate a ring:

$$F/O \ M1 — M2$$
$$\begin{array}{ccc} | & & | \\ M4 & \!\!\!\!——\!\!\!\! & M3 \end{array}$$

The states agree as follows:

```
F/O  M1  23
F/O  M2  13    M1 M2  12
F/O  M3   6    M1 M3   6    M2 M3  7
F/O  M4   7    M1 M4   6    M2 M4  7    M3 M4  9
```

We see that the connections between F/O M1 and M4 and between M2 and M3 are the weakest, and that they are equally weak, so we divide M2 from M3, and F/O M1 from M4, changing *d* to *F O M1:M2:M3:M4.

We can obtain one synthetic simple variation:

```
     M1
     M1:F/O M2 M4:M3      i.
     M1 F/O:M2 M4 M3      e.
    ─────────────────
    *M1:F/O M2 M4 M3
```

From the simple variations we obtain the following preliminary diagram:

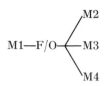

In line 14, *ran* is certainly the correct reading, even if it is an emendation, since it is a rhyme word. In line 35, *hopeless* is probably better than *hapless*, and if so F/O is the archetype. A bibliographical tree would make O a descendant of F but would have to indicate that M1 might be a descendant of either. In addition we know something of the origin of the poem: it was commissioned for musical performance. Dryden must then have supplied a copy to the composer, Draghi, and it is most unlikely that he made him wait for a printed copy. The rules of textual analysis indicate that the prime intermediary for the musical texts must also have had music. If this state were the archetype, a copy must have been abstracted from the score to send to the press, which seems less likely than that Dryden sent a copy of the words alone. External and historical evidence then, not textual or bibliographical, indicates that the archetype in a bibliographical tree would belong between F and the prime intermediary for the texts with music.

F is the natural choice as copy-text, since O is a reprint into which have crept accidental variations not recorded above.

The foregoing examples can all be worked out with pencil and paper without a great amount of trouble. The next cannot, and I therefore arrived at my solution with a computer, using the programs described in Appendix B. I have, however, showed the main lines of the analysis as before, instead of pulling the answer out of a black box. This book has as its main purpose the facilitation of textual criticism of the New Testament, and the next example is therefore a very small sample indeed of what can now be done in this field. We are to consider the Greek text of Philemon in fourteen states recorded in ten uncial manuscripts. The text and collation given below are taken from Tischendorf's eighth edition.[5] Since Tischendorf's notices of the minuscules are often given in summary, they are of no use to the textual analyst. As before, alternate spellings, alternate forms, and other information not ger-

---

[5] *Novum Testamentum Graece*, ed. Constantinus Tischendorf, ed. oct. critica maior (Lipsiae, 1869-1894), II, 895-901; for descriptions of the manuscripts see III, 418-435.

mane to purely textual analysis have been passed over; in other respects, Tischendorf's apparatus has been adjusted only slightly, so that his on the whole admirable system may be illustrated.

The states to be analyzed are as follows: ℵ*, Sinaiticus, fourth century; ℵᶜ, Sinaiticus as corrected, seventh century; A, Alexandrinus, fifth century; C*, Ephraemi rescriptus, fifth century, C² Ephraemi rescriptus as corrected, sixth century; D*, Claromontanus, sixth century; Dᶜ, Claromontanus as corrected, ninth century; E*, Petropolitanus, ninth century; E** Petropolitanus as corrected; F, Augiensis, ninth century; G, Boernerianus, ninth century; K, Moscuensis, ninth century L, Angelicus, ninth century; P, Porfirianus, ninth century. In the collations, it must be remembered that ℵ alone stands for both ℵ* and ℵᶜ, C alone for both C* and C², and so on. It must also be remembered that whatever these sigla represented to Tischenuorf they here represent states of the text.

ΠΡΟΣ ΦΙΛΗΜΟΝΑ

1 Παῦλος δέσμιος Χριστοῦ Ἰησοῦ καὶ Τιμόθεος ὁ ἀδελφὸς Φιλήμονι τῷ ἀγαπητῷ καὶ συνεργῷ ἡμῶν 2 καὶ Ἀπφίᾳ τῇ ἀδελφῇ καὶ Ἀρχίππῳ τῷ συνστρατιώτῃ ἡμῶν καὶ τῇ κατ᾽ οἶκόν σου ἐκκλησίᾳ. 3 χάρις ὑμῖν καὶ εἰρήνη ἀπὸ θεοῦ πατρὸς ἡμῶν καὶ κυρίου Ἰησοῦ Χριστοῦ.

4 Εὐχαριστῶ τῷ θεῷ μου πάντοτε μνείαν σου ποιούμενος ἐπὶ τῶν προσευχῶν μου, 5 ἀκούων σου τὴν ἀγάπην καὶ τὴν πίστιν ἣν ἔχεις πρὸς τὸν κύριον Ἰησοῦν καὶ εἰς πάντας τοὺς ἁγίους, 6 ὅπως ἡ κοινωνία τῆς πίστεώς σου ἐνεργὴς γένηται ἐν ἐπιγνώσει παντὸς ἀγαθοῦ τοῦ ἐν ὑμῖν εἰς Χριστόν. 7 χαρὰν γὰρ πολλὴν ἔσχον καὶ παράκλησιν ἐπὶ τῇ ἀγάπῃ σου, ὅτι τὰ σπλάγχνα τῶν ἁγίων ἀναπέπαυται διὰ σοῦ, ἀδελφέ. 8 Διὸ πολλὴν ἐν Χριστῷ παρρησίαν ἔχων ἐπιτάσσειν σοι τὸ ἀνῆκον, 9 διὰ τὴν ἀγάπην μᾶλλον παρακαλῶ · τοιοῦτος ὢν ὡς Παῦλος πρεσβύτης, νυνὶ δὲ καὶ δέσμιος Χριστοῦ Ἰησοῦ, 10 παρακαλῶ σε περὶ τοῦ ἐμοῦ τέκνου, ὃν ἐγέννησα ἐν τοῖς δεσμοῖς, Ὀνήσιμον, 11 τόν ποτέ σοι ἄχρηστον, νυνὶ δὲ καὶ σοὶ καὶ ἐμοὶ εὔχρηστον, ὃν ἀνέπεμψά σοι, 12 αὐτόν, τοῦτ᾽ ἔστιν τὰ ἐμὰ σπλάγχνα. 13 ὃν ἐγὼ ἐβουλόμην πρὸς ἐμαυτὸν κατέχειν, ἵνα ὑπὲρ σοῦ μοι διακονῇ ἐν τοῖς δεσμοῖς τοῦ εὐαγγελίου, 14 χωρὶς δὲ τῆς σῆς γνώμης οὐδὲν ἠθέλησα ποιῆσαι, ἵνα μὴ ὡς κατὰ ἀνάγκην τὸ ἀγαθόν σου ᾖ ἀλλὰ κατὰ ἑκούσιον · 15 τάχα γὰρ διὰ τοῦτο ἐχωρίσθη πρὸς ὥραν, ἵνα αἰώ-

νιον αὐτὸν ἀπέχῃς, 16 οὐκ ἔτι ὡς δοῦλον ἀλλὰ ὑπὲρ δοῦλον, ἀδελφὸν ἀγαπητόν, μάλιστα ἐμοί, πόσῳ δὲ μᾶλλον σοὶ καὶ ἐν σαρκὶ καὶ ἐν κυρίῳ · 17 εἰ οὖν με ἔχεις κοινωνόν, προσλαβοῦ αὐτὸν ὡς ἐμέ. 18 εἰ δέ τι ἠδίκησέν σε ἢ ὀφείλει, τοῦτο ἐμοὶ ἐλλόγα. 19 ἐγὼ Παῦλος ἔγραψα τῇ ἐμῇ χειρί, ἐγὼ ἀποτίσω · ἵνα μὴ λέγω σοι ὅτι καὶ σεαυτόν μοι προσοφείλεις. 20 ναί, ἀδελφέ, ἐγώ σου ὀναίμην ἐν κυρίῳ · ἀνάπαυσόν μου τὰ σπλάγχνα ἐν Χριστῷ. 21 Πεποιθὼς τῇ ὑπακοῇ σου ἔγραψά σοι, εἰδὼς ὅτι καὶ ὑπὲρ ἃ λέγω ποιήσεις. 22 ἅμα δὲ καὶ ἑτοίμαζέ μοι ξενίαν · ἐλπίζω γὰρ ὅτι διὰ τῶν προσευχῶν ὑμῶν χαρισθήσομαι ὑμῖν. 23 Ἀσπάζεταί σε Ἐπαφρᾶς ὁ συναιχμάλωτός μου ἐν Χριστῷ Ἰησοῦ, 24 Μάρκος, Ἀρίσταρχος, Δημᾶς, Λουκᾶς, οἱ συνεργοί μου. 25 Ἡ χάρις τοῦ κυρίου Ἰησοῦ Χριστοῦ μετὰ τοῦ πνεύματος ὑμῶν.

* προς φιλημονα ut ℵA. Item DEFG αρχεται προς φιλημονα . . . KLP παυλου (L του αγιου αποστολου παυλου) επιστολη προς φιλημονα [C wants the title and the text through vs. 2]

1. δεσμιος: D*E* αποστολος | χριστου ιησου cum ℵADᶜE**FGKP . . . D*E*L ιησου χριστου | ο αδελφος: DEF om ο | αγαπητω: addunt vero D*E αδελφω

2. απφια: D* αφφια, FG αμφια | αδελφη cum ℵAD*E*FGP . . . DᶜE**KL αγαπητη | τω ante συνστρατ.: F om | τη et εκκλησια: D* την et εκκλησιαν

3. πατρος ημων (F υμων) et[iam] ℵᶜ . . . ℵ* om ημων

5. την αγαπ. κ. τ. πιστιν cum ℵACFGKLP . . . DE τ. πιστ. κ. τ. αγαπ. | προς τον cum ℵDᶜFGKLP al[teris] fere omn[ibus] [presumably inluding E] . . . ACD* εις τον | ιησουν: D*E add χριστον

6. οπωσ: FG ινα πωσ | η κοινωνια et. ℵᶜ . . . ℵ* η διακονια | αγαθου: FG praem[ittunt] εργου | του εν cum ℵDEFGKLP . . . AC om του | εν υμιν cum ℵFGP . . . ACDEKL εν ημιν | εις χριστον sine additam cum ℵ*AC . . . ℵᶜ DEFGKLP add ιησουν

7. χαραν cum ℵACDEFG . . . KLP χαριν | πολλην εσχον cum ℵACFGP;. item D*E πολλην εσχομεν . . . Dᶜ (sed πολλ. εχομ.) KL (sed εχωμεν) εχομεν πολλην | και παρακλησιν: ℵ om | επι τη: D*L εν τη

8. εν χριστω παρρησ. εχων: L παρρησ. εν χρι. εχων . . . D* παρρ. εχω εν χρι. ιησου, DᶜE παρρη. εχων εν χρι. (E add ιησου)

9. αγαπην: A αναγκην | νυνι cum ℵCDEFGKLP . . . A νυν | χριστου ιησου cum ℵACP . . . DᶜEFGKL ιησου χριστου . . . D* om utrumque

10. ον cum ℵCDEFGKLP . . . A add εχω | δεσμοις sine μου cum ℵ*AD*FG . . . ℵᶜCDᶜEKLP add μου

11. και σοι cum ℵ*FG . . . ℵᶜACDEKLP om και | ανεπεμψα: D*E* επεμψα | σοι sec[utus] c[um] ℵACD*E* . . . DᶜE**FGKLP om

12. αυτον cum ℵ*AC* . . . ℵᶜC²DEFGKLP praem συ δε | σπλαγχνα sine additam cum ℵ*AFG . . . ℵᶜCDEKLP add προσλαβου

13. μοι διακονη (P -νει) cum ℵACDEFGP . . . KL (-νει) διακονη μοι

14. σης (post της): F om | κατα εκουσιον: D* εκουσιον

15. εχωρισθη: P add σου | απεχης: L -χεις
16. FG om αλλα υπ. δουλ. | αδελφον et. ℵᶜ: ℵ* om | ποσω δε: P om δε
17. με cum ℵACDEFGLP . . . K εμε
18. σε: K om | οφειλει (L ωφειλει): FG add τει
19. αποτισω: D* αποδωσω | προσοφειλεις (L προσωφ-): D*E* add εν κυριω
20. χριστω cum ℵACD*FGLP . . . DᶜEK κυριω. Ceterum desunt reliqua in FG
21. υπερ a cum ℵACP . . . DEKL υπ. ο | ποιησεις: L -σης
22. προσευχ. υμων: L om υμ.
23. ασπαζεται cum ℵACD*EP . . . DᶜKL ασπαζονται
25. του κυριου absque ημων ℵP . . . ACDEKL add ημων | πνευματ. υμων sine αμην cum AD* . . . ℵCDᶜEKLP add αμην

Subscriptio: ℵC προς φιλημονα (in A periit), DE προς φιλημ. επληρωθη . . . P προς φιλημ. εγραφει απο ρωμης, K προς φιλημονα εγραφη απο ρωμης δια ονησιμου οικετου, L του αγιου αποστολου παυλου επιστολη ῥρος φιλημ. και απφιαν δεσποτας του ονησιμου και προς αρχιππον τον διακονον της εν κολοσσαις εκκλησιας · εγραφη απο ρωμης δια ονησιμου οικετου.

In classifying these lengthy variations by type, I adopt a symbol used but not introduced into textual criticism by Greg, the Greek letter Σ, to represent all the items not specifically listed (the unlisted items always form a single group):

a.	type 1:	Σ:ℵ*	6, 16
b.		Σ:D*	8, 14, 19
c.		Σ:A	9, 9, 10
d.		Σ:F	14
e.		Σ:P	15, 16
f.		Σ:L	15, 18, 19
g.		Σ:K	17, 18
h.	type 2:	Σ:C* C²	title-2
i.		Σ:F G	6, 6, 16, 18, 21-subscription
j.		Σ:ℵ* ℵᶜ	7
k.		Σ:D* L	7
l.		Σ:D* E*	11, 19
m.		Σ:K L	7, 13
n.		Σ:D* E* E**	5, 8
o.		Σ:A C* C²	6
p.		Σ:K L P	7, 13
q.		Σ:Dᶜ K L	7
r.		Σ:ℵ* F G	11
s.		Σ:ℵ* A C*	12
t.		Σ:D* Dᶜ E* E**	5
u.		Σ:ℵ* A C* C²	6

v.		$\Sigma:\aleph^*$ A F G	12
w.		$\Sigma:D^c$ E* E** K	20
x.		$\Sigma:\aleph^*$ $\aleph^c$ F G P	6
y.		$\Sigma:\aleph^*$ A D* F G	10
z.		$\Sigma:\aleph^*$ $\aleph^c$ A C* C^2 D* E*	11
aa.	type 3:	$\Sigma:\aleph^*$:F	3
bb.	type 4:	$\Sigma:$L:K P:$\aleph^*$ $\aleph^c$ A:C* C^2	title
cc.		$\Sigma:$K L P:$\aleph^*$ $\aleph^c$ A:C* C^2	title
dd.		$\Sigma:$D* D^c E* E** F G:K L P:C* C^2	title
ee.		$\Sigma:$D* E*:C* C^2	1
ff.		$\Sigma:$D* E* L:C* C^2	1
gg.		$\Sigma:$D* D^c E* E** F:C* C^2	1
hh.		$\Sigma:$D* E* E**:C* C^2	1
ii.		$\Sigma:$D*:F G:C* C^2	2
jj.		$\Sigma:D^c$ E** K L:C* C^2	2
kk.		$\Sigma:$F:C* C^2	2
ll.		$\Sigma:$D*:C* C^2	2, 2
mm.		$\Sigma:$A C* C^2 D*:E* E**	5
nn.		$\Sigma:$D* E* E**:D^c:K L	7
oo.		$\Sigma:$D* D^c E* E**:L	8
pp.		$\Sigma:\aleph^*$ $\aleph^c$ A C* C^2 P:D*	9
qq.		$\Sigma:$D* D^c E* E** K L:F G	21
rr.		$\Sigma:$L:F G	21, 22
ss.		$\Sigma:D^c$ K L:F G	23
tt.		$\Sigma:\aleph^*$ $\aleph^c$ P:F G	25
uu.		$\Sigma:$A D*:F G	25
vv.		$\Sigma:$A:F G	subscription (omission by A)
ww.		$\Sigma:$D* D^c E* E**:P:K L:A:F G	subscription
xx.		$\Sigma:$K L:P:$\aleph^*$ $\aleph^c$ C* C^2:A:F G	subscription
yy.		$\Sigma:$K L P:A:F G	subscription
zz.		$\Sigma:$L:K P:$\aleph^*$ $\aleph^c$ C* C^2:A:F G	subscription

All the type-2 and -4 variations form rings, 235 in all. $\Sigma:D^c$ E* E** K (*w*) and $\Sigma:\aleph^*$ $\aleph^c$ A C* C^2 D* E* (*z*) form the ring with the strongest weakest connection (58 agreements):

$$\aleph^* \ \aleph^c \ A \ C^* \ C^2 \ D^*{-}E^*$$
$$|\qquad\qquad\qquad |$$
$$F \ G \ L \ P{-}D^c \ E^{**} \ K$$

Since the left and bottom connections are the weakest and equally strong, we divide both: $\Sigma:D^c$ E* E** K (*w*) as *$\Sigma:D^c$ E* E** K:F G L P (the Σ now represents $\aleph^*$ $\aleph^c$ A C* C^2 D*), and $\Sigma:\aleph^*$ $\aleph^c$ A C* C^2 D*

E* (z) as *Σ:ℵ* ℵᶜ A C* C² D* E*:Dᶜ E** K (the Σ now represents F G L P).

We have to divide Σ:Dᶜ E* E** K (w) again at once for it forms two rings having the next strongest weakest connections. This variation and three others, Σ:Dᶜ E** K L:C* C² (jj), Σ:Dᶜ K L (q), and Σ:Dᶜ K L:F G (ss), form rings with Σ:K L P (p) and with Σ:K L P:A:F G (yy), all having weakest connections of 55 agreements. Since the weakest connection each time is between K or K L and Dᶜ E** or Dᶜ E* E**, we rewrite the first four variations as follows: *Σ:Dᶜ E* E**:K:F G L P (w), *Σ:Dᶜ E**:K L:C* C² (jj), *Σ:Dᶜ:K L (q), and *Σ:Dᶜ:K L:F G (ss). The same break is indicated for the rings formed by Σ:Dᶜ E* E** K (w) and Σ:Dᶜ E** K L:C* C² (jj) with Σ:D* Dᶜ E* E** F:C* C² (gg). The latter variation and Σ:ℵ* A D* F G (y), however, form a ring that must be differently broken:

$$
\begin{array}{ccc}
\text{D* F} & \text{------} & \text{ℵ* A G} \\
| & & | \\
\text{Dᶜ E* E**} & \text{---} & \text{ℵᶜ K L P}
\end{array}
$$

Here the bottom connection is the weakest, so we divide Dᶜ E* E** from ℵᶜ K L P and both from C* C², writing *Σ :ℵ* A D* F G:Dᶜ E* E**:C* C² (y) in which the Σ now represents ℵᶜ K L P.

We have to divide Σ:ℵ* ℵᶜ A C* C² D* E* (z) and Σ:ℵ* A D* F G (y) again when we come to the rings in which the weakest connections have 53 agreements. These variations and Σ:K L P (p), Σ:K L P:A:F G (yy), and Σ:ℵ* A C* (s) form rings with Σ:ℵ* ℵᶜ F G P (x) and with Σ:ℵ* ℵᶜ P:F G (tt), and some of them also with Σ:ℵ* ℵᶜ (j). Some of these variations have been rewritten and must now be rewritten again. We break the rings by writing *Σ:ℵ* ℵᶜ:A C* C² D* E*:Dᶜ E** K (z), *Σ:ℵ*:A D F G:Dᶜ E* E**:C* C² (y), *Σ:K L P:ℵ* ℵᶜ F G (p), *Σ:K L P:A:F G:ℵ* ℵᶜ (yy), and *Σ:ℵ*:A C* (s). The latter break is also indicated for the rings formed by Σ:ℵ* A C* (s) with Σ:A C* C² (o) and with Σ:A C* C² D*:E* E** (mm).

We must divide Σ:K L P (p) and Σ:K L P:A:F G (yy) again when we come to the rings in which the weakest connections have 51 agreements. This time these variations form rings with Σ:ℵ* ℵᶜ A C* C² P:D* (pp) and with Σ:D* Dᶜ E* E** K L:F G (qq). Each time the weakest connection is between Dᶜ E* E** or D* Dᶜ E** and ℵ* ℵᶜ A C* C². Dividing these elements from each other and from the other sigla in their groups, together with the divisions already made, produces *Σ:K

L P:ℵ* ℵᶜ D*:E*:F G:A C* C² (*p*) and *Σ:K L P:A:F G:ℵ* ℵᶜ:C* C²: D*:E* (*yy*).

When we come to the rings with 49 agreements in their weakest links we find a series that has already been broken, so that we ignore its weakest links. The rest of the analysis only repeats processes already illustrated, and can be treated more summarily.

We have to divide Σ:ℵ* A C* (*s*) again, into *Σ:ℵ*:A:C* because it forms a ring with Σ:C* C² (*h*). We have to divide Σ:Dᶜ E* E** K (*w*) again into *Dᶜ E* E**:K:L:F G P:ℵ* ℵᶜ A:C* C²:D* because it forms a ring with Σ:D* E* L:C* C² (*ff*), which shows that D* L is to be separated from ℵ* ℵᶜ A F G P and both from C* C². We must divide Σ:ℵ* ℵᶜ A C* C² D* E* (*z*) for the third and last time into *Σ:ℵ*:ℵᶜ:A C* C² D* E*:Dᶜ:E**:K:L because it forms a ring with Σ:D* E* E**:Dᶜ:K L (*nn*), which shows that E** is to be separated from F G P and both from Dᶜ and from K L. This rewriting also breaks several other rings formed with Σ:D* E* E** (*n*), Σ:D* Dᶜ E* E** (*t*), and with complex variations in which the same groups appear. Some of these same variations form rings that cause us to divide Σ:Dᶜ E** K L:C* C² (*jj*) a second time into *Σ:Dᶜ E**:K L:C* C²:D* E*.

Σ:ℵ* A F G (*v*) and Σ:ℵ* A D* F G (*y*) form various rings that require us to rewrite Σ:A C* C² (*o*) as *Σ:A:C* C², Σ:ℵ* ℵᶜ F G P (*x*) as *Σ:ℵ* ℵᶜ F G P:A, and Σ:ℵ* ℵᶜ P:F G (*tt*) as *Σ:ℵ* ℵᶜ P:F G:A. Σ:ℵ* ℵᶜ (*j*) forms rings not only with Σ:ℵ* A F G (*v*) and Σ:ℵ* A D* F G (*y*) but also with Σ:ℵ* F G (*r*), which together require us to rewrite it as *Σ:ℵ*ℵᶜ:A:F G and, because one ring has two equally weak connections, to rewrite Σ:ℵ* F G (*r*) as *Σ:ℵ*:F G.

We have to divide Σ:ℵ* ℵᶜ F G P (*x*) again as *Σ:ℵ* ℵᶜ F G P:A:C* C² because of rings with Σ:ℵ* A C* C² (*u*) and with Σ:ℵ* ℵᶜ A C* C² P:D* (*pp*). There are two equally strong weakest connections in the latter ring, but since one of them is the same as the weakest connection in the former, we need to break only the one. Then we have to divide Σ:ℵ* ℵᶜ F G P (*x*) still again because it forms rings with Σ:L:K P:ℵ* ℵᶜ A:C*C² (*bb*) and with Σ:K L P: ℵ* ℵᶜ A:C* C² (*cc*). The two latter variations have to be divided also because all the rings have two equally strong weakest links. The result is *Σ:ℵ* ℵᶜ:P:F G:A:C* C² (*x*), *Σ:L:K P:ℵ* ℵᶜ A:C* C²:F G (*bb*), and *Σ:K L P:ℵ* ℵᶜ A:C* C²:F G (*cc*).

Because of rings with Σ:ℵ* A C* C² (*u*) we must divide Σ:ℵ* A D* F G (*y*) a second time, making *Σ:ℵ*:A:D* F G; we must divide Σ:ℵ* ℵᶜ P:F G (*tt*) a second time, making *Σ:ℵ* ℵᶜ P:F G:A:C* C²;

and we must divide Σ:ℵ* A F G (*v*), making *Σ:ℵ* A:F G. Because of rings with Σ:L:K P:ℵ* ℵᶜ A:C* C² (*bb*) and with Σ:K L P:ℵ* ℵᶜ A:C* C² (*cc*) we must rewrite Σ:Dᶜ E* E** K (*w*) a fourth and final time as *Σ:Dᶜ E* E**:K:F G:P:L:D*.

We must rewrite Σ:D* Dᶜ E* E** F:C* C² (*gg*) as *Σ:D* Dᶜ E* E**: F:C* C² because it forms a ring with Σ:F G (*i*). We must rewrite Σ: D* E* L:C* C² (*ff*) as *Σ:D* E*:L:C* C² because it forms rings with Σ:D* Dᶜ E* E** (*t*) and with similar variations. We must rewrite Σ:ℵ* A D* F G (*y*) for a fourth and last time as *Σ:ℵ*:A:D*:F G: Dᶜ E* E**:C* C² because it forms rings with Σ:D* E* (*l*) and with similar variations, Σ:A D*:F G (*uu*) as *Σ:A:D*:F G for the same reason, and finally Σ:D* L (*k*) as *Σ:D*:L for the same reason.

From the resulting variations we obtain two more type 1, Σ:C* and Σ:Dᶜ, and three more type 2, Σ:ℵ* A, Σ:ℵ* ℵᶜ A C* C², and Σ:ℵ* ℵᶜ A C* C² P. In the first "sum" we use the rewriting of Σ:ℵ* A C*, in the third the rewriting of Σ:ℵ* A F G, and in the fourth (where we are testing the overlap of ℵ* A C* C² with ℵ* ℵᶜ) the rewriting of Σ:ℵ* ℵᶜ A C* C² D* E*.

C*

C:C² ℵᶜ D* Dᶜ E* E** F G K L P:ℵ*:A	*s.* (rewritten)
C* C²:ℵᶜ D* Dᶜ E* E** F G K L P ℵ* A	*h.*
C:C² ℵᶜ D* Dᶜ E* E** F G K L P ℵ* A	

Dᶜ

Dᶜ:D E* E** ℵ* ℵᶜ A C* C² F G P:K L	*q.*
Dᶜ D* E* E**:ℵ* ℵᶜ A C* C² F G P K L	*t.*
Dᶜ:D E* E** ℵ* ℵᶜ A C* C² F G P K L	

ℵ* A

ℵ* A:ℵᶜ C* C² P D* Dᶜ E* E** K L:F G	*v.* (rewritten)
ℵ* A ℵᶜ C* C² P:D*:Dᶜ E* E** K L F G	*pp.*
ℵ A:ℵᶜ C* C² P D* Dᶜ E* E** K L F G	

ℵ* ℵᶜ A C* C²

ℵ ℵᶜ:A C* C²:P K L:F G:Dᶜ E* E** D*	*a.* (rewritten)
ℵ* ℵᶜ A C* C² P:K L F G Dᶜ E* E**:D*	*pp.*
ℵ* ℵᶜ A C* C²:P K L F G Dᶜ E* E** D*	

ℵ* ℵᶜ A C* C² P

ℵ* ℵᶜ A C* C² P:Dᶜ E** F G K L E*:D*	*pp.*
ℵ* ℵᶜ A C* C² P Dᶜ E** F G K L:E* D*	*l.*
ℵ ℵᶜ A C* C² P:Dᶜ E** F G K L E* D*	

And from the simple variations we then obtain the following diagram:

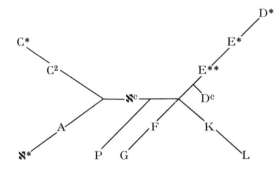

A number of readings seem to have resulted from homoeoteleuton:

2 αρχιππω τω: αρχιππω F
6 αγαθον του: αγαθον A C
11 ον ανεπεμψα: ον επεμψα D* E*
14 της σης: της F
16 δουλον αλλα υπερ δουλον: δουλον F G
16 δουλον αδελφον: δουλον ℵ*
18 ηδικησεν σε: ηδικησεν K
22 προσευχων υμων: προσευχων L

Certain other readings seem to have resulted from a scribe's desire for symmetry of expression:

3, 5 και κυριου ιησου χριστου . . . τον κυριον ιησουν: και κυριου ιησου χριστου . . . τον κυριον ιησουν χριστον D* E
20 εν κυριω . . . εν χριστω: εν κυριω . . . εν κυριω Dᶜ E K

One reading apparently results from harmonization to Paul's usual salutation:

1 δεσμιος: αποστολος D* E*

One reading may have occurred through dittography:

5 εχεις προς: εχεις εις A C D*

One reading appears to be a gloss:

19 σεαυτον μοι προσοφειλεις : + εν κυριω D* E*

One reading may be a grammatical correction by a scribe:

23, 24 ασπαζεται σε επαφρας . . . μαρκος, κτλ.: ασπαζονται σε επαφρασ . . . μαρκος, κτλ. Dᶜ K L

Finally, the omissions in C*, C², F, and G are certainly not original.

Of course this example, while sufficiently complex to challenge the techniques set forth in this book, has far too few manuscripts to provide any firm conclusion about the textual tree of the whole set. With this proviso in mind, however, we may remark that if we knew of no other manuscripts, then, because only אᶜ and P have all the correct readings, we cannot tell whether one of them, or the inferential intermediary between them, is the archetype. The great age of the Sinaitic manuscript would make אᶜ the natural choice as copy-text.

2. HISTORICAL RESEARCH

The historian must often compare witnesses to an event in a effort to determine the details of that event. He is concerned to eliminate witnesses who are only quoting other witnesses and to discover whether the rest testify to the event itself or only to a lost account of the event. If all the witnesses trace back to a single lost witness, the historian is concerned to estimate the accuracy of that witness. In all this the historian works in the same way as a textual critic and may correspondingly take the rules of textual analysis for his guide.

When comparing documents the historian must often reduce them to motifs, in doing which he has two options. He can translate all the documents into his own words, using standardized phrases, or he can translate all but one of the documents into the language of that one. Neither process has simple mechanical rules, which makes the historian's task of comparison harder than the textual critic's. Our first example allows us to illustrate both methods.

We have five accounts of the sale of Oliver Goldsmith's *Vicar of Wakefield*, three of which are versions of Samuel Johnson's account of the event.[6] The family tree of the accounts is not in much doubt; it is

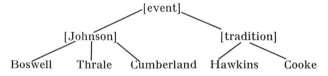

Let us first reconstruct Johnson's story of how he sold the novel for Goldsmith. From other evidence we know that the version in James

[6] I have copied the texts quoted in Richard D. Altick, *The Art of Literary Research* (New York, 1963), pp. 28-30.

Boswell's *Life of Johnson* is quite likely to be in Johnson's very words, and we shall therefore rewrite the other versions in Boswell's language as much as possible.

To begin then with Boswell:

> I received one morning a message from poor Goldsmith that he was in great distress, and, as it was not in his power to come to me, begging that I would come to him as soon as possible. I sent him a guinea, and promised to come to him directly. I accordingly went as soon as I was drest, and found that his landlady had arrested him for his rent, at which he was in a violent passion. I perceived that he had already changed my guinea, and had got a bottle of Madeira and a glass before him. I put the cork into the bottle, desired he would be calm, and began to talk to him of the means by which he might be extricated. He then told me that he had a novel ready for the press, which he produced to me. I looked into it, and saw its merit; told the landlady I should soon return, and having gone to a bookseller, sold it for sixty pounds. I brought Goldsmith the money, and he discharged his rent, not without rating his landlady in a high tone for having used him so ill.

Our next account is that of Mrs. Hester Lynch Thrale Piozzi, in her *Anecdotes of the Late Samuel Johnson*:

> I have forgotten the year, but it could scarcely I think be later than 1765-6, that he was called abruptly from our house after dinner, and returning in about three hours, said, he had been with an enraged author, whose landlady pressed him for payment within doors, while the bailiffs beset him without; that he was drinking himself drunk with Madeira to drown care, and fretting over a novel which when finished was to be his whole fortune; but he could not get it done for distraction, nor could he step out of doors to offer it for sale. Mr. Johnson therefore set away the bottle, and went to the bookseller, recommending the performance, and desiring some immediate relief; which when he brought back to the writer, he called the woman of the house directly to partake of punch, and pass their time in merriment.

And here is Mrs. Thrale's version in Boswell's language:

> At the Thrales' house after dinner *I received a message from Goldsmith begging that I would come to him as soon as possible. I accordingly went, and found that his landlady had arrested him for his rent, at which he was in a violent passion. I perceived that he had got a bottle of Madeira and a glass before him*, and was drinking himself drunk to drown care. *He then told me that he had a novel* which when finished was to be his whole fortune; but he could not get it done for distraction, nor could

he step out of doors to offer it for sale. *I put the cork into the bottle and having gone to a bookseller* recommended the performance, and desired some immediate relief. *I brought Goldsmith the money, and he* called the woman of the house directly to partake of punch, and pass their time in merriment.

Interpreting "enraged author" as "Goldsmith . . . was in a violent passion" has resulted in rearranging the motifs. We must then remember to watch for the same rearrangement in other witnesses, as this would constitute an agreement against Boswell as to the way Johnson told the story (assuming that he told it in the same order each time). It does not, however, affect the contents of the anecdote, which will normally be the historian's prime concern. Some readers may feel that I have given too much or too little weight to others of Mrs. Thrale's phrases as well. All this will suggest that great care is necessary in the choice and expression of motifs if the arguments based on them are to carry conviction.

Our last account of Johnson's anecdote is from Richard Cumberland's *Memoirs*:

> I have heard Dr. Johnson relate with infinite humour the circum-
> stance of his rescuing him [Goldsmith] from a ridiculous dilemma by
> the purchase money of his Vicar of Wakefield, which he sold on his
> behalf to Dodsley, and, as I think, for the sum of ten pounds only.
> He had run up a debt with his landlady for board and lodging of some
> few pounds, and was at his wit's-end how to wipe off the score and
> keep a roof over his head, except by closing with a very staggering
> proposal on her part, and taking his creditor to wife, whose charms
> were very far from alluring, whilst her demands were extremely ur-
> gent. In this crisis of his fate he was found by Johnson in the act of
> meditating on the melancholy alternative before him. He shewed
> Johnson his manuscript of The Vicar of Wakefield, but seemed to be
> without any plan, or even hope, of raising money upon the disposal
> of it; when Johnson cast his eye upon it, he discovered something
> that gave him hope, and immediately took it to Dodsley, who paid
> down the price above-mentioned in ready money, and added an eventual
> condition upon its future sale. Johnson described the precautions he
> took in concealing the amount of the sum he had in hand, which he
> prudently administered to him by a guinea at a time. In the event he
> paid off the landlady's score, and redeemed the person of his friend
> from her embraces.

And here is Cumberland's version in Boswell's language:

> *I found that his landlady* had threatened to arrest *him for his* board
> and *rent,* unless he took her to wife. *He produced to me a novel ready
> for the press,* but seemed to be without any plan, or even hope, of raising
> money upon the disposal of it. *I looked into it, and saw its merit;
> and having gone to* Dodsley, *sold it for* about ten *pounds* in ready money,
> and he added an eventual condition upon its future sale. *I brought
> Goldsmith the money a guinea* at a time, *and he discharged his* board
> and *rent,* and was thus redeemed from his landlady's embraces.

Here we see that it may be possible to condense a text a good deal without
omitting any motifs. I have taken Cumberland's "a guinea at a time"
to correspond to Boswell's "I sent him a guinea." Mrs. Thrale and
Cumberland both say Johnson obtained an advance for Goldsmith,
but there is no convenient way to adjust Cumberland's account to Mrs.
Thrale's; it would be easier to return to hers and substitute "ready
money," Cumberland's phrase, for her "immediate relief."

Assuming that Boswell, Mrs. Thrale, and Cumberland are telling the
truth when they represent their versions as having come directly from
Johnson's own lips, we can reconstruct his version of the event from the
passages in which any two of them agree. Strictly we ought to wait
until we have examined the remaining accounts, since Johnson's is
intermediary between them and the first three, but it happens, as we
shall see, that there are no agreements between these other terminal
accounts and any of the first three in any matter in which all of the
first three disagree.

> I received a message from Goldsmith begging that I would come to
> him as soon as possible. I sent him a guinea and accordingly went
> and found that his landlady had arrested him for his rent, at which he
> was in a violent passion. I perceived that he had got a bottle of Madeira
> and a glass before him. I put the cork into the bottle. He then told
> me that he had a novel ready for the press, which he produced to me.
> I looked into it and saw its merit; and having gone to a bookseller,
> sold it for . . . pounds in ready money. I brought Goldsmith the money,
> and he discharged his rent.

We cannot tell how much, if any, of the variations from this central
core are the result of Johnson's own variations in retelling the story, except for one detail: we know from other evidence that sixty pounds was
the total amount Goldsmith received, so Johnson did not tell Boswell
about getting ready money.

We come, then, to reconstructing the event itself. Here the versions differ so much that we must reduce them to motifs. The two additional accounts are from Sir John Hawkins's *Life of Johnson* and from an article by William Cooke in the *European Magazine*. First Hawkins:

> Of the booksellers whom he [Goldsmith] styled his friends, Mr. Newbery was one. This person had apartments in Canonbury-house, where Goldsmith often lay concealed from his creditors. Under a pressing necessity he there wrote his Vicar of Wakefield, and for it received of Newbery forty pounds.

Then Cooke:

> The doctor [i.e., Goldsmith], soon after his acquaintance with Newbery, for whom he held "the pen of a ready writer," removed to lodgings in Wine Office Court, Fleet-street, where he finished his "Vicar of Wakefield," and on which his friend Newbery advanced him *twenty guineas*: "A sum," says the Doctor, "I was so little used to receive in a *lump*, that I felt myself under the embarrassment of Captain Brazen in the play, whether I should build a privateer or a play-house with the money."

When we reduce Johnson's story and these two accounts to motifs we get something like the following:

> Johnson: Goldsmith was in debt + I sold *The Vicar of Wakefield* for him + for . . . pounds + in ready money.
>
> Hawkins: Goldsmith was in debt + He wrote *The Vicar of Wakefield* at Canonbury House + Newbery bought it + for forty pounds.
>
> Cooke: Goldsmith wrote *The Vicar of Wakefield* at Wine Office Court, Fleet Street + Newbury bought it + for twenty guineas + in ready money.

From these we can reconstruct the tradition upon which Hawkins and Cooke drew: Goldsmith was in debt + Newbury bought *The Vicar of Wakefield* + for ready money.

Both Hawkins and Boswell give the full amount paid Goldsmith and say nothing of an advance. Before we can reconstruct the event itself, therefore, we must attempt to solve the contradiction. On the whole, it seems more likely that Boswell (or Johnson when talking to Boswell) and Hawkins decided independently to give the full amount than that Johnson at other times and Cooke decided to manufacture an advance. Johnson set a high store on truth, especially in biographical matters.

Our knowledge of Johnson's veracity helps us then to reconstruct the event from his account of it and the tradition drawn on by Hawkins and Cooke. We can be satisfied that Johnson sold *The Vicar of Wakefield* for Goldsmith. The tradition supports his story that Goldsmith was in debt at the time, and now that we have solved the contradiction, that he got Goldsmith an advance. Other evidence indicates that the tradition is correct in identifying Newbury as the publisher. We cannot tell the amount of the advance.

We are interested in the possible truth of the miscellaneous details. If Boswell and Mrs. Thrale agree that Goldsmith's landlady had arrested him for his rent, this shows that Cumberland cannot be describing the situation as Johnson told it, unless Johnson varied in his story. Johnson's reputation for truth is higher than Cumberland's. The family tree tells us nothing about the other details in the documents, for the narratives do not run strictly parallel in their omissions, and type-0 variations result. Naturally we shall have our suspicions and trusts, and occasionally these can be corroborated from other evidence (Mrs. Thrale has the date wrong, Hawkins has the place wrong). Still, the tree has helped us with the details a little as well as with the core of the event.

We shall deal more summarily with our second and final example, the four Gospels. Here we shall only establish the family tree of the documents and not attempt to reconstruct the events they record. In the past, the first three have been treated together as "the Synoptic problem" and the fourth by itself as "the Johannine problem." A solution to the Synoptic problem which has been widely accepted, though with individual reservations and modifications of detail, is the so-called four document hypothesis put forward by Canon B. H. Streeter in *The Four Gospels*. Streeter's diagram (p. 150) is essentially as follows:

```
Matthaean source   Mark Q   Lucan source
          \      |  /|  \  /
           \     | / | X "Proto-Luke"
            \    |/  |/ \|
             Matthew  Luke
```

More tentatively Streeter assigns an "Antiochene tradition" as an additional separate source for Matthew and a separate source for the first two chapters of Luke, which he conceives not to have stood in "Proto-Luke." The letter Q represents a body of Jesus' sayings, some of them set in historical contexts. The diagram ought also to have shown lines of descent to Mark and Q from a common ancestor, since Streeter maintains that some of the information in Mark was also found in Q. There should then also be lines of descent from a special Markan source to Mark and from a special Q source to Q to account for the material that is not common to both.

The following tree, according to Streeter and many others before and since, is the major component of the diagram:

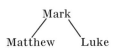

The tree is not intended to indicate that Matthew was written before Luke (as a matter of fact, Streeter [p. 150] puts it five years later).

It is at once clear that such a textual tree does not support the larger diagram. The evidence for it as given by Streeter (pp. 151-152, 157-169) is as follows:

1. Of the material in Mark, about 90 percent appears in Matthew, about 50 percent in Luke, and in both often in the same words.

2. In the passages where the wording is largely identical in all three, Matthew and Mark sometimes agree against Luke, Mark and Luke sometimes agree against Matthew, and Matthew and Luke sometimes agree against Mark.

3. In the ordering of incidents and teachings the three Gospels in general agree, but sometimes Matthew, sometimes Luke, disagrees with the others, and once all three differ.

4. Mark contains details about Jesus that might seem irreverent; these in the other Gospels are given in different wording if at all. Also, Mark's Greek is rougher, almost inviting improvement.

5. The way in which the material not found in Mark is arranged in Matthew and Luke suggests that the authors were working with a more or less inflexible framework, that is, a previously written life of Jesus.

Obviously the agreements of Matthew and Luke against Mark noted under 2 prevent the conclusion that the two former are independently descended from the latter. Streeter therefore sets aside what he calls the "minor agreements of Matthew and Luke" as coincidences (pp. 293-331), and he explains the more considerable agreements of the same sort, as have others before and since, by what is really a separate textual tree:

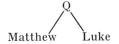

From the textual point of view, the agreements explained as arising from common dependence upon Q are simply clearer and larger manifestations of the state of affairs indicated by the "minor agreements." The pattern is familiar—A:BC, B:AC, AB:C. The general textual diagram indicated by these agreements will have an inferential intermediary between the three Gospels. The possibility that either Matthew or Luke represents a conflation of Mark and the other of the two has been canvassed from time to time by scholars troubled by the "minor agreements," but it may be rejected as unnecessary.

Streeter cites readings (using this term to include motifs as well as individual words) of the following types:

$$\text{Matthew} \leftarrow \text{Mark} : \text{Luke}$$
$$\text{Matthew} : \text{Mark} \rightarrow \text{Luke}$$
$$\text{Matthew} \leftarrow \text{Mark} \rightarrow \text{Luke}$$
$$\text{Matthew} - \text{Luke} \leftarrow \text{Mark}$$
$$\text{Matthew} - \text{Mark} \rightarrow \text{Luke}$$
$$\text{Matthew} \leftarrow \text{Mark} - \text{Luke}$$

Some of the examples cited as illustrative of the third class are not directional, viz., the redundant readings in Mark, where Matthew has one element, Luke the other. These seem to Streeter to be directional, because he is already convinced that Matthew and Luke are independent descendants of Mark.

As Streeter observes, there is also a series of passages that other scholars have supposed indicate Mark's dependence on Q. Once again, Streeter's discussion (pp. 186-191) is based upon his previous conclusion that Matthew and Luke are independent descendants of Mark. Without this antecedent conclusion, more weight may be given to his admission that in these passages the readings common to Matthew and Luke "look more original" and display a "general, though not invariable, superiority" to Mark's. Such readings are of the type:

$$\text{Matthew} - \text{Luke} \rightarrow \text{Mark}$$

Taken together, the directional variations indicate the following textual tree:

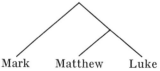

These relationships indicate at the apex of the diagram a body of information concerning Jesus and his sayings. Precise information is wanting about this material, its exact contents, whether it was written down, or the languages in which it was transmitted.

The apex does not represent the original of the three Gospels. The sayings of Jesus came into existence as literary works, and therefore in the usual textual sense each had a separate original. The acts of Jesus, on the other hand, had to be recorded before an original in this sense came into existence. It is most unlikely that any single person could have recorded all Jesus' acts from his own observation, and therefore there was probably a series of originals for these also. On the other hand, although the eleven disciples contended among themselves for primacy while Jesus was with them, they seem at last to have learned the lesson of humility their Master taught and to have come into complete harmony. It is not unreasonable to suppose that they came to agree among themselves as to the majority, if not all, of the events in Jesus' life, and that the discourses of Jesus found their places in the agreed-upon historical context. If so, the different originals became sources for a unified conception of the life and works of Jesus held and taught by the eleven and by those who surrounded them at first. This unified conception would be the original of the Gospels. It seems reasonable that this original would be expressed in the language of the Jews. The word-for-word correspondences of the Synoptics, then, would indicate either that there was a standard Greek translation for at least a part of this material, or that the authors drew upon the same translation, meaning that the apex of the textual diagram represents a development of the material from its original form.

It may well seem that this discussion is a sufficiently cavalier dismissal of a theory that has recommended itself so widely. Certainly, in dealing with the problem in Streeter's terms—that is, in dealing primarily with motifs rather than with words—the methods urged in this book have been bypassed. It is necessary to deal with word-for-word correspondences whenever they occur; to do otherwise is to risk errors in the conclusions. For example, Streeter can dismiss the accounts of the preaching of John the Baptist as an example of "the overlapping of Mark and Q" (pp. 188-189) because he deals with only the general tenor of the passages. Detailed examination shows that Luke gives a long quotation, Matthew a shorter, and Mark a shorter still (*xyz*:

yz:z; a combination of Lk Mt:Mk and Lk:Mt:Mk). The common part is as follows:

Mt 3:11: ἐγὼ μὲν ὑμᾶς βαπτίζω ἐν ὕδατι εἰς μετάνοιαν ·
Mk 1:8   ἐγὼ   ἐβάπτισα ὑμᾶς ὕδατι,
Lk 3:16   ἐγὼ μὲν ὕδατι βαπτίζω ὑμᾶς ·
Mt   ὁ δὲ ὀπίσω μου ἐρχόμενος ἰσχυρότερός μού ἐστιν,
Mk 1:7   ἔρχεται ὁ ἰσχυρότερός μου ὀπίσω,
Lk   ἔρχεται δὲ ὁ ἰσχυρότερός μου,
Mt   οὗ οὐκ εἰμὶ ἱκανὸς τὰ ὑποδήματα βαστάσαι ·
Mk 1:7   οὗ οὐκ εἰμὶ ἱκανὸς κύψας λῦσαι τὸν ἱμάντα τῶν ὑποδημάτων
                                                                    αὐτοῦ.
Lk   οὗ οὐκ εἰμὶ ἱκανὸς   λῦσαι τὸν ἱμάντα τῶν ὑποδημάτων
                                                                    αὐτοῦ ·
Mt   αὐτὸς ὑμᾶς βαπτίσει ἐν πνεύματι ἁγίῳ καὶ πυρί ·
Mk 1:8   αὐτος δὲ   βαπτίσει ὑμᾶς πνεύματι ἁγίῳ.
Lk   αὐτος ὑμᾶς βαπτίσει ἐν πνεύματι ἁγίῳ καὶ πυρί ·

The text is Nestle's,[7] and his notes do not show any strong manuscript support for alternate readings. The following sets of variations occur:

Mt Lk:Mk εγω + μεν; βαπτιζω; order of clauses; δε 1°; om. κυψας; om. δε 2°; υμας 2° before verb; εν 2°; και πυρι.

Mt:Mk Lk υμας 1° before verb; εν 1°; εις μετανοιαν; ερχομενος; εστιν; τα υποδηματα βαστασαι.

Mt Mk:Lk οπισω.

Mt:Mk:Lk οπισωμου: οπισω: ——.

These variations require an inferential intermediary for the general diagram. A full investigation will, therefore, never lead back to Streeter's diagram.

But fuller investigation need not confine itself to the Synoptic Gospels. All four Gospels can, and indeed should, be related to one another. For example, John has a passage paralleling those just quoted from the Synoptics: ἐγὼ βαπτίζω ἐν ὕδατι · μέσος ὑμῶν στήκει ὃν ὑμεῖς οὐκ οἴδατε, ὁ ὀπίσω μου ἐρχόμενος, οὗ οὐκ εἰμὶ ἐγὼ ἄξιος ἵνα λύσω αὐτοῦ τὸν ἱμάντα τοῦ ὑποδήματος (1:26,27).

Following is a sketch of how the analysis of the "Four Gospel Problem" would proceed. For a completely consistent analysis the text cited should be constructed according to the principles set forth in this book, but as no such text exists, Nestle's may serve.

---

[7] *Novum Testamentum Graece*, ed. D. Eberhard Nestle and D. Erwin Nestle, ed. vicesima prima (New York, Stuttgart, [1952]).

There are five levels of agreement and disagreement among the Gospels. The first level is that of genre, biography, and the next that of subject, Jesus Christ. The third level is that of the ordering and inclusion or exclusion of events in Jesus' life or surrounding it, and of his teachings. The fourth level is that of motifs. The last level is that of variations in contexts where the Gospels agree word for word.

At the first two levels, then, the Gospels agree. At the third, as is well known, they differ widely. At this level, only type-1, type-3, and type-0 variations occur.

At the last two levels, type-2 variations also appear, and of every possible sort. In the following list, variations from both levels are lumped together indiscriminately. No parallels have been drawn, however, where Nestle encloses words or passages in brackets.[8]

(1) Mt Mk:Lk Jn. (*a*) Matthew 13:57 and Mark 6:4 record Jesus as saying that no prophet is without honor except in his own country—agreeing in the very words οὐκ ἔστιν προφήτης ἄτιμος εἰ μὴ ἐν τῇ πατρίδι; where Luke 4:24 and John 4:44, while not agreeing nearly so closely, make it a simple positive statement, a prophet has no honor in his own country. (*b*) Furthermore, Luke and John stop here, while Matthew and Mark add καὶ ἐν τῇ οἰκίᾳ αὐτοῦ, "and in his house." (*c*) Describing Jesus' triumphal entry into Jerusalem, all the Gospels record that the welcoming crowd shouted, in the words of Psalm 118, εὐλογημένος ὁ ἐρχόμενος ἐν ὀνόματι κυρίου, "blessed is he who comes in the name of the Lord" (Matthew 21:9; Mark 11:9; Luke 19:38, John 12:13), but Luke and John add ὁ βασιλεύς, "the king," in apposition to ὁ ἐρχόμενος. (*d*, *e*) All four Gospels have accounts of Jesus being anointed

---

[8] This list was compiled from Albert Huck, *Synopsis of the First Three Gospels*, 9th ed. rev. by Hans Lietzmann, English ed. by F. L. Cross (Oxford, 1954), checked against and once supplemented by the parallels noted by Streeter (see Burnett Hillman Streeter, *The Four Gospels* (London, 1930), p. 397, and (2, *d*) in the list). The Greek quotations, however, are from Nestle rather than from Huck. Streeter's list of parallels between John and the other Gospels is mostly not of type-2 variations. For a different list leading to the same conclusion see F. Lamar Cribbs, "St. Luke and the Johannine Tradition," *Journal of Biblical Literature*, XC (1971), 422-450.

Since 1959, when this section was first written, dissatisfaction with Streeter's and similar theories has grown to the point where the Society of Biblical Literature has established a "Task Group on the Sequence of the Gospels"; for some of their discussions see Charles H. Talbert and Edgar V. McKnight, "Can the Griesbach Hypothesis Be Falsified?" *Journal of Biblical Literature*, XCI (1972), 338-368, and citations there.

with costly ointment by a woman while he was at a banquet (Matthew 26:6-13; Mark 14:3-9; Luke 7:36-50; John 12:1-8); if these accounts are all versions of the same event, as some scholars would have it, then Matthew and Mark agree the woman anointed Jesus' head, while Luke and John agree that she anointed his feet, and Luke and John add that she wiped his feet with her hair. (*f*) At Jesus' arrest, the Gospels all tell how one of his followers cut off the ear of one of those arresting him (Matthew 26:51; Mark 14:47; Luke 22:50; John 18:10); Luke and John add that it was the left ear, τὸν δεξιόν. (*g*) All four Gospels tell of Peter's triple denal that he knew Jesus (Matthew 26:69-74; Mark 14:66-72; Luke 22:56-60; John 18:17, 25-27); Matthew and Mark add that at his third denial he cursed. (*h*) All four Gospels agree that Pilate asked Jesus, σὺ εἶ ὁ βασιλεὺς τῶν Ἰουδαίων, "are you the king of the Jews," and that Jesus replied, σὺ λέγεις, "you say . . ." (Matthew 27:11; Mark 15:2; Luke 23:3; John 18:33-37—John has some intervening dialogue); but Matthew and Mark continue, using much the same phrasing, with an account of how Jesus caused Pilate to wonder at his refusal to answer his accusers, whereas Luke and John continue instead, using nearly the same words, with Pilate's finding that Jesus had committed no crime. (*i*) Luke and John agree that Pilate repeated this finding for the third time after the mob demanded Jesus' crucifixion (Matthew 27:23; Mark 15:14; Luke 23:22; John 19:6). (*j*) All four Gospels say that the mob cried out twice for Jesus' crucifixion, but only Matthew and Mark add the detail that the second time they shouted louder, περισσῶς (Matthew 27:23; Mark 15:14; cf. Luke 23:23; John 19:15). (*k*) Just before Jesus was crucified, he was offered wine to drink, according to Matthew 27:34 and Mark 15:23; Luke and John omit this detail, which would follow Luke 23:33*a* and John 19:17. (*l*) In the sentence telling of the women who followed Jesus to the place of crucifixion, Matthew 27:55 and Mark 15:40 begin ἦσαν, "there were," and Luke 23:49 and John 19:25 begin εἰστήκεισαν, "there stood." (*m*) In describing the tomb where Jesus was laid (Matthew 27:60; Mark 15:46; Luke 23:53; John 19:41), only Luke and John conclude by saying that no one had been buried there before (not quite the same thing as saying that it was new). (*n*) And in describing Jesus' burial (as before, and John 19:42), only Matthew and Mark close their accounts with Joseph closing the door of the tomb with a stone; Matthew has καὶ προσκυλίσας λίθον μέγαν τῇ θύρᾳ τοῦ μνημείου ἀπῆλθεν; Mark has καὶ προσεκύλισεν λίθον ἐπὶ τὴν θύραν τοῦ μνημείου.

(2) Mt Lk:Mk Jn. (*a*) In recording John's saying that he baptized only in (or with) water, Matthew 3:11 and Luke 3:16 begin ἐγὼ μὲν βαπτίζω, "I indeed baptize," while Mark 1:8 and John 1:26 begin simply ἐγὼ . . . , "I. . . ." (*b*) All the Gospels give an account of the feeding of the five thousand (Matthew 14:15-21; Mark 6:35-44; Luke 9:12-17; John 6:5-13), but only Mark and John record a protest from among the disciples, when faced with the task of feeding the multitude, that two hundred denarii would not buy bread enough (this detail would come in Matthew 14:16 and Luke 9:13*b*). (*c*) In the four accounts of the woman anointing Jesus, Matthew and Luke simply say she used ointment, employing different forms of μύρον, where Mark and John specify that she used oil of nard or spikenard, agreeing in the words μύρου νάρδου πιστικῆς. (*d*, *e*) All the Gospels say that Peter followed Jesus into the high priest's house or palace, where he sat among the servants and was questioned by them (compare Matthew 26:58, 69; Mark 14:54, 67; Luke 22:55, 56; John 18:18, 25) but only Mark and John say he warmed himself at a fire there, both using ὁ Πέτρος . . . θερμαινόμενος in the first passage, Mark using τὸν Πέτρον θερμαινόμενον and John using Σίμων Πέτρος . . . θερμαινόμενος in the second. (*f*) In recording the second of the mob's outcries for Jesus' crucifixion Matthew 27:23 and Luke 23:23 have passive constructions, but Mark 15:14 and John 19:15 have the active construction σταύρωσιν αὐτόν, "crucify him!"

(3) Mt Jn:Mk Lk. (*a*) In citing Isaiah 40:3, Matthew 3:3 and John 1:23 read that Isaiah said these words (Matthew has λέγοντος, John εἶπεν), where Mark 1:2 and Luke 3:4 read "it is written," γέγραπται, in Isaiah. (*b*, *c*) In recounting John's explanation of his baptizing and his prophecy of the one who was to come after him (Matthew 3:11, Mark 1:7, 8; Luke 3:16; John 1:26, 27), Matthew and John have ἐν ὕδατι, "in water," and ὁ . . . ἐρχόμενος, "the one who is coming," where Mark and Luke have ὕδατι, "with water," and ἔρχεται, "comes." (*d*) Describing how Jesus came to ride into Jerusalem in his triumphal entry (Matthew 21:1-7, Mark 11:1-7; Luke 19:28-35; John 12:14-15), only Matthew and John say that this act was a fulfilment of the prophecy in Zechariah 9:9. (*e*) In Jesus' dialogue with Pilate, only Mark and Luke introduce σὺ λέγεις with a participial phrase, ἀποκριθεὶς αὐτῷ, "answering him," as well as with a verb. (*f*) In describing Jesus' death on the cross, Matthew 27:50 and John 19:30 read, respectively, ἀφῆκεν τὸ πνεῦμα and παρέδωκεν τὸ πνεῦμα, "he gave up the ghost"; Mark 15:37 and Luke 23:46 say it in one word, ἐξέπνευσεν. (*g*) Finally,

in saying that Jesus was laid in a tomb, Matthew 27:60 and John 19:41
have different forms of one word for "tomb," $\mu\nu\eta\mu\varepsilon\tilde{\iota}o\nu$, and Mark 15:46
and Luke 23:53 have another word, $\mu\nu\dot{\eta}\mu\alpha\tau\iota$, although only Sinaiticus
and Vaticanus among the manuscripts cited by Nestle have $\mu\nu\dot{\eta}\mu\alpha\tau\iota$
instead of $\mu\nu\eta\mu\varepsilon\dot{\iota}\omega$ here in Mark.

These variations show three rings:

```
Mt—Mk      Mt—Mk      Mt—Lk
|    \      |     |      |     |
Lk—Jn      Jn—Lk      Jn—Mk
```

The far greater degree of correspondence between the Synoptic Gospels
shows us that the weakest connections will be those on either side of
John, without our having to make a full pair count. And we have just
seen that John agrees most often with Luke. Therefore the variations
Mt Lk:Mk Jn and Mt Jn:Mk Lk are to be rewritten as *Mt Lk:Mk:Jn
and *Mt:Mk Lk:Jn. The preliminary diagram will then be:

Two of the type-2 variations seem directional. The addition of $\dot{o}$
$\beta\alpha\sigma\iota\lambda\varepsilon\dot{\upsilon}\varsigma$ listed under (1, *c*) looks like a gloss on the quotation from the
Psalm. The omission of reference to Peter's cursing listed under (1, *g*)
looks like a pious alternation. If these are directional variations, they
are of the type

Mt   Mk→Lk   Jn

But apparent elaboration does not really provide satisfactory directional variations. It cannot be emphasized strongly enough that a
sound method of determining direction when motifs vary is yet in
its infancy. We are not, then, driven to suppose that John's simpler
accounts of the disciples' fear when they saw Jesus walking on the
water (John 6:19; Mark 6:49, 50; Matthew 14:26-31) and of the ass
ridden by Jesus on his triumphal entry into Jerusalem (John 12:14;
Matthew 21:1-3, 6, 7; Mark 11:1-7; Luke 19:28-35) came to this Gospel
by conflation with earlier forms of the stories than those found in the
Synoptics.

From the foregoing evidence, then, we should establish the following
tree for the four Gospels:

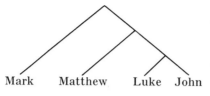

Mark   Matthew   Luke   John

The Gospel of John is traditionally the last to have been written—written, too, according to tradition, to supplement the others—and modern scholars often, perhaps customarily, regard it as a derivative work. The foregoing tree supports that general position. It is important to remember, however, that the archetype here is not a lost gospel; it is a body of information about a set of events. It does not follow, therefore, that the whole of the material peculiar to any Gospel is necessarily a departure from the facts, for it is reasonable to suppose that the body of general knowledge about Jesus grew for a time as individual recollections were added to it. The tree cannot, then, be used as evidence for or against the authorship of a Gospel or the historicity of its unique contents.

Appendix A

Labor-Saving Devices

The pencil-and-paper methods of textual analysis so far illustrated are really satisfactory only for fairly small projects, but it is not absolutely necessary to use computers except for very large projects. An intermediate range of problems can be solved with the help of edge-notched cards in sorting variations and in making counts of texts that agree (pair counts), and with the help of an abacus in identifying rings and in constructing synthetic simple variations.

Edge-notched cards are used for a process called key sorting. The cards have holes punched along one or more edges, in the same positions on each card, so that when the cards are assembled into decks a rod, called a key, can be run through any hole from the front of the deck to the back. Some of these holes are opened into notches. When one inserts and then lifts the key, therefore, the cards with a notch in the key position remain behind. Cards can be bought ready punched, and then notched individually as desired; can be punched by anyone with a drill press (the commercial standard is four 1/8-inch holes to the inch), and notched as desired; or can be individually punched and notched in one operation by a keyboard machine. Notching can be done with scissors, if necessary, but various kinds of specially designed notching punches are available, from the simple ticket-punch type through a whole range of more complicated devices. The punches may run around all four sides of the cards in a single or double row. One corner of the cards will be, or should be, cut off to allow immediate recognition of any that have been inserted upside down or back to front in the pack. It will be easiest to use the cards if they have printed or otherwise reproduced on them the meaning of the holes, but if the cards are notched subsequent to punching and the identification of the holes is not printed or mimeographed on the face of each card, a master guide may be prepared by laying one of the punched cards over an unpunched card of the same dimensions and writing through the holes the number or letter represented by each. The cards may then be laid over this guide in turn, and the holes to be opened into notches may be quickly marked. When sorted, the cards should be held without excessive pressure so that those to be lifted out will withdraw easily and not bring with them any that ought to remain. If the cards are small, they can be placed between two blocks of wood. If the cards show any tendency to stick to or catch on each other, the key should be vigorously shaken.

The following account of key sorting assumes a single row of holes around the edges of the cards. A double row would allow the same information to be entered more compactly.

For the purposes of textual analysis it is best to number the first holes 4, 2, 1, 8, 4, 2, 1, 8, 4, 2, 1 (the second series of 8, 4, 2, 1 may not be needed as we shall see) and assign one of the rest to each of the states of the text. The first three holes are for variation type numbers and can be additionnally labeled as such. A notch at hole 4 represents type 4, notches at holes 2 and 1 represent type 3, and so on. As we shall see, we shall want a list of the true groups in the type-4 variations; these groups may be given a "type-5" designation by notches at holes 4 and 1.

The next eight holes represent two-digit decimal numbers, the first four holes for the first digit, the second four holes for the second digit. A single-digit number will be represented by the second four holes, except that if there are no two-digit numbers, a second series of four holes is not needed. The holes may be additionally labeled to indicate their purpose. They are for the counts of the states in the smaller groups of the simple variations, or in the first group if both are the same size, and in the "type-5" groups. Notches at holes 8 and 1 represent 9, a notch at hole 8 alone represents 8, notches at holes 4, 2, and 1 represent 7, notches at holes 4 and 2 alone represent 6, and so on.

We write the variations on the cards and then notch the cards. Assuming that we have more than twelve states, a type-1 variation will have a notch at the first hole 1, a notch at the third hole 1 because the smaller group has only one state, and a notch at the hole for the state in the smaller group. A type-2 variation in which the smaller group has three states will have a notch at the first hole 2, notches at the third holes 2 and 1, and notches at the holes for the three states in the group.

Type-3 and type-4 variations will have notches at the first holes 1 and 2 or the first hole 4 and at the holes for the singleton groups.

We copy the "type-5" groups on separate cards, writing also on each the variation from which it comes. We notch each of these cards at the first holes 4 and 1, at the next eight holes to indicate the number of states in the group, and elsewhere according to the states in the group. The cards for type-0 variations are not notched.

We sort the cards as follows: starting at the third hole 1, or the second if there are only two, we insert the key, lift out the cards with no notch in this position, and put them in front of the other cards. We repeat this operation with each hole in turn, working toward the first hole 4. When we have repeated the operation with this hole, the cards will be ordered with the type-0 variations first and the type-5 groups last, and in addition, the type-2 variations will be in order of the size of the smaller group, and the "type-5" groups will be in order of size.

We then write a list of the states and check off those that stand alone in type-1 variations. If there are any type-0 variations we put a cross beside the states that do not have a check and then set aside the cards for the type-0 variations. Otherwise we take the cards for the type-3 and type-4 variations. If a state in the list has not been checked we insert the key in the hole for that state and lift out the cards with no notch at that position. If any card remains we put a cross beside the state in the list. The list thus tells us which states are terminal (checks) and which are singleton groups in complex variations (crosses).

We are now ready to test the variations for rings, an operation in which we can use an abacus to advantage. An abacus consists of a row of wires fixed in a rectangular frame; a transom, through which the wires pass; and a set of movable beads, seven to the wire in a Chinese abacus, two on one side of the transom, five on the other. The Japanese abacus, having only six beads to the wire, cannot be used in the following routines without adding a seventh bead of some sort, such as a ring of pipe cleaner. In use, the abacus lies flat, and the beads are slid along the wires with the fingers, a pencil, or something similar. As the abacus is used in textual analysis, each wire represents a state of the text and should be tagged on the transom with a self-adhesive label. The wires should be labeled in the same order as the states have been written in the variations. If the textual critic buys his calculator, he can clamp two or more abacuses in a row if necessary. If he builds his own calculator, he should have seven beads to the wire, divided two and five, and as many wires as possible without making reach or inspection difficult.

When the abacus is referred to below, only those wires for which texts have been assigned are to be understood. A wire to which a text has been assigned will be called the wire for that text. Similarly reference will be made to the wires for a group, and so on. The shorter segments of the wires will be said to be above the transom, or simply above; the longer segments, below. Clearing the abacus will mean moving all the beads away from the transom, clearing above, moving all the beads away above the transom, and so on. Adding will mean moving beads to the transom, adding above will mean moving them to the transom above, and so on. Subtracting will mean moving beads away from the transom. Subtracting may result in clearing. When a wire is said to have so many beads, beads at the transom are meant, that is, beads added and not subtracted or cleared; both beads above and beads below are meant unless one or the other class is specified. Beads and wires will not be specifically mentioned in phrases such as "add one above for the group," that is add one bead above on the wires for the group.

Given n texts, wires, and so on, the word "some" means 1 to $n-1$ inclusive, the word "any" means 1 to n inclusive, whether the noun and verb following are singular or plural.

The two sections of the abacus, above and below the transom, correspond more or less to the variations taken two at a time in the pencil-and-paper calculus described in chapter 2. But because the same wire must always represent the same state of the text, the operation with the abacus is somewhat different. Also, it is generally impossible to represent more than two groups in a variation at a time, a one-bead group and a two-bead group. This limitation results in a certain amount of intermediate pencil-and-paper record keeping when overlap sequences must be developed, for it is generally possible to distinguish by beads only the first and last groups in a sequence. Records of the sequences should not be thrown away, for as we shall see they have more than one use.

The same limitation makes an account of the calculus almost unbelievably tedious to read even in the sketchy form here. My apologies. And my defense: if the reader ever decides to use an abacus in this way he will be grateful I have left nothing out. On the other hand, there is nothing sacred about this calculus, and the reader may find more interest in the account if he accepts it as a challenge to improve the routines.

With the abacus, testing for rings takes three steps:

I.   Test type-2 variations together.
II. Test type-2 against type-4 variations.
III. Test type-4 variations together, and if overlap sequences develop test the sequences against type-2 variations and against type-4 variations.

I. The first test for rings tests groups from type-2 variations two by two. Only the first group from each variation is tested.

In the first test for rings, we clear the abacus and add one bead above on the wires for a group from a type-2 variation. Then we add one below on the wires for a group from another type-2 variation. If some wire has no bead, some one above only, some two, and some one below only, a ring is indicated. The four ring elements in series have beads as just listed. To work out the rings in a standard way, we start with the element to which the left-hand wire belongs and to its right put the element next in the sequence (reading the sequence either way) that has the more nearly left-hand wire. Thus if we have

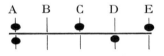

giving elements B, CE, A and D, we write

$$\begin{array}{ccc} A & — & CE \\ | & & | \\ D & — & B \end{array}$$

Ring or no, we clear the abacus below and add another group. If none remain, we clear the abacus and begin the step again. If there are three variations, the test order is first variation above, second below; first above, third below; second above, third below. More variations are tested similarly.

To aid in testing we stack the cards for the type-2 variations as a base stack. The variations added above go into a discard stack, the others into a temporary discard stack. When no cards remain in the base stack, the temporary discard stack becomes the base stack for the next cycle.

II. The second test for rings tests groups from type-2 and groups from type-4 variations. Only the first group from each type-2 variation is tested but all true groups from type-4 variations are tested.

In the second test for rings we clear the abacus and add one bead above on the wires for a group from a type-2 variation. Then we add one below on the wires for a true group from a type-4 variation. Unless some wire has no bead, some one above only, some two and some one below only, we clear the abacus below and repeat with another true group from a type-4 variation. Otherwise we find an untested true group from the same variation and add two beads below on its wires. If we now have some wire with one bead below only, some with one above and one below, some with one above and two below, and some with two below only, a ring is indicated. The four elements in sequence have beads as just described. States whose wires have no beads at the transom are not part of the ring. The following represents AE:BCD and AB:C:DE

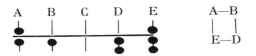

Ring or no, we clear below the wires with two beads below, and add two below for another untested true group from the same variation. When no such groups remain we clear the abacus and repeat the step. If we have two type-2 variations and two type-4 variations with three groups each, the order is:

1. first type 2 above, first group of first type 4 below (one bead), second group of first type 4 below (two beads)
2. same but first and third type-4 groups
3. same but second and third type-4 groups
4. same but first and second groups of second type-4 variation

. . . .

7. second type 2 above, first and second group of first type 4 below. And so on.

To aid in testing, we stack the cards for the type-2 variations as the simple base stack and the cards for the type-4 as the complex base stack. Cards from the simple base stack go into a simple discard stack. Cards from the complex base stack go into a complex discard stack when their groups are entered with one bead, and into a temporary discard stack when entered with two beads. When the last relevant two-bead group has been cleared, the temporary discard stack goes back on the complex base stack.

III. The third step in testing for rings tests true groups from type-4 variations. The groups are tested two by two, and if an overlap instead of a ring results, the overlap is tested against all the type-2 variations and all the other type-4 variations to see if a ring results. Whether or not rings result, if an overlap has resulted, a search is made for a group that will extend it, and if one is found the new overlap is tested for rings.

This step has four substeps, (1), (2), (3), and (4). When we cannot repeat (4), we repeat (3) and start (4) again. When we cannot repeat (3), we repeat (2) and start (3) and (4) again. When we cannot repeat (2) we repeat (1) and start (2), (3), and (4) again. When we cannot repeat (1) the step is finished. (1) We clear the abacus and add one bead above on the wires for a true group from a type-4 variation. (2) We add one bead below on the wires for a true group from another type-4 variation. If we do not have some wire with no beads, some with one bead below only, some with two, and some with one above only, we repeat (2). Otherwise (3) we find an untested true group from the first variation and add two beads above on its wires. If we do not have some wire with two beads above and one below and some wire with two beads above only, we subtract two beads above on the wires with two above and repeat (3). (4) We find an untested true group from the second variation and add two beads below on its wires. If this results in some wire with one bead above and one below, some with two above and one below, some with two above and two below, and some with two below and one above, a ring is indicated. If no wire has two below and one above, but some have two below only, an overlap is indicated. Otherwise we repeat (4). When we cannot repeat (4) we go directly to (3) only if we have found neither ring nor extension; otherwise we go to a back-up routine described below.

(A) If a ring is indicated, the elements in series have beads as just described. No other states are part of the ring, even if their wires have beads at the transom.

The following represents AB:CD:EF and AE:BDF:C. White beads were added and subsequently subtracted in step (3).

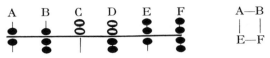

After we have written the ring we clear the wires with two beads below and repeat (4).

(*B*) If an overlap is indicated, we are off on a long and complicated process. In the first place, an overlap can have an odd or an even number of elements as we find overlapping groups. Each time we find a new group, and so a new element, we must test for rings. The tests differ with odd and even elements.

(*i*) The first overlap sequence and every second extension of the sequence thereafter will be formed by an even number of groups and will have an odd number of elements. The first element in the sequence will have one bead above only; the last element will have two below only.

(*a*) To test for rings, we begin with type-2 groups, testing both groups in each variation unless the first group shows a ring. We add three below on the wires for the group. If any has four or five beads below and one or two above, we subtract three below on wires with more than two below and repeat (*a*). When this happens, the three-bead group is part of a smaller ring. If we do not have some wire with one bead above and three below and some with five below only we also subtract and repeat. Otherwise we have a ring. Four of its elements in sequence have two beads above and one below, two above and two below, five beads below only, and one above and three below. The wires with one above and one below may represent one or more elements; we must consult our record of the overlap to see.

After writing the ring we subtract three beads below on the wires with more than two below and repeat (*a*).

(*b*) After testing for rings with type-2 groups we test with type-4 groups, testing all true groups in each variation. The process is the same as in (*a*) except that a ring-closing variation must also have a group that includes members from two elements in the overlap which are not both the first and the last. There is no way to test for this second group with the abacus; we must visually compare the variation with our record of the sequence.

After testing for rings with type-4 groups we attempt to extend the overlap, as described below.

(*ii*) The first extension of the overlap sequence and every second extension of the sequence thereafter will be formed by an odd number of groups and will have an even number of elements. The test for rings is the same as before, except that the last element in the sequence will now have two beads above only on its wires instead of two below only. Also, a group from one of the variations making up the sequence may close the ring. A ring will be indicated then when some wire has three beads below and one above, and some wire has three below and two above. The next element in sequence will have two above and one below. The wires with one above and one below represent three or more elements.

The following represents ABC:DE:FG and ABF:CD:EG. White beads were added and subsequently subtracted in extending the overlap C—AB—F—G—E—D as explained below.

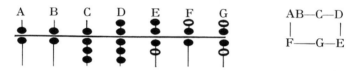

(*C*) After a sequence has been tested for rings it must be tested for extension.

(*i*) If the sequence has an odd number of elements, the last element will have two beads below only on its wires. First we subtract one bead above on all wires with two above. Then we look at the variation whose groups have been represented by two beads above to see if it has a true group, some but not all of whose wires have presently two beads below. If so, we add two beads above on the wires for this group. If not, we determine visually whether the sequence can be extended by groups from another variation by double overlap as explained in chapter 2. We must look for both kinds of possible double overlap, which means looking at both variations currently making up the sequence. If we can extend the overlap this way, we do, except that we do not add above on any wire that already has one above. If we can extend the overlap in any way we test it for rings. Otherwise we go to the back-up routine described below.

(*ii*) If the sequence has an even number of elements, the last element will have two beads above only on its wires instead of two beads below. The extension process is the same, *mutatis mutandis*.

(*D*) The back-up routine is required because if a group is large enough it may also be part of another sequence or ring. We work backward through the groups making up the sequence (each group will have states in two elements) until we find one that has some state not part of an element. As we go, we mark off the states of the groups that do not meet the requirement by putting a paper clip or some other marker on their wires. Marked wires are not to be used hereafter. If the remaining sequence has more than four elements, we go back to (*B*). If it has four elements we go to (4), if three to (3). Otherwise we remove the markers from the wires and go to (2).

To aid in all this testing we make the type-4 variations the base complex stack, and the type-2 variations and separate groups from the type-4 variations ("type 5s") the ring-closing stack. The first type-4 variation to have a group entered on the abacus goes onto a discard stack, the others onto a temporary discard stack. Whenever we repeat (1) we first restore the contents of the temporary discard stack to the base complex stack. We run through the ring-closing stack as often as required.

In the event that rings are found, we return to key sorting to get the necessary pair counts. The number of times one state agrees with another is the sum of their agreements in the type-1, -2, and -3 variations and separately listed "type-5" groups. The process with the type-1 and type-3 variations is as follows: insert the key in the hole for the first state and set aside the cards left behind when the key is lifted; with the remaining cards do the same at the hole for the second state. Count the cards on the key the second time. The process with the "type-5" groups is the reverse: insert the key in the hole for the first state and set aside the cards that lift out when the key is lifted; with the remaining cards do the same at the hole for the second state. Count the cards left behind the second time. The process with type-2 variations is a combination of the foregoing, resulting in two counts: insert the key in the hole for the first state and separate the cards left behind from those lifted out when the key is lifted; insert the key at the hole for the second state; if the cards are those that were left behind before, count the ones left behind this time; if the cards are those that were lifted out the first time, count those that are lifted out this time. Add the separate counts.

If rings have been found, repeat the search for rings after the variations have been rewritten. If more rings are found, use the pair counts made from the original variations. If there are no rings, or when the variations have been satisfactorily rewritten, we return to the abacus to identify the synthetic simple variations.

Only one example of each variation and of each true group from identical type-4 variations is needed in identifying synthetic simple variations. In the following it is assumed that duplicates have been eliminated. Be careful not to eliminate a "type-5" group unless the variation written on its card is also a duplicate; for example, if the group is AB and the variation is AB:CD:E, do not eliminate the card if the only other card for AB has the variation AB:C:DE written on it.

To find synthetic type-1 variations, we work from the list of states, which has been marked with checks and crosses. If a state has been marked with a cross, we clear the abacus and add two beads above on the wire for this state. We then work through the cards for the type-2, -3, and -4 variations. From the first card we come to we take a true group that does not contain the state with two beads above on its wire, and we add one bead above on the wires for this group. We take all the other true groups in each variation in turn, adding one bead below on the wires for the group. If no wire has one bead above and one below, or if any has three at the transom or none has one below only, we clear the abacus below and go to the next group. Otherwise, we add a bead above on the wires with one bead below and none above. If this puts beads above on all wires, the state with two beads above is a group in a synthetic type-1 variation, and we change the cross by this state to a check to signal this fact. Otherwise, we continue with the variations as before, or, if there are no more, we start over with the next state marked with a cross.

Finding synthetic type-2 variations is a longer process.

(1) First we work through the "type-5" groups. The cards for those that are already the same as a group in a type-2 variation are discarded, the cards for those that prove to be intermediary go into an intermediary stack.

It is probably easy enough to see by looking whether the "type-5" group is the same as one of the simple groups, or whether it overlaps both groups in a simple variation, in which latter case it is intermediary. If one wishes to use the abacus, the procedure is as follows:

Clear the abacus and add one bead above on the wires for the "type-5" group. Go through the type-2 variations, taking only one group from each, and add one bead below for the group. If no or all wires have one bead, the "type-5" group is the same as a group in a type-2 variation. If some wire has one above only, some two, some one below only, and some none, the "type-5" group is intermediary.

(2) Next we go through the "type-5" groups remaining. We add one bead above on the wires for each group, and two beads below on the wires for another group in the same variation, which, of course, is written on the card along with the group. Then we go through the type-2 variations and the other type-4 groups. We take both groups in the type-2 variations, except that if either group is wholly included in the test group we pass the variation by. We have listed the overlap sequences we have found, so if the variation on a "type-5" card divides off and divides up the test group, we can see whether any of its groups extends a sequence away from the test group. If the group on the card is not one of these, we pass it by. Otherwise we add one below on the wires for the type-2 or "type-5" group. If we do not have some wire with one bead below, some with two below, and some with three below, we subtract one below on the wires with one or three below and go on. If all wires have beads, the group we are testing is terminal. We discard its card and instead make a card for the necessary synthetic type-2 variation and put it with the other type-2 cards. Otherwise we subtract one below on the wires with three beads and add one below on those with one, so that all wires with beads below have two below, and repeat. starting with the first type-2 variation.

(3) Last we go through the "type-5" groups in the intermediary stack. We clear the abacus and add two beads above on the wires for the group. Then we go through the type-2 variations, taking both groups in each variation. We add one bead below on the wires for the group. If some wire has beads above and below, some a bead below only, some a bead or beads above only, and some no beads, we add one bead above on any wire with one below and none above. In any event we clear the abacus below and repeat with a new type-2 group, except that if we have added one above we do not take a second group from the same variation.

The first time we add one bead above, we mark the type-2 variation and the group added. If subsequent addition of beads above puts beads above on all wires, we clear the abacus below, subtract one bead on all wires with one above, and go back to the next group after the one we had marked. If we finish the type-2 variations without adding one bead above we start over with a new "type-5" group. Otherwise the wires with beads above represent an overlap of the "type-5" group with type-2 groups. We then proceed as in (2), except that we do not count a variation as dividing off and dividing up the overlap unless it divides the group with two beads above on its wires, and when we have finished we clear the abacus below, subtract one above on the wires with one above, and go back to the next group after the one we had marked.

It is so much easier to test by inspection for the remaining circumstances in which groups and overlaps can be terminal that abacus routines are not worth working out. More specifically, overlaps of more than one "type-5" group, and "type-5" groups such as AB in the variations AB:C:D:EF and AB:CD:E:F, where C, D, E, and F are terminal, are not discussed here.

When the synthetic simple variations have been determined, the preliminary diagram can be built in the usual way, working from the checked states in the list of states and the cards with the type-2 variations. At the end, the complex variations should be examined to see if any are anomalous. Also, any states apparently duplicates must be checked against the list of states, for they are not true duplicates if either has a cross by it in the list, and against the "type-5" groups, for they are not true duplicates unless they appear together in all these groups. For this last check, take the cards for the "type-5" groups insert the key in the hole for the first of the duplicates, and set aside the cards left behind when the key is lifted. With the remaining cards do the same at the hole for the second of the duplicates. If the states are true duplicates, no cards will be left behind when the key is lifted again. If there are more than two duplicates, repeat the process with either of the first two and a third. If neither the first test nor the second produces true duplicates, repeat the process with the other of the first two and the third. Continue in this way until all the duplicates that are not true duplicates have been tested against each other.

Appendix B

Notes on Computer Programs

Whether computer programs ought to be published is a moot point. Computer programmers are often reluctant to seek publication because they do not feel that their programs reflect their abilities, and publishers are often reluctant to publish because they foresee very small markets. The latter reasoning may seem more obvious than the former to someone who has never written a computer program. The intellectual labor of writing even a fairly short program is such that one seldom has time or energy to do more than obtain satisfactory results with it. To take full advantage of all one learns while writing a program would often require rewriting it almost completely. To go further, to think through a number of alternative ways of writing the program so as to be reasonably sure of choosing the best, is nearly impossible. Still, I should have published my computer programs here if I could have justified the expense to the publisher, because of the labor that others might save by adopting or adapting them. Instead I have deposited a number of copies of the longer programs in the Research Library of the University of California, Los Angeles, whence those interested may borrow them and have them reproduced.

I have published a proofreading program written for me by William P. Anderson and discussed my collating program in "Computer Aids to Editing the Text of Dryden," in *Art and Error: Modern Textual Editing*, edited by Ronald Gottesman and Scott Bennet (1970), pages 254-278.[1]

---

[1] For more information on collating programs see Penny Gilbert, "Automatic Collation: A Technique for Medieval Texts," *Computers and the Humanities*, VII (1972-73), 139-47, and references there.

The proofreading program can be used to collate texts two at a time if they are reasonably similar. I have also contributed four short programs for stylistic analysis to *Literary Data Processing*, an IBM publication (form no. GE20-0383), pages 37–59 (see also p. 71).

The most generally useful kind of program for stylistic study is a concordance program. One can most easily make a concordance suitable for private use by obtaining a KWIC (Key Word in Context) Index program such as IBM uses for indexing its publications. Instead of inputting titles with bibliographical references, one can input lines of text with their titles and line numbers. The output will be similar enough to David Packard's four-volme concordance to Livy to be entirely useful, that is, the alphabetized key words will be in a column down the center of the page with context on each side and the reference information at the right. An experienced programmer can easily make adjustments to the program so that it will produce alphabetizing as though the words were spelled backward, which facilitates the study of suffixes and inflectional endings. Should one wish something more elaborate, he can correspond with those who have written concordance programs (addresses can be obtained from the annual list of projects in *Computers and the Humanities*), or he can write his own program. One simple way to proceed is to input the whole text, or as much of it as possible, find the head of each word in turn and record its location, and compare each word with enough of the other words to determine its alphabetical order. I give below a very fast and simple routine for alphabetizing. Then, starting with the first word in alphabetical order, output the first, say, 60 characters to the left of the word followed by the next, say, 60 characters, depending on the maximum line length that can be printed. One need only store a corresponding number of blank characters ahead of and behind the input text to keep the print routine very simple. If the input is cards, for example, one can read in a blank card at the head of and at the end of the cards with text. If all the text cannot be stored at once, the results of earlier inputs may be stored temporarily outside the computer and merged with the results of the last input before printing. Alphabetizing of the words as if spelled backward requires only working through the text from back to front. This method I learned from my colleague, Professor Earl Rand, who has used it with very small computers. I have myself always worked with large machines and have written my more recent programs in the COBOL language, a combination that provides a reasonably efficient and very flexible sort routine. I have not needed recently, then, to write detailed instructions as to how to sort large amounts of data. Instead, I make up what I call sort-units, and sort them by the COBOL routine. My sort-units consist of a word from the text; identifying title, line number, and so on; the word in context; and, if I desire, any of a number of other things: a word or phrase to the left or right of the word in context, which provides a subhead for dividing the contexts of common words into shorter but still meaningful subsections; another word nearby, which allows the study of word associations; the number of occurrences of the word; the word in modern spelling, or spelled backward, or both; the class of the word, as for instance, personal name, italicized, in a stage direction; and so on as needed. Each item goes into a space of a standard length, say 20 characters for the word, 70 for the context, with the unused space filled with blank characters. The computer sorts the units in any order and as many different orders as desired. For example, normal alphabetical sorting makes it easy to count the occurrences of the words and store the counts with one example of each word, after which the words can be sorted in order of frequency. If contexts are omitted, the "concordance" becomes a word list that can be used for the study of spelling, for example. In the program I used to study Dryden's spellings, I also sorted words according to the occurrence in them of letter-pairs which I specified, so that I could see how many times and where "friend" and "freind" occurred, and so on. I have not kept a copy of this program, but I have deposited copies of two more recent concordance programs, under the titles GUFFEY and MARLOWE, in the library at UCLA.[2]

I have deposited under the title MSFAMTRE the program I used to perform the probabilistic studies described in chapter 4. Such a program is simple enough to write. Input must specify the number of trees to be "grown," the number of "gain-loss" cycles in the growth of each tree, and the number of manuscripts to be "gained" (given an ancestor) and "lost" in each cycle. Gain must precede loss in each cycle, for a manuscript cannot be lost before it comes into existence, that is, has an ancestor. Trees of six manuscripts with two survivors, for example, might be given three cycles of the following sort: gain 4, lose 1; gain 1, lose 1; gain 1, lose 2. Zero gains or losses have no effect and so are not used. The computer will then generate the necessary random numbers for the

---

[2] For more information on concordances, see *Literary Data Processing*, pp. 14–36.

ancestors and the losses. The computer will generate the same series of numbers for each run unless part of the input is a starting number for the series and a different starting number is supplied for each run; this corresponds to starting at different places in a book of random numbers. A convenient way of recording the results internally is to set up storage spaces representing manuscripts 1, 2, and so on, and to put in each space the number of the ancestor of the manuscript represented. The contents of the storage space for manuscript 2 will always be 1, since manuscript 2 in any tree must be a descendant of manuscript 1, and so need not be generated. "Lost" manuscripts may be represented by making the contents of their storage spaces negative. Manuscript 1 will have no ancestor, but needs a dummy that can be set negative in case manuscript 1 is lost (a zero here will not work, as a general rule, since it is seldom possible to get a computer to distinguish between postive and negative zero). Each totally new tree must be separately stored and tallied, and each duplicate must be tallied. Storing the trees in what is called a binary tree speeds comparison and allows the trees to be sorted for output in standard order. I shall explain binary trees and their use below. The format of the output is not so important as the sorting. If the new trees are output in order as generated at random, the results of one run are harder to compare with the results of another, especially when many different trees are possible.

My program prints the ancestors in rows directly above their descendants, with negative values representing lost manuscripts. Manuscript 1 has no ancestor, so it appears in the ancestors row only. Thus

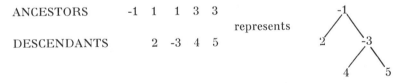

ANCESTORS   -1   1   1   3   3

                                          represents

DESCENDANTS   2   -3   4   5

Each tree is followed by its tally and probability. The probability is the tally divided by the total number of trees grown, including all duplicates.

The trees do not include lost texts with no or only one ancestor. These are deleted as follows. First, we work through the storage spaces representing the trees from right to left, that is, from the last manuscript to the first. If a manuscript has a negative value in its storage space, indicating that it is a "lost" manuscript, we look for the number of the manuscript (not the number in its storage space, which is the number of its ancestor) in any spaces to the right and record the first we find. If its number is not to be found elsewhere, it had no descendants, and we put zero in its space. If its number is found only once elsewhere we put zero in its space after we put the number in its space (its ancestor's number) in place of its own number in the other space, as a positive number if the other number was positive, otherwise as a negative number (the negative refers to the space, not to the contents of the space; a negative value means a lost descendant, not a lost ancestor). Suppose we have a tree with seven texts, as follows:

$$-2 \quad -1 \quad -1 \quad -3 \quad 3 \quad 4 \quad -5$$

(the first number is a dummy ancestor for the first manuscript). In this tree, manuscripts 1, 2, 3, 4, and 7 have been lost; manuscript 1 is the ancestor of 2 and 3; manuscript 3 is the ancestor of 4 and 5; manuscript 4 is the ancestor of 6; and manuscript 5 is the ancestor of 7. When we test manuscript 7, which has no descendants, we change the contents of the storage spaces as follows:

$$-2 \quad -1 \quad -1 \quad -3 \quad 3 \quad 4 \quad 0$$

Manuscripts 6 and 5 are not lost. When we test manuscript 4, which has only one descendant, we change the contents of the storage spaces as follows:

$$-2 \quad -1 \quad -1 \quad 0 \quad 3 \quad 3 \quad 0$$

Manuscript 3 has more than one descendant. When we test manuscript 2, which has no descendants, we change the contents of the storage spaces as follows:

$$-2 \quad 0 \quad -1 \quad 0 \quad 3 \quad 3 \quad 0$$

And when we test manuscript 1 we find that while it had two descendants before it has only one now, and change the contents of the storage spaces as follows:

$$0 \quad 0 \quad -2 \quad 0 \quad 3 \quad 3 \quad 0$$

Second, we work left to right through the storage spaces, replacing each zero space with the contents of the next nonzero space to the right, and renumbering the references to the spaces accordingly. In our example, we move the contents of the third space to the first space and change 3 to 1 wherever it occurs (we should change -3 to -1 if it occured). Thus we change the storage spaces to:

$$-2 \quad 0 \quad 0 \quad 0 \quad 1 \quad 1 \quad 0$$

Then we move texts 5 and 6 one at a time, with the final result:

$$-2 \quad 1 \quad 1 \quad 0 \quad 0 \quad 0 \quad 0$$

The computer would then print the tree as:

ANCESTORS   -1   1   1

DESCENDANTS   2   3

representing

The manuscript now numbered 1 is not the first manuscript "grown," corresponding to the fact that in a real textual tree the archetype is not necessarily the author's original.

Under the title PRELIMDI I have deposited a program for determining the preliminary diagrams for textual and bibliographical trees. As it is a long and complex program I shall describe its operation according to the sections into which it is divided. The terminology used assumes a textual tree is in prospect.

The program-control section starts the program, controls transfer to subordinate sections, which transfer back to it in turn, tests whether a further problem is to be solved, and if not, stops the program. A section like program-control is sometimes called a "driver." It allows the program to be built up or revised part by part.

The store-data section reads, prints, and stores the variations. The input variations need not be entirely standardized. One group in any one variation can be omitted; for example, the larger group in a type-1 variation. On the other hand, states omitting a passage where other states vary must be input as part of the variation; they can, however, be lumped together at the end after a special symbol, if desired, in which case the computer will recognize each as a singleton. The other groups and sigla can be in any order. The store-data section prints out the variations as input, each preceded by a serial number which the computer will use thereafter instead of the line number or other input identification of the variation and which it will print out thereafter instead of the variation itself. The sigla are also given serial numbers for internal use but are always printed out as input. The store-data section also supplies the serial numbers for the sigla in each variation that were not input, arranges the groups and sigla in a standard order, and stores the variations. Therefore a list of all the sigla in a problem must be input before any of the variations. It is stored in an array called sigla-list. An array is a storage area with subdivisions of equal size, which may be visualized as arranged in a row or a series of rows.

The internal formats for the variations are as follows. Simple variations are reduced to their smaller groups of sigla or to the ones beginning with the first siglum in the standard order if both their groups are the same size. The type-1 variations also have a 1 entered in the positions assigned to their singleton sigla in an array called type-1-list. Storing only one group in simple variations saves space, but complicates the program, which must recognize that for every stored group there is another consisting of the remaining sigla.

Complex variations are reduced to their true groups. The singletons have -1 entered in their positions in the type-1-list unless a 1 has already been entered there. The entries in the list are of basic importance. Sigla marked with 1 belong to terminal states, the rest belong to intermediary states; those with 0 do not appear as singletons in any variation, those with -1 appear as singletons in complex variations. Later, -2 will be entered if sigla belong to duplicates of other states or have been printed out in the preliminary diagram.

The variations are entered *seriatim* in a large array called variation-store and the starting position of each is recorded in an array called keylist. Each variation begins with its type number, from 0 to 4, followed by its length-count, that is, the number of positions in the variation-store occupied by its type number, length-count, sigla, and group dividers. The sigla are assigned numbers beginning with 1, so 0 is used as the group-divider symbol. For example, suppose there are five sigla in a problem, A-E, which have been assigned numbers 1-5. Then the internal form of the following variations will be as shown:

type 1:	A:BCDE	1	3	1				
	B:ACDE	1	3	2				
type 2:	AB:CDE	2	4	1	2			
type 3:	A:B:CDE	3	5	3	4	5		
type 4:	A:BC:DE	4	7	2	3	0	4	5
type 0:	A:B:C:D:E	0	3	0				

The type-0 variations are dummies and, with the type-1 variations, will be eliminated after the duplicate variations have been printed. The type-1-list preserves the information contained in the type-0 and type-1 variations.

The key-list is arranged in four columns, each variation being assigned a row. The first two columns will be used later in sorting the variations, the third column contains the starting locations of the variations in the variation-store, the fourth column holds the serial numbers of the variations. The first two positions are set zero at first, and the whole first row is also set zero, as it has a special purpose after the variations have been sorted. The second row contains the information about the first variation. If the variations shown above were stored in the order given, the relevant contents of the variation-store would be

1 3 1 1 3 2 2 4 1 2 3 5 3 4 5 4 7 2 3 0 4 5 0 3 0

and the corresponding contents of the key-list would be

0	0	0	0
0	0	1	1
0	0	4	2
0	0	7	3
0	0	11	4
0	0	16	5
0	0	23	6

The store-data section also makes tests to insure that the input data conforms to various requirements; for example, that no unexpected siglum appears, that no siglum appears twice in the same variation, that there is an end-of-problem marker, and that there are not too many variations in the problem to fit in the variation-store or to be recorded in the keylist. If it finds errors it prints diagnostic statements and reports to the program-control section that the problem must be aborted. The variation-store and key-list are used later for storing rings and synthetic simple variations; and similar tests are then made and similar diagnostic statements and reports result if either storage area would be overloaded. When a problem is aborted, the program-control section bypasses the rest of the sections and tests at once to see if a further problem is to be processed.

If the store-data section finds no errors in the data, the sorting section sorts the variations, using the binary-tree method explained below. The contents of the variations are compared from left to right, so that the variations are ordered by type, then by length, and finally by sigla and group dividers. The sorted order is recorded in the second column of the key-list, where each variation has the row number for the next in the order, except the last, which has 0. The row number of the first variation in the order is entered in the second column of the first row of the key-list. In our example, the type-0 variation would sort first, followed by the others in order as input, so the resulting key-list would be

1)	0	7	0	0
2)	0	3	1	1
3)	0	4	4	2
4)	0	5	7	3
5)	0	6	11	4
6)	0	0	16	5
7)	0	2	23	6

The list-duplicate section prints out a table of duplicate variations in which the assigned serial numbers of the variations appear instead of the input identifications. It also marks the duplicates and all type-0 and type-1 variations internally by putting negative values in the fourth column of their key-list rows. In our example, we should have -1, -2, and -6. The occurrence counts of the variations go in the first column of the key-list in the row belonging to the first occurrence of each, and, if the variations are type-1, in the singleton sigla's positions in an array called text-list.

The eliminate-marked-variations section deletes the marked variations from the key-list and variation-store, to leave maximum space for further processing. In our example, variations 1, 2, and 6 will be eliminated, leaving the relevant contents of the variation-store as follows:

2 4 1 2 3 5 3 4 5 4 7 2 3 0 4 5

and the relevant contents of the key-list as follows:

1)	0	2	0	0
2)	1	3	1	3
3)	1	4	5	4
4)	1	0	10	5

There will also be a 1 in the positions for A and B in the text-list.

The store-type-4-groups section first sets up three more empty rows in the key-list and records their row numbers in spaces called type-3-entry, type-4-entry, and type-5-entry. Next, it cuts off the type-3 and type-4 variations and puts into the second column of their entry rows the row number of the first variation in order of each kind. In our example, then, the relevant contents of the key-list become

1)	0	2	0	0
2)	1	0	1	3
3)	1	0	5	4
4)	1	0	10	5
5)	0	3	0	0
6)	0	4	0	0
7)	0	0	0	0

Finally, it reproduces the groups in the type-4 variations separately, giving them 5 as their type-number in the variation-store, and putting the occurrence count of their parent variations in the first column of their key-list rows, and the row number of their parent variations in the fourth column. Groups with the same value in their fourth column are thus from the same variation, and the values allow recovery of the parent variation as needed. In our example, the relevant contents of the variation-store will become

2 4 1 2 3 5 3 4 5 4 7 2 3 0 4 5 5 4 2 3 5 4 4 5

and the relevant contents of the key-list become

1)	0	2	0	0
2)	1	0	1	3
3)	1	0	5	4
4)	1	0	10	5
5)	0	3	0	0
6)	0	4	0	0
7)	0	0	0	0
8)	1	0	17	5
9)	1	0	21	5

The values in the first column of the "type-5" rows will be used instead of those in the rows of the parent variations should it prove necessary later to count the agreements of each siglum with each of the others.

The test-for-rings section is very similar in its operations to the abacus routines described in Appendix A. It makes use of two arrays, test-1 and test-2, that correspond to the wires above and below the transom of the abacus. A 1 in a siglum's position in test-1 corresponds to one bead above on its wire in an abacus. The major difference from the abacus routines comes from the fact that there is effectively no limit to the size of the values that can be stored, as though one had an abacus with a very large number of beads.

Only groups with 2 or 5 as their group numbers are tested, and these are often distinguished by the fact that their rows are above and below the type-3-entry row, respectively. The groups are tested in order as stored, by working down the key-list. The basic groups are called 1st and 2nd. The first 2nd is always the first type-2 or "type-5" group after 1st. When the last 2nd has been tested, the first 2nd becomes the new 1st.

Each 1st is recorded in test-1, each 2nd in test-2. As each new 1st is chosen, a value called last-group-in-test-1 is set zero and test-1 is cleared.

As each new 2nd is chosen, a value called last-group-in-test-2 is set zero and test-2 is cleared. Just before a group is recorded the corresponding last-group value is incremented by 1 and this value is stored in the positions belonging to the sigla in the group. Each 2nd is tested for overlap with 1st, and is not recorded if it does not overlap.

If 2nd overlaps 1st and both are from type-2 variations, the variations form a ring of the type

A B: C D E   A——B
                       | |
E A:B C D   E— CD

If 2nd overlaps 1st and only 1st is from a type-2 variation, then if another group from the same variation as 2nd also overlaps 1st, the variations form a ring of the type

A B: C D E   A—B
                       | |
E A:B C:D   E—C

If 2nd overlaps 1st and neither are from type-2 variations we need the following to form a ring:

(1) Another group from the same variation as the last group in test-1 which overlaps the last group in test-2.

(2) Another group from the same variation as the last group in test-2, or, if the ring would have more than five elements, from any type-2 or type-4 variation, which overlaps 1st and the last group in test-1. Also, if the ring-closing group does not come from the same variation as the last group in test-2 we need another group from the same variation as the ring-closing group which includes members of any two elements in the overlap sequence except both the first and the last. The double-check section, which is subordinate to the test-for-rings section, tests for this last group. Rings formed in this way have an even number of elements, of the type

A B: C D:E   A—B
                       | |
D A:B C :E   D—C

(3) Another group from the same variation as the last group in test-2 that overlaps the last group in test-1.

(4) A group from a third variation that overlaps 1st (in test-1) and the last group in test-2, and another group from the same variation

which includes members cf any two elements in the overlap sequence except both the first and the last. The double-check section tests for this last group. Rings formed in this way have an odd number of elements, of the type

$$
\begin{array}{ll}
\text{A B: C D:E} & \text{A—B—C} \\
\text{A:B C:D E} & \quad|\qquad\quad| \\
\text{E A:B C D} & \text{E———D}
\end{array}
$$

If the search for (1) cannot be made because all sigla have already been recorded in test-1 or test-2 or both, or if the search for (1) fails and 1st is the only group in test-1, the computer chooses a new 2nd.

Otherwise, if the search for (1) fails, the double-overlap section subordinate to the test-for-rings section tests for a variation that will extend the overlap because it has a group that overlaps the last two groups in test-2 and has another group that will overlap the last group in test-2, or because it has a group that will overlap both the last group in test-2 and another group not yet recorded from the same variation as the last group in test-2 and has another group of its own that will overlap this unrecorded group. If the test fails, the computer goes to a backup routine, to be described below.

If the search for (2) fails, the computer tries to find (3).

If the search for (3) cannot be made because all sigla have already been recorded in test-1 or test-2 or both, the computer chooses a new 2nd.

If the search for (3) fails, the double-overlap section tests for a variation that will extend the overlap sequence because it has a group that overlaps the last two groups in test-1 and has another group that will overlap the last group in test-1, or because it has a group that will overlap both the last group in test-1 and another group not yet recorded from the same variation as the last group in test-1 and has another group of its own that will overlap this unrecorded group. If the test fails, the computer goes to a backup routine.

If the search for (4) fails, the computer tries to find (1).

When the first ring is found, the count-pairs section subordinate to the test-for-rings section stores and prints a table of the number of times each siglum is found with every other in the true groups in the variations. The test-for-rings section then prints the ring. It also sorts the numbers of the key-list rows of the groups in the ring, using a bubble sort routine, stores the sorted numbers in the variation-store, and records the location of storage in a new key-list row. A bubble sort compares each item in a series with the next and if they are not in the desired order reverses them; the series is run through repeatedly until no more reversal is required. Subsequent rings have the numbers of the key-list rows of their groups sorted and compared with those previously stored. The rings are only printed if they are made up of different groups than any previous ring, in which case the numbers of the key-list rows of their groups are stored as before. To speed comparison, the entries in the first two columns of the key-list rows for the rings are used to build a binary tree, as explained below.

Rings are printed out as follows. First the serial number of the ring is printed. Next, the groups causing the ring are printed in rows, according to their order around the ring, starting with 1st and 2nd in that order, each group preceded by the serial number of the variation in which it occurs. Finally, the elements in the ring are printed out in corresponding rows and order, with the strength of the connection between each pair printed in intervening rows. The latter are drawn from the table stored by the count-pairs section. No attempt is made to represent the rings physically. For example:

144 RING FORMED BY VARIATIONS AND GROUPS AS SHOWN
  77 M2, M5, M7, M9, M10
134 M1, M4, M9
  77 M1, M3, M4, M6, M8, Q1, F, Q2, Q3, Q4, Q5, Q6, Q7, Q8, O1, O2, O3
134 M2, M3, M5, M6, M8, M10, Q1, F, Q2, Q3, Q4, Q5, Q6, Q7, Q8, O1, O2, O3
THE RING ELEMENTS ARE AS FOLLOWS (THE FIRST ELEMENT IS TO BE CONSIDERED AS FOLLOWING THE LAST)
  M9
GREATEST AGREEMENT BETWEEN PRECEDING AND FOLLOWING IS 149
  M1, M4
GREATEST AGREEMENT BETWEEN PRECEDING AND FOLLOWING IS 188
  M3, M6, M8, Q1, F, Q2, Q3, Q4, Q5, Q6, Q7, Q8, O1, O2, O3
GREATEST AGREEMENT BETWEEN PRECEDING AND FOLLOWING IS 190
  M2, M5, M10
GREATEST AGREEMENT BETWEEN PRECEDING AND FOLLOWING IS 146

The ring's serial number (144 in the example) and weakest connection (146 in the example) are stored temporarily outside the computer for subsequent sorting.

When a ring has been found, if both 1st and 2nd are from simple variations the search for rings resumes with a new 2nd. Otherwise the ring-closing group is deleted from test-1 or test-2, as the case may be, and search continues for another ring-closing group by a return to (2) if the ring was found there, and otherwise by a return to (4).

The backup routines mark off the last group in test-1 or test-2, whichever has been recorded last, and then test the group before that, which will be in the other array. When a tested group has a siglum that is not recorded in both test-1 and test-2, return is to (1) if the tested group is in test-2, and to (3) if the tested group is in test-1. Otherwise the tested group is marked off and the last group before that tested, until only two groups remain. At that point, the search for rings resumes with a new 2nd.

When a group is entered in test-1 or test-2 the number of its key-list row is stored for later recovery as needed in a last-in-first-out array called push-down. When a group is deleted from or marked off in test-1 or test-2 its number is removed from push-down. Groups are marked off by changing their group numbers in test-1 or test-2 from positive to negative. Tests for negative values prevent using the same overlapping group twice in a ring. This procedure insures that if the overlap sequence starting with 1st and 2nd has any forks every branch of every fork will be followed up to see if it is part of a ring, but no branch more than once. The variations AB:CDE:FG:HI and A:BC:DF:EH:GI provide an example of a forked sequence: starting with A we have both A—B—C—D—F—G and A—B—C—E—H—I, the fork coming between C, D, and E.

If rings occur, the ring serial numbers and weakest connections, which have been temporarily stored outside the computer, are sorted by the COBOL sort and printed with the strongest weakest connection first, as an index to the rings for use when breaking them. The test-for-rings section then returns the computer to the program-control section, which searches at once for another problem. Breaking the rings is a tedious and exacting process that is also best done by computer. The present program assumes, however, that many users will prefer to look at the variations causing the rings and to rewrite the variations according to their own assessment of the nature and cause of each ring.

When the rings have been broken and the problem resubmitted with synthetic complex variations in place of some of the original variations, rings may be found again, as explained in chapter 2. In that event, the table of pair counts from the first submission should be used to establish the strength of the connections; the table, strengths, and index to the rings printed on resubmission will reflect the synthetic variations, not the originals. In recalculating the strengths start with the apparently weakest connection and stop as soon as it is clear that the weakest connection has in fact been located.

If no rings occur, the find-synthetic-variations section prints out and stores any synthetic simple variations. This section has four major routines, which once again are very similar to those with an abacus. Here the principal difference is that the computer can transfer to some of the routines in the test-for-rings section and back again; it does not need a completely different set of instructions.

(1) First, each siglum having -1 in its position in the type-1-list is tested to see if its state is terminal. The first true group from a type-2, type-3, or type-4 variation which does not include the siglum being tested is recorded in test-1, followed by any other such groups that overlap or wholly include the previous contents of test-1. If the overlap is extended, the groups are run through again in case a variation passed over will now extend the overlap. If all sigla except the one being tested are thus recorded in test-1, the siglum being tested has a 1 entered in its position in test-1-list, and is printed with the notation that it is a group in a synthetic simple variation.

(2) Next the true groups from the type-4 variations are tested, using their separate "type-5" listings. As a preliminary, the first column of the "type-5" rows in the key-list is cleared and the groups are sorted in the same way as but separately from the variations proper. The number of the key-list row of the first group in sorted order is entered in the second column of the type-5-entry row in key-list. To return to our earlier example, the relevant key-list rows will now be:

$$\cdot \; \cdot \; \cdot \; \cdot \; \cdot \; \cdot \; \cdot \; \cdot$$

7)	0	8	0	0
8)	0	9	17	5
9)	0	0	21	5

The groups are processed in sorted order, which means working with the smallest first. 1st and 2nd groups are chosen from the "type 5s," and all groups except 1st itself are taken in turn as 2nd with each 1st.

Each 1st is tested against the type-2 variations. If it is the same as a type-2 group, the sorted order is adjusted to bypass it thereafter. If it is overlapped by a simple group, it cannot be terminal and a new 1st is chosen. Otherwise 1st is tested against each 2nd for possible overlap. If more than one overlap could be obtained from groups in the same variation, 1st cannot be terminal and a new 1st is chosen. Otherwise, if an overlap has occurred, the overlapping group is chosen as 2nd for the next operation and is recorded in test-2. The computer then transfers to the test-for-rings section, where it searches for (1) and (3), bypassing (2) and (4), until the test-for-rings section would choose a new 2nd. At that point, the computer returns to the find-synthetic-variations section. Now, if any siglum has not been recorded either in test-1 or test-2, the find-synthetic-variations section chooses a new 2nd. Otherwise, 1st is terminal, and so is each larger overlap sequence that includes it. (Identifying the including overlaps is a separate operation in the other calculi.) In other words, if we have AB:CD:E and A:BC:DE, where AB is 1st and BC is 2nd, we have 11220 in test-1 and 01122 in test-2, indicating a sequence A—B—C—D—E, in which AB and the overlap *ABC are terminal. The next to the last overlap, in this case *ABCD, is not counted, nor is the unoverlapped part of 1st, in this case A. Both of these are terminal also, but their terminality will already have been discovered or will be discovered in (3) below. If a sequence forks, it is followed only to the fork nearest to 1st. Eventually all groups at the ends of forks will be chosen as 1st, and in (3) below the computer will work with groups at the centers of forks. The synthetic terminal groups thus identified are printed, and are stored in the variation-store in the usual format for type-2 variations. The entries in the second column of the key-list are adjusted to include the new variations at the right places in the sorted sequence of simple variations. Also the sorted order for the "type-5" groups is adjusted to bypass 1st hereafter. Then a new 1st is chosen, until the end of the sorted order is reached.

(3) 1st is reset to the first "type-5" group still in the sorted order and testing continues. Each 1st is tested for overlap with simple groups. If one group in a simple variation overlaps 1st, so does the other, and each of the resulting overlaps is tested separately. Once the overlap has been started, however, only one overlapping group from any other simple variation will not overlap or wholly contain the simple group or groups already in the ovrrlap, and only these wholly different groups will be chosen to enlarge the overlap. If a completed overlap proves to have the same sigla as a type-2 or a type-4 group or to be overlapped by two groups from the same type-4 variation, a new 1st is chosen. If no overlap with simple groups is found, but 1st is overlapped by two groups in the same type-4 variation, a new 1st is chosen. Otherwise,

the complementary-overlap-test section subordinate to the find-synthetic-variations section determines whether the remaining sigla can be comprised in an overlap made up of type-2 or type-4 groups that do not contain any sigla in the group or overlap being tested. Such a complementary overlap must start with a group from the same variation as 1st. If the overlap is extended the groups are run through again in case a variation passed over before will now extend the overlap. This routine will recognize that the variations AB:CD:E and AB:C:DE indicate that AB is terminal, and that the variations AB:CDEFGH, CD:ABEFGH, A:BC:D:EF:GH, and A:B:CD:E:FGH, which indicate a forked overlap sequence, also indicate that *ABCD is terminal. If a complementary overlap is obtained, the group or overlap is printed and stored and the sorted order for the "type-5" groups is adjusted to bypass 1st, as before. Then a new 1st is chosen, until the end of the sorted order is reached.

(4) 1st is reset to the first "type-5" group still in the sorted order and testing continues. The first 2nd is the first group after 1st. If 2nd overlaps 1st an attempt is made to build another overlap from the same variations which is complementary to the first or which will become complementary when both are extended by groups from the same type-4 variation (all the type-4 variations are tested repeatedly until no more extension of the overlaps occurs), or when either of the overlaps or both are extended by a group or groups from type-2 variations. If complementary overlaps are found, one is printed and stored as before. This routine will recognize that the variations A:BC:D:EF and AB:C:DE:F indicate that *ABC is terminal.

No attempt is made in the program to locate variations of the type AB:CD:E:F and AB:C:D:EF, which, it will be recalled, indicate that AB is terminal provided C, D, E, and F are all terminal.

The final-tests section first prints out the sigla of the duplicate and effective-duplicate states, and puts -2 in the positions of all but one of each set of duplicates in the type-1-list. Then it lists the anomalous type-4 variations, first those that have two or more true groups that are comprehended in a simple group when the simple group has no smaller simple groups within it which divide up the sigla in the type-4 groups. The rest are identified as follows. A nonterminal group, or, if no group remains to test, a nonterminal state, is recorded in test-1. Then two simple variations are sought with groups which include the contents of test-1 and whose non-including groups have no siglum in common. If found, the first non-including group is recorded in test-2 using 1s and the second using 2s. If any simple group includes a state with 1 in its test-2 position and a state with 2 in its test-2 position but no state recorded in test-1, search continues for groups to enter in test-2. Otherwise, any nonterminal group that includes at least one state with a 1 in its test-2 position and one state with a 2 in its test-2 position, but no state recorded in test-1, is part of an anomalous variation.

The build-tree section, with the print-tree section which is subordinate to it, either prints the preliminary diagram indicated by the simple variations or reports that no tree can be constructed because there are no simple variations, original or synthetic. When there are type-2 variations, the procedure is to read through the stored groups in their sorted order, which means starting with the smaller groups and proceeding through the larger. Any sigla in a group which have a 1 in their type-1-list positions are entered in an array called terminal-list, any with 0 or -1 are entered in an array called intermediary-list. As the sigla are entered, -2 is entered in their positions in the type-1-list. If all are entered in the terminal-list, an inferential intermediary is chosen as "ancestor" and printed out with each of the sigla in turn as "descendant." Of course, these terms are for convenience only, as the archetype has not yet been located. Inferential intermediaries are given negative numbers, starting with -1, as sigla. The other sigla are output from the sigla-list where they were stored when input. The siglum for the inferential intermediary then replaces the first "descendant's" siglum in the sigla-list, and a 1 is put in the "descendant's" position in the type-1-list. If there is an entry in the intermediary-list, it is chosen as "ancestor," and printed out with the entries in terminal-list as "descendants." Then the "ancestor" siglum has a 1 put in its position in the type-1-list. The result is that after a group has been processed, only one of its sigla will be recognized as part of any larger group, and if the group has been assigned an inferential intermediary the siglum of the inferential intermediary will be printed instead of the original siglum. For instance, if we have a group AB with A terminal and B intermediary, B will be printed out as the "ancestor" of A, A will be ignored thereafter, and B will be treated as if it were terminal. If we have a group CD with both states terminal, both will be printed out as "descendants" of, say, -1, D will be ignored thereafter, and -1 will be printed instead of C. In this way the diagram is built up segment by segment through repetitions of the same simple routine.

When all the stored type-2 groups have been processed, or if there were none to start with, all sigla with 1 in their type-1-list positions are printed out as "descendants" of a siglum with 0 or -1 in its type-1-list position; or if there are none of the latter, then as "descendants" of a last inferential intermediary, unless there are only two of the former, in which case one is printed as "ancestor." The result might be

"ANCESTORS"   -0001   -0001   -0002   -0002   -0002

"DESCENDANTS"   A   B   C   D   -0001

The preliminary diagram thus represented is

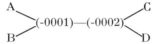

Diagnostics report out variations from the expected: "only one text left in type-1-list; dummy supplied," "more than one intermediary left in type-1-list; took first," "terminal group with no terminal texts treated as terminal text," "more than one intermediary in group from variation (here the serial number appears); took first listed candidate," and "found no terminal texts remaining."

Under the title ARCHETYP I have deposited a program for locating the archetype in a preliminary diagram. The first part of this program operates much like the store-data section of PRELIMDI. The input list of sigla, however, must include sigla for the inferential intermediaries in the diagram, and these sigla must be included as appropriate in the input groups from the variations. Only groups from which arrows point in fully directional or synthetic fully directional variations are input. The program does not evaluate the evidence of partially directional variations, which, as we have seen, may influence the location of archetypes.

If any two input groups overlap, there has been a mistake in the input and a diagnostic statement will be printed out. Otherwise, if any siglum is found in all groups it is listed as "the archetype," even if there is more than one. In the latter event, any siglum listed may equally well be the archetype, requiring more than one tree, or annotations to the one tree chosen. If no siglum is found in all groups but two groups are complementary and any others are either the same as or wholly include one of the two, the archetype is an additional inferential intermediary between the complementary groups. The two groups are printed out with an explanation. Otherwise, the message that "the archetype is not in the tree" is printed. This message indicates that the directional variations show a ring in the tree unrecognized before, and that the whole problem will have to be begun again with the archetype included in the variations submitted to PRELIMDI.

All the foregoing programs have been used with success, and, in different versions, with continuing success over many years, but still not under every possible circumstance. The collating program, for example, has served me satisfactorily with the poems and some of the prose of John Gay, and many of the poems and plays (in prose and verse) of John Dryden, but further use may show that the program still needs or would profit from modification. A wise user of these programs, therefore, will test them with every variety of data he can conceive of needing to process before trusting them for the solution of his problems. I shall be happy to correct any errors reported to me and to deposit revised copies of the programs for subsequent users.

Finally, the long promised binary-tree method of sorting and searching data, which I learned from Martin Kay. The method requires two arrays or two columns in one array to record the connections between the items in the tree, and three indexes to specify positions in the arrays. Each position except the first in the arrays or the columns of the array corresponds to an item to be sorted. The first positions are saved for a pointer to the first item in the sorted order. A major advantage to this method of sorting is that the items themselves need not be reordered but can be keyed to their positions in the arrays by a third array or a third column in the same array in which the storage locations of the items can be recorded. The items can be stored before sorting begins, or one by one as the first step in the sorting process takes place. Before the second step in the sorting process has been performed, items stored can be very quickly located; afterward they can only be located by starting at the beginning of the sorted order. Let us think of the sorted order as a long row of items and think of the items in the order as to the left or to the right of other items. Then we can call the positions in the first of the arrays or columns in the array left-pointers and those in the second right-pointers. A nonzero value in the left-pointer belonging to an item will be the location of the left- and right-pointers of the next item to its left, and a nonzero value in the right-pointer belonging to an item will be the location of the left- and right-pointers of the next item to its right. In the first part of the sorting process, each item may have one item to its left and one to its right, but after the second part each item will have an item to its right only. For example, if B, A, D, and C are stored in that order, the first part of the sorting process will produce a binary tree, that is, a tree having no more than two branches descending from any branch-point, with A to the left of B, D to the right of B, and C to the left of D.

		left	right
1)	starter	0	2
2)	B	3	4
3)	A	0	0
4)	D	5	0
5)	C	0	0

starter
B
A   D
C

The second part of the sorting routine will produce a sequence with B to the right of A, and so on.

		left	right
1)	starter	0	3
2)	B	0	5
3)	A	0	2
4)	D	0	0
5)	C	0	4

starter—A—B—C—D

We start the sorting process by comparing the second item with the first (as noted above, the second item can be already stored, or waiting to be stored). If the second item belongs to the left of the first, we put the location of the second item's pointers in the left-pointer of the first item; if the second item belongs to the right of the first we put the location of the second item's pointers in the right-pointer of the first item. Subsequent items are also compared with the first, but if they belong to the left of the first and another item has already been chosen as to the left they are compared with the other item, and similarly if they belong to the right of the first item. Thus each new item is traced through the tree until an earlier item is found which has no other to its left, if the new item belongs to its left, or no other to its right if the new item belongs to its right. If two items prove to be the same, the new one can be eliminated or treated as belonging to the right of the old. If a tree grows symmetrically, it is possible to place new items in it very rapidly. A perfectly symmetrical tree would hold over a million items in twenty levels, requiring then only twenty tests at most to place an item in it and only twenty tests at most to find an item in it. In fact, the trees will not grow absolutely symmetrically, but the more the items are out of the desired order when stored, the more the tree will tend to be symmetrical.

The algorithm for producing a series from the tree is even simpler. Let us call the indexes 1st, 2nd, 3rd. If the value of 1st is 3, by "left-pointer (1st)" we mean the third position in the array of left-pointers, if the value of 1st is 4 we mean the fourth position. We begin by giving 1st and 2nd the value 1. Then we proceed as follows:

(1) If left-pointer (2nd) has the value 0 go to (6); otherwise go to (2).

(2) Give 3rd the value of left-pointer (2nd). Give left-pointer (2nd) the value 0. Give right-pointer (1st) the value of 3rd. Go to (3).

(3) If right-pointer (3rd) has the value 0 go to (5); otherwise go to (4).

(4) Give 3rd the value of right-pointer (3rd). Go to (3).

(5) Give right-pointer (3rd) the value of 2nd. Give 2nd the value of right-pointer (1st). Go to (1).

(6) If right-pointer (2nd) has the value 0, stop; otherwise go to (7).

(7) Give 1st the value of 2nd. Give 2nd the value of right-pointer (2nd). Go to (1).

In step (4) the computer will use the old value of 3rd to find right-pointer (3rd) before it gives 3rd a new value; in step (7) it will use the old value of 2nd to find right-pointer (2nd) before it gives 2nd a new value.

Appendix C

Direction with Motifs

Directional variations of the kinds illustrated in chapter 2 are more certainly directional when they result from well-defined physical processes than when they result from ill-defined mental processes. Variations where the variants are motifs result from mental processes only, and it has been a question whether any of these mental processes are well defined enough to support rules for identifying directional variations. None of the rules in common use is satisfactorily based, but I have discovered one that is, and this discovery gives me hope there may be others as well.

Once the purpose of a narrative motif has been lost in retelling, its recovery is difficult, if not impossible, except by consulting an earlier state of the narrative. The same is true of motifs in any form of discourse. From this fact it follows that a variation in which the variants are motifs is directional if one of the variants is purposive and another not. The purposive motif is the earlier.

For example, in the ancient near-eastern flood stories, the hero is usually said to be sealed in his ark or boat. The exceptions are the stories of Ziusudra and Sisithros. After the deluge, the hero is usually said to send out birds on three or four occasions. The exceptions are the stories of Ziusudra again and Atra-hasis, in the latter case perhaps because of lacunae in the records. Now in the stories of Noah and Xisuthros we infer that the hero cannot see the water when he is sealed in, for he determines from the actions of his birds whether it is safe to break the seal: at the conclusion of his tests, Noah removes the top of the ark and sees that the ground is dry, Xisuthros pries open the seams of his boat and sees that it is aground on a moutain. In the story of Utnapishtim, on the contrary, the hero opens a window in his boat and sees not only the water but land in the distance; furthermore his boat runs aground a week before he sends out his birds. The motif of sending out the birds is thus not purposive in the story of Utnapishtim. In the story of Sisithros, the motif is still more vestigial: Sisithros floats in his boat to Armenia; he sends out his birds; there is no more to the story. It follows that the motif of sending out birds in the stories of Noah and Xisuthros is earlier than the motif of sending out birds in the stories of Utnapishtim and Sisithros.

Since the stories of Noah and Xisuthros were recorded after the story of Utnapishtim, a bibliographical tree would show a lost archetypal narrative of which the Noah/Xisuthros and the Utnapishtim stories were independent descendants. Textually speaking, however, the Noah/Xisuthros stories are effective duplicates, the ancestor of the Utnapishtim story—at least until we develop rules that will allow us to recognize directional variations in the other motifs and these variations are found to point in the opposite direction.

For the purposive-vestigial rule to be set aside, it must be shown that the author of the discourse with the purposive motif regularly takes pains to supply purposive connections between wandering motifs in his sources.

As we increase our ability to distinguish earlier motifs from later, we correspondingly refine our analysis of variations that have resulted from consulting similar writings. Thus the first example in chapter 2 of the latter kind of analysis depends upon whether Mark is a source of Matthew. If the two Gospels have a common source in a body of information about Jesus, then the normal reading of Mark in the example may be the later instead of the earlier.

Topical Index

abacus, 9, 204-14, 224, 229

add-omission: definition, 26; rules, 26-34. *See also* variation

adscript: definition, 52; examples, 6, 11, 181, 186

agreement, 4-5, 19, 21-22, 28, 36-37, 61, 66. *See also* count, pair; group; variation, agreement-defined

algorithm: definition, 9

ambiguities: rules, 35-37. *See also* variation, anomalous

anagrammatism, 46-47

analysis, textual: definition, 1-2, 13, 58, 83, 85; goal, 2; difference from bibliography, 14-19, 153; place of probability in, 123

ancestry. *See* descent

—prime, 16, 66, 98

annotation: trees, 37; preliminary diagrams, 77; emendations, 160

apparatus criticus: definition, 5; rules, 28-29, 34, 146-147, 153, 158-60; examples, 6, 58, 163, 167, 170, 176, 180-81. *See also* variant, press, listing of

archetype: definition, 7, 42, 124-25; location, 2, 6-8, 10-12, 77-80, 90-91, 108-12, 153, 233-34 (computer program); reconstruction, 2, 7, 11, 80; examples, 164-66, 169, 173, 178, 187, 191-92, 194-95

array: definition, 220; examples, 219-36

arrows in directional variations: rules, 56, 59, 77-80, 108-12, 114, 233; examples, 194, 200

asterisk: explanation, 56, 146; use with synthetic variations, 56, 64, 68, 87; use with overlaps, 71; use with sigla, 146; examples, 164, 168, 173, 177, 179-87, 200

axioms and corollaries, 14, 16, 84-91, 110

bibliography: definition, 13; difference from textual analysis, 14-19, 153; rules, 23, 38-40, 42-43, 55, 66-67, 75-76, 84, 89, 98-99, 115; probability in, 114-35, 217-20 (computer program); examples, 169, 173, 178

calculus: definition, 9; kinds, 14; rules, 59-74, 202-14 (abacus routines), 220-36 (computer routines); examples, 164, 168, 173, 177, 182-85

cards, edge-notched. *See* keysorting

—Manly's and Rickert's, 151-52

—punched, 152, 216

collation. *See* comparison

collection of texts and documents, 24-25, 138-43

comparison: number of printed copies to compare, 139-41; methods, 147-53; computer programs, 215-16

computers, 25, 58, 67, 152-54, 215-36

concordance, computer programs for making, 216-17

conflation: definition, 15, 18; rules, 15-19, 66-67, 98-99. *See also* reading, conflated; ring

connections in rings. *See* strength of ring connections

contamination: definition, 17. *See also* conflation

PRINCIPLES AND PRACTICE
OF TEXTURAL ANALYSIS

VINTON A. DEARING

When a document of any sort—literary, historical, musical, cartographic—exists in copies that differ among themselves, it is often of interest to determine the derivation of the copies, and if necessary to reconstruct lost copies from which the extant have descended. Most scholars are interested in identifying or reconstructing a copy that best reflects the author's intentions.

Textual analysis concerns itself with such variant states of documentary evidence. It is both a very general discipline, with a wide range of applications, and a purely logical discipline, with axioms and corollaries that may be precisely formulated.

This book explains the operations of textual analysis in general, and specifically how to carry them out using a new notation that is manipulable like simple arithmetic. It gives a full explanation of the logic of the operations in a formal theory of textual analysis. It examines other methods that have been proposed for obtaining the same ends, particularly statistical and probabilistic methods. It discusses the whole process of editing texts and documents: analyzing the project, collecting the manuscripts or other records, comparing the records, recording the differences, arriving at a "best text," emending it, and printing the results. This book gives sample solutions of literary and historical problems. Finally, it explains how more complex problems may be solved with the help of an abacus or a computer.

VINTON A. DEARING is Professor of English at the University of California, Los Angeles. He is the textual editor of the California edition of *The Works of Dryden*, and edited *Poems and Prose of John Gay* (1973).